Betty Crocker's

GOOD

AND

EASY

COOK BOOK

SKYHORSE PUBLISHING

First published by General Mills, Inc. in 1954

First Skyhorse Publishing Edition 2017

Foreword Copyright © 2017 by Skyhorse Publishing
Text by Amy Sherman

Skyhorse Publishing books may be purchased in bulk at special discounts for sales promotion, corporate gifts, fund-raising, or educational purposes. Special editions can also be created to specifications. For details, contact the Special Sales Department, Skyhorse Publishing, 307 West 36th Street, 11th Floor, New York, NY 10018 or info@skyhorsepublishing.com.

Skyhorse® and Skyhorse Publishing® are registered trademarks of Skyhorse Publishing, Inc.®, a Delaware corporation.

Visit our website at www.skyhorsepublishing.com.

10 9 8 7 6 5 4

Library of Congress Cataloging-in-Publication Data is available on file.

Cover photographs: iStockphoto

Print ISBN: 978-1-5107-2413-6
Ebook ISBN: 978-1-5107-2416-7

Printed in the United States of America

Foreword

We celebrate Betty Crocker more for what she stands for than who she was. Around a decade ago I came as close to meeting Betty Crocker as might be possible. When blogging was still new and shiny, I was part of a group of food bloggers invited to General Mills headquarters in Minneapolis. We toured the test kitchens, tasted products, visited the food photography studios, and admired an entire wall of Betty Crocker portraits. I admit, those portraits made quite an impression on me. Who was this mythical woman? Her style changed with the times. In years past she looked serious, wearing pearls and a bouffant hair-do, more recently she wore a more casual sweater and has a friendly smile.

Of course, Betty Crocker never really existed. She was dreamt up by an advertising agency in 1921 and in a few short years became a household icon, inspiring legions of cooks. She changes as America changes, but she was and still is a reassuring source for reliable recipes and cooking guidance.

Betty Crocker is as American as apple pie. Both are not only familiar symbols of America, but they each have a lot in common. They stir up feelings of comfort and home, and memories of meals cooked from scratch by mom and enjoyed by the whole family. Imagine a Norman Rockwell scene of a family sitting around the dinner table. It used to be a common sight, but is it still? Year in and year out we are told that no one cooks anymore, that meals are eaten on the run, and certainly not at the table as a family. Mom is not the one cooking every night, if at all. So what's going on? There seems to be a cooking conundrum. People are cooking from scratch less than ever before, as the food media continues to churn out new recipes and cooking celebrities all the time. New cookbooks are being published at an astonishing pace. We can't seem to get enough. So what is it we are hungry for anyway? Are we looking for something new and different? Or are we looking for something nostalgic and comforting? Have we forgotten the basics? Is it possible to look forward by looking back?

Betty Crocker's Good and Easy Cookbook was published in 1954 during the baby boom, and convenience foods were making their way into the American kitchen like never before. Today we are somewhat ambivalent about processed foods. We want everything to be good and easy and quick as well, but processed foods have been demonized. Looking back, the recipes in the book are a reflection of the time. There's a reliance on things like canned soup, baking mix, and cake mix. Exotic ingredients are limited to the likes of artichoke hearts, water chestnuts, Roquefort cheese, Worcestershire sauce, soy sauce, and chili powder. There's no quinoa, no kale, no miso, no smoked paprika. There are no recipes for avocado toast or whole grain bowls. The supposedly ethnic recipes are far from authentic, merely authentically American.

According to the introduction, *Betty Crocker's Good and Easy Cook Book* was designed for the "homemaker." It's a term we don't really use anymore. But that doesn't mean the book isn't relevant for today's home cooks. Recently I've read articles in magazines and online on the following topics: salads packed in wide mouth jars, crackers doctored with butter and dried herbs, homemade chocolate syrup and hot cocoa, endless variations on cake mixes, pressure cooker recipes and tips for making juicy burgers. Each and every one of these topics is also in this classic from 1954 and clearly just as top of mind today as they ever were. While some recipes go in and out of fashion, others remain classics. The value of *Betty Crocker's Good and Easy Cook Book* resides in the stalwarts, the tried and true recipes for things like New England Boiled Dinner, Deviled Eggs, Old-Fashioned Macaroni and Cheese, Tossed Green Salad, Coleslaw, Butterscotch Brownies and Hermits— all are American classics that should be part of everyone's repertoire. So, too, are the techniques for things like roasting a chicken, making soft boiled eggs, and whipping up salad dressings from scratch. The book has plenty of recipes for anyone just getting interested in cooking, young or old.

My blog *Cooking with Amy* received considerable attention when it first launched back in 2003 and helped to propel my career as a food writer and cookbook author. I genuinely love to eat and love to cook and I describe myself as a culinary enthusiast. I enjoy expressing my creativity by developing recipes for brands and cookbooks. When I go to a thrift shop or a used book store, I make a beeline for the cookbook section. I'm always on the hunt for inspiration and to learn more about a particular subject that ends up becoming endlessly fascinating to me. I want to know how people cook today and how their parents cooked. I want to be surprised and delighted and to get hungry as I peruse recipes from different cultures and different eras. The *Betty Crocker Good and Easy Cook Book* is the kind of book I love to read. But after spending some time with it, I realize why I never found it on the shelves. This is the kind of book people hang onto and rarely discard.

I don't expect every recipe I find to be to my taste, but the promise of finding a special one makes it all worthwhile. *The Betty Crocker Good and Easy Cook Book* should be approached in the same way. Don't assume every recipe will be perfect for today. Rely on it for the timeless classics, dig deep for the hidden gems and treasure it for being iconic, just like Betty Crocker.

—Amy Sherman

Betty Crocker's

GOOD

AND

EASY

COOK BOOK

Dear Friend,

Three times a day, and sometimes more, every homemaker asks herself, "What can I serve that my family and friends will enjoy?"

To help make the answer easier for you, we have divided this book into four sections: one for breakfast, one for lunch, one for dinner, and one for between-meal snacks, which we call the fourth meal.

A glance through any section will suggest many delicious possibilities —— good foods, easy to prepare. We hope they will make mealtimes happy times in your home.

Sincerely,
Betty Crocker

P.S. Every recipe in this book has been carefully tested for you.

Breakfast Today

A good breakfast is the foundation for a happy day.

Not only can the breakfast table be a happy family meeting place, but a well balanced breakfast, including one-fourth to one-third of the whole day's food requirement, makes us work better, play better, feel better. And it keeps us more cheerful all day long.

Today fixing a good breakfast is so easy, too. Set the table the night before. Take advantage of all the fine modern time-savers—the prepared mixes, ready-to-eat cereals, canned and frozen fruits and juices to interchange with the fresh. Use the handy automatic cooking appliances.

We have planned our breakfast-getting with time in mind, so you will find the breakfasts on the following pages good and easy—and quick to fix, as well. Then there are always those special touches that only you can give that will make breakfast in your home something for your family to remember fondly.

PRETTY AS A PICTURE

Brown-eyed Susan: Orange slices or sections around cooked prunes.

Frosty Raspberry Cup: Chill glass sherbet cups in refrigerator overnight. In morning, fill frosted cups with raspberry sauce or juice. Serve at once.

Grapefruit New Orleans: Grapefruit half on glass plate with vine-like garnish of mint or watercress around it and crushed strawberries on top.

Sparkling Grapes: Serve each guest a small bunch of grapes in a glass of cold water, stem at top.

From the Strawberry Patch: Fasten partly slit strawberry over the rim of a glass of fruit juice served on a green strawberry or grape leaf — or leaf doily.

ATTRACTIVE GO-TOGETHERS

Two fruits are often better than one—and a fine way to turn leftovers into breakfast treats. Try these, then branch out into your own combinations...

Sliced Bananas in Fruit Juice	Applesauce with Raisins
Strawberries and Pineapple Cubes	
Sliced Peaches and Blueberries	Grapes with Orange Slices

GLAMORIZING STAND-BYS

Garnish orange juice with—
½ slice orange or
one prime strawberry or
a pineapple cube or
little seedless grapes or
a sprig of fresh mint

To tomato juice add—
Worcestershire sauce or
lemon juice or
lemon wedge

JUICES
Rich in Vitamin C
(necessary for growth)

Grapefruit   Lemon   Lime
Orange   Tangerine   Tomato

Try these for variety:
Apple   Apricot   Carrot
Cranberry   Grape   Prune
Pineapple

CEREAL SUNDAES
WITH MILK OR CREAM
See picture, p. 17.

Berry: Mix cereal lightly in bowl with fresh, frozen or canned raspberries.

Maple Nut: Use maple syrup or shaved maple sugar on cereal for sweetening. Sprinkle with chopped or crushed nuts.

Chocolate: Pour chocolate milk over crispy corn puffs. No sugar is needed.

Tutti-frutti: Top cereal bowl with mixed fruit (such as canned fruit cocktail).

Happy Thought: Sprinkle cereal with chopped dates, nuts.

Peach Melba: Top cereal bowl with fresh, frozen or canned sliced peaches and raspberries.

White House: Cereal bowl topped with fresh or canned sweet cherries (pitted).

CORN MEAL MUSH
1 cup cold water
1 cup corn meal
3 cups boiling water
1 tsp. salt

Mix cold water and corn meal. Stir in boiling water and salt. Cook, stirring, until it boils. Cover and cook 30 min. in double boiler over boiling water, stirring occasionally.

FRIED CORN
MEAL MUSH
An old-time treat for a stay-at-home holiday.

Pack Corn Meal Mush into a greased loaf pan the night before using. Cover and chill until firm. Slice ½″ thick. Dip slices in flour and brown on both sides in greased frying pan. Serve hot with maple syrup or jelly . . . sausage, bacon or ham.

A WEEK OF TREATS

Do breakfast appetites at your house lag? Surprise them with cereal treats, both hot and cold. Try the combinations with milk or "half and half."

SUNDAY
Fried corn meal mush with jelly, little sausages

MONDAY
Bowl filled half with red berries, half with Cheerios

TUESDAY
Apricot halves on Sugar Jets

Raisin Face
on cooked cereal

Child's Own Bowl—
Berries on cereal
forming child's initial

TASTE TEMPTERS
for the Children

Teddy Bear in a Bowl—
Half pear on Wheaties
with raisin face and
banana ears

Jack Horner Bowl
with hidden prune

Try Your Own—such as
three date "bears"
in "porridge house"

WEDNESDAY

Blueberries and Kix

FRIDAY

Cooked wheat cereal
with brown sugar
in colored bowl

THURSDAY

Warm baked apple
in center of a bowl
of crunchy Wheaties
or hot oatmeal

SATURDAY

Bowl of favorite cereal
ringed with sliced bananas

HOW TO SOFT-COOK EGGS

Have eggs at room temperature. Cover eggs completely with hot or cold water (see below); do not pile them on top of each other. Don't let them boil!

Cold water start: Heat until water boils, then remove from heat, cover, let stand 2 to 4 min.

Boiling water start: Lower eggs into boiling water on spoon, reduce heat to simmer, cook 3 to 5 min., turning several times.

Coddled Eggs: Start in boiling water, lowering eggs carefully on spoon; cover pan tightly and remove from heat. Let stand 4 to 6 min.

HOW TO POACH EGGS

In greased skillet, bring to a boil enough water (or milk) to cover eggs. Reduce heat to simmer, and slip in, one at a time, each egg you have broken into saucer. Cover pan and cook at simmer for 3 to 5 min. Lift eggs from water one at a time with slotted spoon, drain. Salt and pepper lightly and serve at once.

HOW TO FRY EGGS

Heat a thin layer of butter or bacon fat in heavy skillet until mod. hot. Break eggs, one at a time, into saucer; slip into skillet. Reduce heat to cook slowly, and spoon fat over eggs until whites are set (3 to 4 min.). Turn if desired and cook until done as you want them.

DIFFERENT—AND GOOD

Poach-fried Eggs: Immediately after slipping eggs, one at a time, into hot fat in skillet, add ½ tsp. water or cream for each egg, cover tightly and cook to firmness desired.

EGGS IN A FRAME

Cut out center of bread slice with biscuit cutter; butter bread generously on both sides, place in hot buttered skillet, drop egg into center, cook slowly until egg is set; turn, brown on second side; season, and lift out with broad spatula or pancake turner.

FOR VARIETY
SERVE POACHED EGGS ON . . .

Fried bread (butter each side, brown lightly in skillet) or Split and toasted English Muffins or
Codfish Cakes (p. 11), or hash cakes, or
Ham-covered toasted bread rounds (use slice of cooked ham or deviled ham spread).

HOW TO SCRAMBLE EGGS

Break eggs into bowl. Add 1 tbsp. milk or cream, dash of salt and pepper for each egg. Beat with fork, slightly (for gold and white effect) or well (for uniform yellow). Heat ½ tbsp. fat for each egg in mod. hot skillet. Pour in mixture and reduce heat to low. Cook slowly, turning gently as mixture sets at bottom and sides of pan. Avoid constant stirring. When cooked through but still moist (5 to 8 min.), serve at once.

POPULAR VARIATIONS

With Mushrooms: Sauté 2 tbsp. sliced mushrooms per egg in the hot fat before scrambling eggs.

With Tomatoes: Sauté 2 tbsp. cut-up fresh or canned tomatoes in the hot fat before scrambling eggs.

With Deviled Ham: Spread hot buttered toast with deviled ham, top with scrambled eggs.

With Dried Beef or Ham: Frizzle cut-up dried beef or cooked ham in the hot fat before scrambling eggs.

HOW TO BAKE OR SHIRR EGGS

See picture, p. 23.

Heat oven to 350° (mod.). Slip each egg into a greased individual baking dish. Dot with butter; salt and pepper. Cover with 1 tbsp. sweet or sour cream. Bake 15 to 20 min., until set. Serve at once in the baking dish.

THESE, TOO, ARE DELICIOUS—

Shirred Eggs with Mushrooms: Use undiluted canned cream of mushroom soup instead of cream.

Shirred Eggs with Tomato: Cover with tomato juice or sauce instead of cream.

Baked Eggs on Corned Beef Hash: Heat oven to 400° (mod. hot). Spread warmed, moist corned beef hash in well greased shallow baking dish. Heat. With bottom of custard cup make deep hollows in hash. Slip eggs into these and proceed as above.

OMELET

For each egg use:
1 tbsp. milk or cream
salt and pepper
1 tsp. butter

Beat eggs until fluffy. Beat in milk or cream, salt and pepper. Pour into sizzling butter in skillet over low heat. Cook slowly, keeping heat low. As undersurface becomes set, lift it slightly with spatula to let uncooked portion flow underneath and cook.

As soon as all of mixture seems set, fold or roll it; serve immediately.

TRICKS WITH TOAST

Toast bread first, then butter; never put buttered bread into a toaster.

For Toasted Bread-and-Butter: Toast buttered side only under broiler.

One- or two-day-old bread makes the best toast.

Split and toast your leftover rolls, muffins, biscuits and unsugared doughnuts.

Slice a package of unbaked Brown 'n Serve rolls like bread and toast long slices.

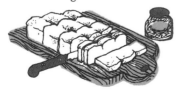

FRENCH TOAST

6 slices stale bread
2 beaten eggs
¼ tsp. salt   ½ cup milk

Mix eggs, milk and salt. Dip each slice of bread into mixture. Brown both sides in butter or other fat on hot griddle. Serve hot with maple syrup, jelly or honey.

Quick French Toast: Use French bread so more of the small slices can be fitted onto your griddle at one time.

FOR A LOT OF SLICES

Oven French Toast: Heat oven to 500° (very hot). Place dipped slices on greased baking sheet. Bake about 10 min., until browned.

FISHERMAN'S LUCK

Sliced Peaches and Blueberries
with Milk or Cream
Pan-fried Fish
Corn Bread (p. 25)

Milk   Coffee

A BOSTON BREAKFAST

Baked Apple and Wheaties
Codfish Cakes
with Egg Sauce
Hot Muffins
Currant Jelly

Milk   Coffee

MORNING ON THE POTOMAC

Cherry Circle on Cheerios
Salt Mackerel
with Minced Parsley Garnish
Tiny Boiled Potatoes
Little Hot Biscuits

Milk   Coffee

PAN-FRIED FRESH FISH

(Use trout, perch, sunfish, crappies, etc.) Dip cleaned fish in cold water or milk. Drain. Sprinkle with salt and pepper. Dip in flour, corn meal or Bisquick. Cook in hot fat ⅛" deep in skillet over med. heat until browned on both sides (about 10 min. in all). Drain and serve.

CODFISH CAKES

    1 cup flaked salt codfish, freshened (see pkg.)
    2 cups diced raw potatoes
    1 egg, beaten
    salt and pepper
    1 tsp. butter or margarine

Cook freshened fish and potatoes in boiling water, covered, until potatoes are tender. Drain. Mash. Beat in remaining ingredients. Form into flat cakes or drop from spoon. Fry in hot fat until brown (5 min. to a side). Serve with Egg Sauce (p. 122).

BROILED SALT MACKEREL

Soak mackerel fillets in cold water overnight. Drain, wipe dry and brush with butter on both sides. Place skin side down on hot greased broiler rack 2" under heat. Broil until well browned (about 6 min.), turn and broil until browned on other side. Baste each side with melted butter once as fish cooks. Arrange skin side down on hot platter, pour melted butter over fish. Serve at once.

BACON...
AND CANADIAN BACON
Quick Ways to Cook It

Pan-fried: Place separate slices (have Canadian bacon ⅛" thick) in a cold skillet. Don't crowd. Cook over low heat 5 to 8 min., turning to brown evenly. Place cooked slices on absorbent paper to drain.

Broiled: Arrange separate slices (have Canadian bacon ¼" thick) on broiling rack 3" from heat. Turn slices after 3 to 4 min. to brown evenly.

Baked: Heat oven to 400° (mod. hot). Arrange separate slices on wire rack set in a baking pan. Bake until brown, about 10 min.

BACON AND EGGS
OR HAM AND EGGS

Pan-fry bacon or ham; remove from skillet and keep hot. Drain excess fat from skillet and cook eggs slowly in the rest. Serve eggs with bacon or arranged around ham on hot platter.

A BREAKFAST TREAT

Sliced Bananas in Orange Juice
Bowls of Cheerios
Ham and Eggs (p. 12) or Frizzled Ham (p. 13)
Hot Muffins (p. 25) Marmalade
Beverage

ALL YOU HAVE TO DO:

To turn bacon, sausages, chops and other small meats easily, use wire tongs.

To improvise a broiling or baking rack, set a wire cake cooling rack in cake or pie pan.

HAM—Quick Ways to Cook It

Broiled: Slash edges of fat on ½ to 1" thick slice of ham. Place on broiling rack 3" below heat. Broil until tender, 5 to 10 min. on each side. Serve on hot platter garnished with peach or apricot halves, broiled a few minutes.

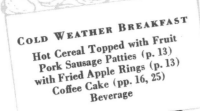

COLD WEATHER BREAKFAST

Hot Cereal Topped with Fruit
Pork Sausage Patties (p. 13)
with Fried Apple Rings (p. 13)
Coffee Cake (pp. 16, 25)
Beverage

SUMMER BREAKFAST
ON THE PORCH

Berries in Cantaloupe Rings
Bacon and Egg Platter
(p. 12)
Cinnamon Rolls (p. 29)
Beverage

PORK SAUSAGE LINKS

Pan-fried: Place links in cold skillet. Add a small amount of water. Cover and simmer 5 min., but do not boil or prick! Then drain off water and cook slowly until browned, turning once.

Baked: Heat oven to 400° (mod. hot). Simmer as above, then drain and bake 20 to 30 min. in an open pan, turning once.

PORK SAUSAGE PATTIES

Pan-fried: Place ½" thick patties in cold skillet. Cook over low heat 12 to 15 min., until evenly browned with no trace of pink remaining. Turn with wire tongs or broad spatula. Pour off fat as it gathers.

Baked: Heat oven to 400° (mod. hot). Bake patties 20 to 30 min. in an open pan, turning once as in frying.

Fried Apple Rings: Use ½" slices of cored tart apples. Sprinkle with sugar and sauté in sausage drippings after sausage has been removed from skillet (or in butter or bacon fat.) Turn once with broad spatula while cooking, cook until tender. Serve with pork sausages for breakfast, chops or roast for dinner.

Pan-fried: Slice ham ¼ to ½" thick. Trim off some fat to rub hot skillet. Cook ham slowly until brown on one side, 4 to 8 min. Turn and brown on second side.

Frizzled: Lay boiled ham in lightly greased hot skillet. Pan-fry quickly until edges curl and cook crisp. Remove to hot platter. Eat with fingers.

LIGHTNING-QUICK PANCAKES
of old-fashioned goodness

See picture, pp. 20-21.

Just follow the directions on the Bisquick pkg. Then try these:

Blueberry Pancakes: Fold 2 tbsp. sugar and 1 cup drained fresh, frozen or canned blueberries gently into Bisquick Pancake batter. Bake. Serve with honey or confectioners' sugar.

Nut Pancakes: Mix ¾ cup of finely chopped toasted pecans, peanuts or walnuts into your Bisquick Pancake batter. Bake. Serve with syrup.

Corn Meal Pancakes: Use ½ cup corn meal in place of ½ cup of the Bisquick. Bake. Serve with syrup or jelly and frizzled ham or bacon, or with grilled sausage and apple rings.

PUFF PANCAKES
So plump and light!

2 eggs
1 cup milk
2⅓ cups Bisquick
2 tbsp. sugar
¼ cup melted shortening

Beat eggs with rotary beater or mixer until soft peaks form. Blend in milk; add Bisquick and sugar. Mix just until well dampened, then fold in shortening. Spoon onto ungreased medium-hot griddle. Turn when puffed up and bubbles begin to break. Cook on other side. *15 to 20 pancakes.*

SILVER DOLLAR PANCAKES

Add a little more milk than usual to Bisquick Pancake batter. Spoon the thin batter a tablespoonful at a time to fill your griddle with tiny tasty pancakes. Serve a plateful to each person.

HINTS THAT HELP

To save dishes, mix pancake or waffle batter in wide-mouthed pitcher ready to pour onto griddle.

Leftover batter can be stored, covered, in refrigerator and thinned with milk when used again.

Remember — modern griddles need no greasing.

LIGHTNING-QUICK WAFFLES

Just follow the directions on the Bisquick pkg. Then try the variations suggested for pancakes across the page. Nuts and blueberries are just as much at home in the waffle iron as on the griddle.

A SPECIAL TREAT

Bacon Waffles: Lay short strips of bacon over the grids of a heated waffle iron. Close about 1 min. Then pour Waffle batter—minus butter—over cooked bacon and bake.

ALL YOU HAVE TO DO:

To bake waffles correctly, close the iron quickly after pouring on the batter, and bake until steaming stops.

NORTH WOODS PANCAKE BREAKFAST

Fruit Juice
Ready-to-Eat Cereal
Blueberry Pancakes (p. 14)
Pan-fried Bacon (p. 12)
Strained Honey
Beverage

KENTUCKY BLUE-GRASS BREAKFAST

Southern Melon Halves
Corn Meal Waffles
Damson Plum Jelly
Fried Country Ham (p. 13)
Beverage

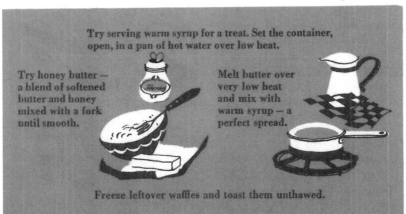

Try serving warm syrup for a treat. Set the container, open, in a pan of hot water over low heat.

Try honey butter — a blend of softened butter and honey mixed with a fork until smooth.

Melt butter over very low heat and mix with warm syrup — a perfect spread.

Freeze leftover waffles and toast them unthawed.

DOUBLE-QUICK COFFEE BREAD
See picture, pp. 18-19.

You can make it the day before, warm it for breakfast, serve hot and fragrant.

First, choose topping (opposite) and have it ready.

>   ¾ cup warm water—
>   not hot (110 to 115°)
>   1 pkg. active dry yeast
>   ¼ cup sugar
>   1 tsp. salt
>   2¼ cups sifted
>   Gold Medal Flour
>   1 egg
>   ¼ cup soft shortening
>   or butter

Mix — In mixing bowl, dissolve yeast in warm water. Add sugar and salt and about half the flour.

Beat — thoroughly 2 min. Then add egg and shortening. Beat in rest of flour gradually until smooth.

Spoon — Drop small spoonfuls over entire bottom of greased pan. Cover and let rise in warm place (85°) 50 to 60 min., until double in bulk. Heat oven to 375° and bake 30 to 35 min., until brown. Immediately turn out of pan to avoid sticking. Serve warm.

Pick Your Favorite
They're all easy . . . all delicious!

Cherry Butterscotch: Melt in 9″ ring mold ⅓ cup butter and ½ cup brown sugar with 1 tbsp. corn syrup. Decorate with walnut or pecan halves and candied or maraschino cherries. Cool to just warm before spooning in dough.

Tutti-frutti Buns: Mix into finished dough ½ cup candied fruit and ¼ cup chopped nuts. Fill half full 16 to 20 greased medium muffin cups. Let rise. Bake 15 to 20 min. When baked, ice with a mixture of ¾ cup sifted confectioners' sugar and 1 to 2 tbsp. cream. Decorate tops with more candied fruit and nuts.

Cinnamon Streusel: Mix thoroughly 2 tbsp. butter, ⅓ cup granulated or brown sugar, 2 tbsp. flour, 2 tsp. cinnamon, ½ cup chopped nuts. Spoon dough into 8 or 9″ sq. pan. Sprinkle with the Streusel mixture.

Breakfast fruits (p. 5) and cereal sundaes (p. 6) can look gay and delicious.

16

Double-Quick Coffee Bread

Hot coffee bread (p. 16) makes any occasion festive.

Dissolved yeast, sugar, salt, half the flour are beaten till batter sheets off spoon.

Add egg, shortening and rest of flour. Beat together until smooth. Beating takes the place of kneading the dough.

With spatula, push dough by teaspoonfuls into greased pan.

Pancake Time

A happy breakfast treat for the family — easy on mother, too (p. 14).

Make your own cereal sundae (p. 6), along with the scrambled eggs.

When friends come
in for brunch, let
glamorous strawberry
shortcake (p. 71) take
the spotlight.

Pretty Breakfasts

Breakfast should always be
an attractive meal, both for
the family and for guests.

For a holiday breakfast, try juice,
cereal with fruit, and shirred eggs (p. 9).

The Breakfast Tray

Indulge in a few pretty dishes and choice
linens for a breakfast tray to please
a house guest, the sick-a-bed or
Mother on Mother's Day.

SPECIAL BREAKFAST
Double Orange—Slices in Juice
Soft-cooked Egg
Toasted Raisin Bread
Coffee

LIGHTNING-QUICK COFFEE CAKES

For a homey treat — just follow the easy directions for Coffee Cake on the Bisquick pkg. Then try these:

Cinnamon Coffee Cake: When Bisquick Coffee Cake batter is in the pan, sprinkle over it a mixture of ½ cup brown or granulated sugar and 1½ tsp. cinnamon. Bake.

Berry or Fruit Coffee Cake: Fold into Bisquick Coffee Cake batter 1 cup fresh berries or ¾ cup well drained canned berries, or 1 cup cut-up dates or figs. Bake.

Prune, Apricot or Pineapple Coffee Cake: When Bisquick Coffee Cake batter is in the pan, spread over it 2 tbsp. melted butter and sprinkle with ¼ cup granulated or brown sugar (add ¾ tsp. cinnamon for prune variation). Arrange over top 1 cup chopped drained cooked prunes or apricots or 1 cup drained crushed pineapple. Bake.

LIGHTNING-QUICK MUFFINS

For light, tender muffins to win you praise, just follow the easy directions on the Bisquick package, and then try these:

Blueberry Muffins: Fold carefully into Bisquick Muffin batter, 1 cup fresh berries or ¾ cup well drained canned berries. Bake.

Date, Fig or Raisin Muffins: Fold into Bisquick Muffin batter 1 cup finely cut-up dates, figs or raisins. Bake.

Wheaties Muffins: Fold into Bisquick Muffin batter 1½ cups Wheaties. Bake.

Corn Muffins, Corn Sticks or Corn Bread: Substitute ¾ cup corn meal for ¾ cup Bisquick in Muffin batter. Fill muffin or corn-stick pans ⅔ full, or pour into 8″ round pan. Bake just until set, about 15 min. in hot oven (450°).

> **EVEN-QUICKER MUFFINS:** different and intriguing flavors— such as wild blueberry, orange, date, raisin bran and corn—each in its own package. Make them with Betty Crocker Muffin Mix. Delicious!

JIFFY-QUICK BREAKFAST SWEET ROLLS

Just buy a package of Brown 'n Serve rolls from your neighborhood grocer. Before you pop them into the mod. hot oven (400°) to brown for serving (6 to 8 min.), sometimes try these:

Cinnamon - topped Rolls: Butter rolls, then sprinkle with sugar-and-cinnamon mixture (¼ cup granulated or brown sugar to 1 tsp. cinnamon).

Streusel-topped Rolls: Spread rolls with a mixture of 2 tbsp. butter or margarine, 5 tbsp. sugar, 2 tbsp. flour and ½ tsp. cinnamon.

Or, after browning, try these:

Orange-glazed Rolls: Bring to a boil and simmer for 5 min. ½ cup sugar, 2 tbsp. water, ¼ cup orange juice; stir in grated rind of 1 orange and cool. Spread on fresh rolls while still warm.

Frosted Rolls: Mix sifted confectioners' sugar with cream or milk to spreading consistency. Add flavoring, if desired. Spread over freshly baked rolls while still warm.

POPOVERS

These magical-looking crusty shells will win you the rank of expert cook. And they're now so easy to make!

1 cup sifted Gold Medal Flour
½ tsp. salt
1 cup milk
2 eggs

Heat oven to 425° (hot). Beat ingredients together with rotary beater *just* until smooth. Over-beating will reduce volume. Pour into well greased deep muffin cups (¾ full) or oven-glass cups (½ full). Bake until golden brown, 40 to 45 min. If not baked long enough, they will collapse. Serve at once. *5 to 9 popovers.*

ANY EXTRA POPOVERS?

Leftover popovers take well to freezing.
No need to thaw—just pop into oven.

To reheat popovers, place in paper bag or aluminum foil and set in hot oven (425°) for 5 min.

Try them split and toasted, too.

STIR-N-ROLL BISCUITS

A new method—speedy, easy, sure. Created for *you*. You'll have rich and flaky biscuits with tender, crisp crusts this good and easy way.

2 cups sifted Gold Medal Flour
3 tsp. baking powder
1 tsp. salt
⅓ cup cooking (salad) oil
⅔ cup milk

Heat oven to 475° (very hot). Sift dry ingredients together into bowl. Pour oil and milk into measuring cup, without stirring. Then pour all at once into flour, and stir with fork until mixture cleans sides of bowl. Then:

... **for Rolled or Patted Biscuits:** Smooth by kneading dough about 10 times, without additional flour. Roll or pat out ¼ to ½″ thick between waxed papers. Cut out. Place on ungreased baking sheet.

... **for Drop Biscuits:** Drop from spoon onto ungreased baking sheet or into ungreased muffin cups.

Bake 10 to 12 min. Serve hot from the oven with butter and jelly, honey or jam—or dunk in individual dishes of maple syrup. *16 biscuits.*

HONEY BUTTER
Beat ½ cup honey into ½ cup soft butter. Add 1 tsp. grated orange rind and beat until fluffy.

SOME VARIATIONS

Corn Meal Biscuits: Sift ½ cup yellow corn meal with 1½ cups flour. Proceed as above.

Bacon Biscuits: Reduce salt to ½ tsp. Add ⅓ cup well drained crisply cooked bacon bits to dry ingredients. Proceed as above.

ALL YOU HAVE TO DO:

To save time in cutting, roll dough into rectangle and cut into squares with sharp knife—or roll into cylinder and cut off ½″ slices.

LIGHTNING-QUICK ROLLED BISCUITS

Follow the easy Rolled Biscuit directions on Bisquick pkg. Then to add a special flourish to your meals try these:

Cinnamon Rolls: Heat oven to 425° (hot). Roll out Bisquick Rolled Biscuit dough into 7x16″ rectangle. Spread with 2 tbsp. soft butter. Then sprinkle with ¼ cup sugar and 1 tsp. cinnamon, mixed. Roll up tightly. Cut into 1″ slices. Bake on greased baking sheet, or in greased muffin cups about 15 min. *About 16 rolls.*

Butterscotch Pecan Rolls: Same as Cinnamon Rolls, but bake slices in greased medium muffin cups. First, mix ½ cup melted butter, ½ cup brown sugar (packed). Spoon into 16 muffin cups with 2 or 3 pecan halves in each cup.

DROP BISCUITS

Just follow the easy Drop Biscuit directions on Bisquick pkg. Then for variety try:

Cinnamon Biscuit Balls: Heat oven to 450° (hot). Make small balls of Bisquick Drop Biscuit dough and roll them in mixture of 2 tbsp. sugar and 1 tsp. cinnamon. Bake on lightly greased baking sheet 8 to 10 min. *About 2 doz. biscuits.*

Jolly Breakfast Ring: Heat oven to 400° (mod. hot) while you mix Bisquick Drop Biscuit dough. Shape dough into 12 balls. Melt ⅓ cup butter and pour about 3 tbsp. of it into a 9″ ring mold. Sprinkle over the butter 3 tbsp. brown sugar, 12 cherries (candied or maraschino) and ¼ cup nuts. Roll balls in rest of melted butter, then in a mixture of ½ cup sugar, 1 tsp. cinnamon, 3 tbsp. chopped nuts. Place in ring mold and bake 25 to 30 min. Remove from pan while warm.

DOUGHNUTS

Light, crispy doughnuts used to be a real test for a skilled cook. Now they're quick and easy—especially if you have an automatic fryer.

2 cups Bisquick
¼ cup sugar
⅓ cup milk
1 tsp. vanilla
1 egg
¼ tsp. each of cinnamon and nutmeg, if desired

Heat fat to 375° (temperature at which a small bread cube browns in 50 sec.). Mix ingredients together until well blended. Turn dough onto lightly floured surface and knead about 10 times. Roll out ⅜″ thick. Cut with floured doughnut cutter. Drop into hot fat. Fry until golden brown on both sides, about 1 min. to a side. Remove from fat and drain on absorbent paper. *About 12 doughnuts.*

ALL YOU HAVE TO DO:

To sugar doughnuts, just before serving, shake one at a time in a small paper bag containing a little confectioners' or granulated sugar—perhaps with a dash of cinnamon.

GENERAL RULES FOR MAKING COFFEE

1. Use fresh coffee. Keep tightly covered for freshness.
2. Use the right grind for your maker—drip for dripolators and vacuum makers, regular grind for steeped coffee and percolators.
3. Keep coffee maker sparkling clean.
4. Start with fresh cold water.
5. Use enough coffee—1 to 2 level tbsp. for ¾ measuring cup of water. Find your favorite strength and stick to it.
6. Time carefully.
7. Serve as soon as possible. Do not let coffee stand on grounds or boil; keep warm over very low heat or by standing pot in hot water.

Warning: Adding water to used grounds never makes good coffee. For a second brewing, rinse out coffee maker and start fresh.

PERCOLATOR

Measure fresh cold water into the pot and coffee into the basket. Let water boil until it has "perked" 5 to 10 min. for desired strength.

DRIPOLATOR

Measure coffee into filter section, fresh boiling water into upper container. Cover and set over very low heat until water has dripped through coffee. Remove upper section. Stir. Serve.

VACUUM MAKER

Measure fresh cold water into lower bowl. Fit top bowl on with filter adjusted. Put coffee in top. Place on heat. When water rises, lower heat. Stir once. Remove from heat in 1 min. When coffee is back in lower section, remove top and serve coffee.

STEEPED IN POT

Allow 2 level tbsp. coffee (regular grind) to each ¾ cup fresh cold water. Place over heat. Stir. Bring just *to* boil. Stir again. Take off heat. Add dash of cold water. Strain. Serve.

FROZEN COFFEE

Mix in cup according to directions on container.

INSTANT COFFEE

Place Instant Coffee in serving cup, using 1 or more tsp., depending on strength desired. Fill cup with boiling hot water and stir as directed.

"COME OVER FOR BREAKFAST"

The best party is the one the hostess can enjoy too. More and more young hostesses are finding breakfast is this kind of party — breakfast, or a leisurely noontime combination brunch.

Breakfast entertaining doesn't take formal "fixings" or long hot hours in the kitchen. It's inexpensive — and it's fun. It can be as pretty as you please, too. See the color pages following for some ideas on that.

Why not have folks in for breakfast on a lazy day? Try one of these...

COUNTRY BREAKFAST
Bunches of Grapes
Cereal with Top Milk
Eggs Baked on Corned
Beef Hash (p. 9)
Quick Cinnamon Coffee Cake
(p. 25)
Beverage

STRAWBERRY FESTIVAL
Orange Juice Flip
(beat orange juice into lightly
beaten eggs; add sherry flavor-
ing, if desired)
Strawberry Shortcake (p. 71)
Crisp Bacon (p. 12)
Beverage

HOLIDAY BREAKFAST
Sparkling Red Fruit Juice
Kix with Raisins
Shirred Eggs (p. 9) with Bacon
Jolly Breakfast Ring (p. 29)
or Holiday Coffee Cake
(from neighborhood baker)
Beverage

BREAKFAST BUFFET
Choice of Juices
Make-Your-Own Cereal Sundaes
(p. 6)
Toasted Bread-and-Butter (p.10)
Scrambled Eggs with
Mushrooms (p. 9)
Little Pork Sausages (p. 13)
Beverage

See the color pages 17 through 24 for more breakfast entertaining ideas. The fruit and cereal treats shown on page 17 are described on pages 5, 6 and 7.

Lunch...or Supper

In some American homes the noon meal is lunch, and dinner comes at night. In many other homes, dinner is at noon and supper is the light meal of the day. We've called this section of our book Lunch, but any of the ideas or recipes will be just as good for supper if that is what you have in your home.

Here are dishes that take very little time to prepare, for we know how busy you are. There are "put-togethers" and "made-overs" because this is a good time for using up food from other meals. And there are suggestions for a too-often-overlooked meal: the lunch to pack and carry.

For the times when you have guests for lunch or supper, you will find some simple, easy dishes and menus to give the meal a company air but still leave you free to enjoy the occasion and be a charming hostess, too.

EASY TO MAKE AT HOME

Soup has become the mainstay of the lunch at home. Years ago good soup took hours to make, but not today—not with packaged, canned and frozen soups and vegetables, and pressure cookers to speed and ease the homemaker's work.

QUICK VEGETABLE SOUP

10½-oz. can bouillon or
  consommé
½ pkg. frozen mixed vege-
  tables, cooked, or 10½-oz.
  can mixed vegetables
2 tbsp. minced parsley
1 tbsp. butter

Dilute soup as directed on can. Add rest of ingredients; cover, cook slowly until vegetables are heated through. *4 servings.*

SOPHISTICATED SOUP LUNCHEON

Chilled Quick Potato Soup
(Vichyssoise)

Fruit Salad   Beverage

QUICK POTATO SOUP

1 tbsp. grated onion
1½ cups chicken broth
  (your own or canned)
2 cups milk
½ cup packaged instant
  mashed potato
1 tsp. salt
¼ tsp. pepper

Add onion to chicken broth; bring to boiling. Slowly add milk, potato, seasonings. Heat to boiling. Top each bowl with cut chives from that pot in the window. *4 to 6 servings.*

CHICKEN-RICE SOUP

¼ cup uncooked rice
2 cups chicken broth (your
  own or 14½-oz. can; or 4
  chicken bouillon cubes in
  2 cups boiling water)
salt and pepper

Add rice to chicken broth; bring to boiling and simmer covered until rice is tender, about 20 min. *2 to 3 servings.*

Note: ¾ cup cooked rice may be used and just heated in the broth.

Chicken-Noodle Soup: Follow recipe for Chicken-Rice Soup, using ¾ cup uncooked noodles in place of rice. *2 to 3 servings.*

Cream-style Chicken Soup: Melt 2 tbsp. butter; add 1 tbsp. flour and allow to bubble. Gradually add finished Chicken-Rice or Chicken-Noodle Soup. *2 to 3 servings.*

PEASANT SOUP

4 cups water
1 small smoked ham hock
1 cup split peas or lentils,
    soaked several hr. or
    overnight
½ cup finely grated carrots
¼ cup chopped celery
¼ cup finely chopped onion
1 sprig parsley, cut fine
1 bay leaf, crumbled
⅛ tsp. thyme
salt and pepper to taste

Combine all ingredients in pressure cooker; cook at 10 lb. for 45 min. Remove ham hock; skin and dice; add to soup. *6 servings.*

AUTUMN SOUP

1 lb. ground beef
1 cup chopped onions
4 cups hot water
1 cup cut-up carrots
1 cup cut-up celery
1 cup cut-up potato
2 tsp. salt
½ tsp. pepper
1 tsp. meat extract
1 bay leaf and pinch basil
6 whole fresh tomatoes,
    stems removed

Brown beef slowly in hot fat in a heavy kettle. Add onions and cook 5 min. Loosen meat from bottom of kettle. Add remaining ingredients, except tomatoes; bring to boil, cover and simmer 20 min. Add the tomatoes; simmer 10 min. more.

    Serve a whole tomato in each bowl. Nutritious for dieters; add a hearty dessert for others. *6 servings.*

NEW-FASHIONED VEGETABLE SOUP

1 soup bone with meat
4 cups water
1 medium onion, chopped
1 cup sliced carrots
1 cup cut-up celery and
    leaves
no. 2 can tomatoes
3 sprigs parsley, cut fine
1 tbsp. salt
1 bay leaf, crumbled
5 peppercorns
½ tsp. marjoram
½ tsp. thyme
green beans, diced potatoes,
    cabbage may be added, if
    desired

Cut meat off soup bone; brown meat in hot fat in pressure cooker. Add water to meat and bone; cook at 10 lb. for 15 min. Open cooker (according to directions). Add vegetables and seasonings; cook at 10 lb. for 10 min. *6 servings.*

Note: Vegetable Soup may be cooked in the deep well of range. Increase cooking of meat to 2 hr., vegetables to 30 min. Cook Peasant Soup in deep well 3 hr.

START WITH A CAN OF SOUP

Canned soup offers good, wholesome nourishment. Add a bit of garnish and you have a colorful treat. Or let your imagination go and combine two or more soups for an infinite variety of good and easy dishes.

Swedish Split Pea: Add bacon fat and a pinch of ginger to 1 can split pea soup. Top with strips of ham slightly browned in butter. *4 servings.*

Spicy Cream of Tomato: Heat 1 can tomato soup with a slice of onion, pinch of cinnamon, clove and bay leaf. Add an equal amount of rich milk. Heat again. *4 servings.*

Lobster Bisque: Heat 1 can cream of chicken soup and 1 cup rich milk. Add 6½-oz. can lobster cut in pieces, ½ tsp. paprika, ¼ tsp. nutmeg and a few grains cayenne pepper. *4 servings.*

Savory Cream of Chicken: Mix together 1 can each of cream of chicken soup and chicken with rice. Add ½ cup rich milk and 1 tsp. tarragon. Heat over low heat, stirring occasionally. Garnish with whipped cream sprinkled with paprika. *4 servings.*

Boola-boola Soup: Mix together 1 can each of turtle soup and green pea soup. Heat and add sherry flavoring to taste. Top with a spoonful of whipped cream. *4 servings.*

Quick Russian Borsch: Add 2 finely shredded small raw beets, 1 cup finely shredded cabbage and 2 to 4 tbsp. chopped onion to 1 can bouillon, diluted according to directions on can. Bring to boiling and simmer 10 min. Serve topped with a spoonful of sour cream. *4 servings.*

French Onion Soup: Lightly brown 2 cups sliced onion in 2 tbsp. butter; add 10½-oz. can consommé, ½ soup can water, 1 tsp. salt. Bring to boiling and simmer 15 min. Top each bowl with a toasted slice of French bread; sprinkle with grated Parmesan cheese. *4 servings.*

Clam-Tomato Bisque: Combine 1 can tomato soup and 7½-oz. can minced clams. Add salt, pepper, lemon juice to taste. Simmer 5 min. Just before serving, add ½ cup rich milk. Heat but do not boil. *4 servings.*

Crabmeat Mongole: Combine 1 can pea soup and 1 can tomato soup diluted according to directions. Add ½ cup rich milk and 6½-oz. can crabmeat, flaked. Use sherry flavoring, if desired. Heat over low heat. *6 to 8 servings.*

TO MAKE SOUPS MORE HEARTY, ADD:

Bits of cooked ham or bacon to split pea or navy bean soup.

Noodle, barley or rice to vegetable soup or meat soup.

Tiny browned meat balls to vegetable soup.

Slices of bologna or frankfurter to pea or bean soup.

KEEP ALL THESE ON YOUR SHELF

Condensed soups in cans to which you add water or milk before heating.

Canned soups which you heat and serve as they are.

Clear soups that can be chilled in the refrigerator and served jellied.

Packaged dried soups easy to store and ready to eat in a few minutes.

Beef and chicken bouillon cubes which with boiling water make a simple soup or a hearty soup base.

ADDITIONAL USES FOR READY-MADE SOUPS

As sauce on soufflés, casseroles and leftover meats use cream of tomato and cream of mushroom soups. Thin as you like and heat.

Add bouillon cubes to gravies, sauces, stews to increase depth of flavor.

When short of meat or chicken stock, fill out with bouillon cubes dissolved in water.

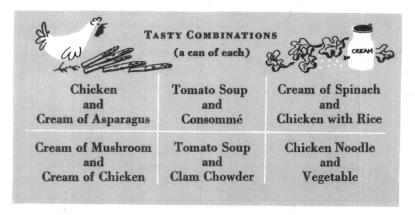

TASTY COMBINATIONS
(a can of each)

Chicken and Cream of Asparagus	Tomato Soup and Consommé	Cream of Spinach and Chicken with Rice
Cream of Mushroom and Cream of Chicken	Tomato Soup and Clam Chowder	Chicken Noodle and Vegetable

SOMETHING CRISP

Croutons: Cut day-old bread in ½" squares. Fry in butter until golden brown. Shake skillet or toss with fork.

Melba Toast: Heat oven to 300° (slow). Slice day-old bread thin as possible; remove crusts. Heat in oven until golden brown.

Parmesan Rounds: Butter ½" slices French or Vienna bread. Sprinkle generously with grated Parmesan cheese and paprika. Just before serving, pop under broiler until butter and cheese bubble.

Cheese Spread Toast: Blend 2 parts cream cheese with 1 part Roquefort-type cheese; moisten with milk and spread on hot buttered toast or toasted split buns. Nice with tomato soup.

CREAM OF SPINACH

1 lb. chopped fresh or frozen spinach (tough stems removed)
1 medium onion
(¼ cup water if food blender is used)
6 tbsp. butter
6 tbsp. Gold Medal Flour
6 cups rich milk
sherry flavoring

Put spinach and onion through food blender or chop fine. Melt butter; blend in flour and cook until it bubbles vigorously. (This is the secret of good creamy soups.) Stir in spinach-onion mixture. Bring to boiling. Add milk. Season to taste; heat and serve. *6 servings.*

OYSTER STEW

2 cups milk
½ cup cream
1 pt. oysters (with oyster liquid)
¼ cup butter
1 tsp. salt
dash each of pepper and cayenne
1 tsp. Worcestershire sauce

Heat milk and cream to boiling. Heat oysters, butter and seasonings until edges of oysters curl. Pour into hot milk and serve at once. *4 servings.*

FOR FLAVOR PLUS

Chicken broth, chicken fat or chicken bouillon cubes added to any cream soup will enhance its flavor.

CREAM OF TOMATO SOUP

2½ cups cooked tomatoes
(no. 2 can)
1 small onion, sliced
¼ tsp. cinnamon
¼ tsp. celery salt
⅛ tsp. cloves
3 cups Thin Cream Sauce
(p. 122)

Cook tomatoes, onion and seasonings 15 min. Press through sieve, if desired. Heat strained tomatoes to boiling; add slowly to cream sauce. Serve at once without reheating. *6 servings.*

QUICK CREAM OF VEGETABLE SOUP

Use 1 can diluted cream of chicken soup or make 2 cups Thin Cream Sauce (p. 122), using chicken broth or consommé as part of liquid. Add ½ pkg. frozen mixed vegetables, cooked, or half of 1-lb. can mixed vegetables. (Use the other half pkg. or can for salad on another day.) Heat to boiling. *4 servings.*

TASTY GARNISHES

Toasted slivered almonds or crisp cereals . . . on creamed soups.

Lemon slice . . . on black bean, jellied soup, clear tomato.

Salted whipped cream or cheese popcorn . . . on tomato soup.

Minced parsley or chives . . . on any cream, vegetable or jellied soup.

OUT OF THE CRACKER BOX

For Crispier Crackers: Heat oven to 300° (slow). Brush crackers with salad oil or melted butter. Heat in oven until lightly browned.

To Freshen Crackers: Toast large crackers in the automatic toaster—set at *Light*—or in slow oven.

Top-a-Cracker: Heat oven to 300° (slow). Brush crackers with salad oil or melted butter; sprinkle with paprika, celery seed, caraway or poppy seed. Heat in oven and serve warm.

Cheese Crackers: Heat oven to 300° (slow). Place thin slice of cheese or grated cheese on cracker. Heat in oven until cheese melts.

Try different crackers from the wide variety on your grocer's shelf.

SOUP-SANDWICH-SALAD
Quick Potato Soup (p. 34)
Deviled Ham Sandwich
Peach-Cottage Cheese Salad

SOUP-SANDWICH-DESSERT
Cream of Tomato Soup (p. 39)
Toasted Peanut Butter Sandwich
Baked Apple

SOUP PATTERNS FOR LUNCH

Soup and sandwich, soup and salad, soup and fruit—all these are popular lunch patterns of to-day. Start with these good and easy ideas, then branch out on your own.

SOUP-ROLL-DESSERT
Autumn Soup (p. 35)
Toasted Split Rolls
Fruit Cobbler

SOUP-SALAD-DESSERT
Peasant Soup (p. 35)
Hot French Bread
Lettuce Wedges—French Dressing
Fruit Cup

SOUP-RELISH-DESSERT
New-fashioned
Vegetable Soup (p. 35)
Crisp Celery   Pickles
Crackers
Sliced Orange and Banana

SANDWICH-MAKING

The Bread: Use fresh or day-old bread. Leave crusts on (prevents drying). Use slices next to each other in the loaf for a good fit. Try different breads.

The Spread: Have butter or margarine soft. Keep a covered bowl of odds and ends. Spread all the way to the edge on both slices to prevent fillings' soaking. Cream cheese or peanut butter keeps filling from soaking.

The Filling: Have filling well seasoned before spreading (moist but not wet). Keep fillings fresh and moist in covered bowls or plastic containers in refrigerator. Use several thin slices of meat rather than one thick slice. Wrap lettuce separately.

The Making: Line up matching slices—spread butter on all. Spoon on filling, then spread evenly to the edges. Wrap individually in waxed paper (below).

For Packing a Number of Sandwiches: Place a damp towel in shallow pan, line with waxed paper. Make double fold of paper over sandwiches, then bring towel over top (left).

Single Wrap: Place sandwiches in center of oblong of waxed paper. Bring edges together, fold down several times, turn under corners, then ends.

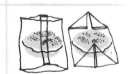

If you have a freezer, a week's supply of sandwiches can be made up at one time. Wrap in waxed paper as above, slipping name of sandwich under top fold. Avoid sandwiches with mayonnaise or lettuce. Sandwiches will be thawed by lunch time if taken from freezer at breakfast time.

FILLING SUGGESTIONS

Sandwich fillings are seldom made from written recipes but rather from ingenuity, imagination and whatever is on hand. Season to taste.

MEAT

Leftover beef roast (ground), chopped pickle and celery, prepared mustard or horse-radish, mayonnaise.

Leftover baked ham (ground), chopped pickle, mustard, mayonnaise.

Ground cooked ham or canned luncheon meat, cheese, sweet pickle and mayonnaise.

Liverwurst, slice of tomato, lettuce, mayonnaise.

FISH

Flaked tuna or salmon, sweet pickle, celery and mayonnaise.

Crabmeat, chopped celery, lemon juice and mayonnaise.

UNUSUAL

Baked bean, chili sauce, thinly sliced onion.

Sliced radishes on rye or whole wheat.

Peanut butter and chopped crisp bacon.

EGG

Chopped hard-cooked egg, pickle relish, pimiento, salad dressing.

Chopped hard-cooked egg, ripe olives, mayonnaise.

Chopped hard-cooked egg, chopped ham, minced onion and green pepper, salad dressing.

Fried or scrambled egg on whole wheat bread with catsup.

CHEESE

Cream cheese, chopped stuffed olive and nuts.

Sliced American cheese, thinly sliced fried ham, prepared mustard.

Swiss cheese, ham and pickle.

Cream cheese, Roquefort cheese and chopped nuts.

Cream cheese, drained crushed pineapple, chopped pecans.

Swiss cheese and mustard on rye bread.

Cottage cheese, minced green pepper and onion on whole wheat bread.

FROM THINGS ON HAND

CARROT-PEANUT

Combine 1½ cups grated raw carrots, ½ cup finely chopped salted peanuts, ¼ cup pickle relish, ⅓ cup salad dressing. *8 sandwiches.*

RAISIN-PEANUT BUTTER

Mix together ¾ cup crunchy peanut butter, 6 tbsp. chopped seedless raisins, 6 tbsp. orange juice. *5 sandwiches.*

FROM THAT CAN ON THE SHELF

CORNED BEEF AND EGG

Combine ¼ lb. corned beef (coarsely ground), 2 hard-cooked eggs (chopped), 1 tbsp. sweet pickle relish, ¼ cup rich milk, 1 tbsp. lemon juice, ¼ tsp. salt, pepper. *8 sandwiches.*

EGG AND DEVILED HAM

Combine 1 hard-cooked egg (chopped), ¼ cup deviled ham, 1 tbsp. Worcestershire sauce, 2 tbsp. chopped pickle. *3 sandwiches.*

SALMON SALAD

Combine 1 cup flaked salmon, ¼ tsp. salt, ½ cup finely chopped celery, ¼ cup finely chopped green pepper, 2 tbsp. mayonnaise and 2 tbsp. lemon juice. *8 sandwiches.*

SARDINE AND EGG

Combine ¼ cup mashed sardines, 2 hard-cooked eggs (chopped), 1 tbsp. pickle relish, 2 tsp. sardine or olive oil, dash of salt, 1 tbsp. salad dressing. *3 sandwiches.*

VARIETY FROM COLD CUTS

DEVILED FRANKFURTER

Mix together ½ lb. frankfurters (coarsely ground), ½ tsp. dry mustard, 3 tbsp. sweet pickle relish, 2 tbsp. rich milk and ⅓ cup salad dressing. *6 sandwiches.*

BOLOGNA-CHEESE

Grind together ¼ lb. bologna, ¼ lb. American cheese. Add ⅓ cup rich milk, 2 tbsp. sweet pickle relish, ¼ tsp. dry mustard, ⅛ tsp. salt, dash pepper. *8 sandwiches.*

FROM THE GRILL

Cheese, meat and fish sandwiches, and almost any leftover sandwiches may be grilled. Brush lightly with melted butter or spread with soft butter on both sides, and bake until golden brown on electric grill or heavy skillet.

MAKING A GOOD HAMBURGER IS AN ART!

WHAT TO BUY

Ground beef and ground round steak are both sold for hamburger. Ground beef made from chuck or trimmings and sold by a reliable meat dealer is less expensive, has even more flavor and is juicier than ground round because it has some fat through it. A pound of ground beef makes 4 thick patties or 8 thin ones.

Hamburgers come packaged and frozen or canned (plain or in mushroom sauce).

HOW TO STORE

For use same day or next, wrap loosely and refrigerate at once. To keep longer, shape into patties, place between waxed paper and keep in freezer. Patties can be wrapped in freezer paper and stored up to three months.

HOW TO MAKE JUICY HAMBURGERS

1 lb. ground beef
1 tsp. salt
1/4 tsp. pepper
2 tbsp. chopped onion

1/2 cup water or milk
flavor extender (p. 124)
Worcestershire sauce
horse-radish or mustard

Toss together lightly with a fork. Divide and form into 4 thick patties or 8 thin ones. Handle as little as possible.

Pan-fried: Fry in small amount of hot fat in skillet or without fat on electric grill until as rare or well done as you like—8 min. for rare, 12 for medium and 16 for well

done. Turn once but do not flatten—this presses out juice.

Broiled: Arrange thick patties on cold broiler pan. Broil 3″ from heat, turning once. Time same as for pan-fried.

Quick Barbecued: Broil, turning once. Spread with catsup or chili sauce after turning and continue broiling.

VARIATIONS

Cheeseburgers: When second side is half broiled, top with thin slice of cheese. Broil until cheese melts.

California Hamburger: Top cooked hamburger in bun with slice of tomato, onion, lettuce and mayonnaise.

NICE FOR LUNCH, SUPPER OR QUICK SNACKS

CORNED BEEF HASHBURGERS

Remove both ends from no. 2 can corned beef hash; push out hash and cut in 4 thick slices. Spread slices lightly with prepared mustard. Top each with a thin slice of cheese. Broil 5" from heat until cheese melts. Serve on hot buttered toasted split buns with pickles and crisp vegetable relishes. *4 servings.*

CRABMEAT SPECIAL
Broiled Crabmeat Buns
Tossed Green Salad
Fruit   Beverage

BROILED CRABMEAT BUNS

6 hamburger buns
6½-oz. can crabmeat, flaked
¼ cup mayonnaise
1 tsp. Worcestershire sauce
¼ cup diced celery
1 dill pickle, diced
6 thin slices cheese

Split and butter buns. Toast on split side. Mix remaining ingredients (except cheese); spoon onto lower half of buns; top with cheese slices. Broil 5" from heat until cheese melts. Place top on each bun. *6 servings.*

For Appetizers: This same mixture can be used on dollar-sized toast rounds with smaller pieces of cheese on top.

BACON-AND-TOMATO SANDWICH

Toast bread on one side; toast lightly on other side; spread half the slices with soft butter and mayonnaise. Top with thick tomato slices and 2 slices bacon, fried until almost crisp. Add leaf of lettuce. Place second slice of toast on top. Secure with toothpicks.

BROILED BACON-AND-TOMATO SANDWICH

Toast bread on one side and lightly on second side. Butter second side and top with thick tomato slices. Place 2 slices bacon, fried until almost crisp, on each sandwich. Top with thin slice of cheese. Broil 5" from heat until cheese melts.

CRUMBLED HAMBURGER

½ cup chopped onion
2 tbsp. fat
1 lb. ground beef
2 tbsp. flour
6 tbsp. catsup
1 tbsp. prepared mustard
½ tsp. salt
¼ tsp. pepper
1 cup sour cream
8 hamburger buns

Brown onion in hot fat; add and brown meat. Mix in remaining ingredients, except buns; simmer 5 to 10 min. Serve hot on toasted split buns. *8 servings.*

HAM-FILLED ROLLS

½ lb. cheddar-type cheese
½ lb. minced ham
2 sweet pickles
1 tsp. grated onion
2 tbsp. mayonnaise or
    salad dressing
8 to 10 buns, split and
    buttered

Heat oven to 350° (mod.). Put cheese, ham and pickles through food chopper. Add onion and mayonnaise. Spread between bun sections. Place on baking sheet; heat in oven 15 min. *8 to 10 servings.*

TOASTED BACON-CHEESE SANDWICHES

4 slices bread
8 slices bacon
1 egg, slightly beaten
¾ cup grated cheese
¼ tsp. paprika
½ tsp. Worcestershire sauce

Place bread and bacon on broiler rack. Toast bread on one side. Broil bacon until crisp. Combine remaining ingredients; spread over untoasted side of bread. Broil until cheese melts. Serve with 2 strips of bacon on each slice. *4 servings.*

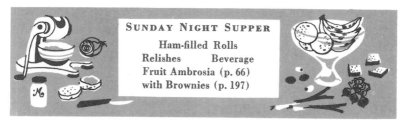

SUNDAY NIGHT SUPPER
Ham-filled Rolls
Relishes   Beverage
Fruit Ambrosia (p. 66)
with Brownies (p. 197)

SURE-FIRE SPECIAL

Slices of cold roast beef, Bermuda onion and 2 or 3 anchovy fillets between whole wheat or light rye bread slices.

PUFFY CHEESE SLICES

½ lb. cheddar-type cheese
1 egg, slightly beaten
½ tsp. each dry mustard, salt
6 slices bread, toasted one side

Cut up cheese; blend in egg and seasoning. Spread on untoasted side of bread. Broil 3″ from heat until cheese bubbles. Serve with slice of tomato, if desired.

DENVER OR WESTERN SANDWICH

For each sandwich:

1 egg, beaten
1 tbsp. minced onion
1 tbsp. minced green pepper
2 tbsp. minced cooked ham
2 tbsp. milk
salt and pepper

Combine ingredients; drop by spoonfuls into hot fat in large skillet or on greased grill. Make shape of bread slice. Turn when set and golden brown on one side; cook second side. Serve between buttered slices of bread or toast.

Fancy sandwiches accompany a bowl of soup or a fruit salad for simple entertaining. The family will like them, too, for special treats.

CREAM CHEESE- MARMALADE

Mix together thoroughly 3-oz. pkg. cream cheese, 1 to 2 tbsp. orange marmalade (for desired consistency) and grated rind of one orange. Spread on bread, toast rounds or pastry rounds. Sprinkle with chopped peanuts.

CREAM CHEESE- PINEAPPLE

Mix together thoroughly 3-oz. pkg. cream cheese, 2 tbsp. drained crushed pineapple and 1 tbsp. minced chives or young onion tops. Spread on bread or toast rounds or pastry rounds. Garnish with watercress.

CHICKEN, CRABMEAT OR TUNA

1 cup diced cooked chicken
   or 6½-oz. can crabmeat
   or tuna, flaked
½ cup finely chopped celery
1½ tsp. lemon juice
salt and pepper to taste
1 or 2 hard-cooked eggs,
   chopped
¼ cup mayonnaise

Combine all ingredients lightly. Spread on buttered bread or toast (cut in fancy shapes). Garnish with pimiento, or top with bread or toast for double sandwich.

BIT O' BACON

3-oz. pkg. cream cheese
1 tbsp. milk
2 tbsp. chopped green pepper
3 slices crisp bacon,
   crumbled
1 tsp. finely chopped onion

Soften cheese with milk. Add remaining ingredients and mix until blended.

APRICOT-NUT

3-oz. pkg. cream cheese
¼ cup apricot purée (try
   strained baby food)
dash of salt
¼ cup chopped pecans

Soften cheese; add remaining ingredients and blend.

Either of the above is excellent filling for nut bread sandwiches.

AVOCADO-BACON

1 ripe avocado
1 tsp. finely minced onion
1 tbsp. lemon juice
½ tsp. salt
dash cayenne pepper
2 strips bacon, fried crisp

Peel and mash avocado; blend in onion, lemon juice and seasonings. Spread on fancy shapes of bread or toast (no butter needed). Crumble bacon and sprinkle over top.

UNCOOKED   COOKED

1 cup macaroni = 2 cups

1 cup rice = 3 cups

Follow cooking directions on pkg.

OLD-FASHIONED MACARONI AND CHEESE

4 cups cooked macaroni
(8-oz. pkg.)
2 tbsp. butter, cut in pieces
1¼ cups cubed sharp cheese
½ tsp. salt
¼ tsp. pepper
2 eggs, beaten
3 cups milk

Heat oven to 350° (mod.). Combine macaroni, butter, cheese and seasonings. Place in greased 2-qt. baking dish. Combine eggs and milk; pour over macaroni. Sprinkle with paprika or buttered crumbs. Bake 40 to 50 min. *6 servings.*

Tomato Macaroni: Substitute 2 cups canned tomato for 2 cups of the milk in Old-fashioned Macaroni and Cheese. Add with cheese.

Meaty Macaroni: To Old-fashioned Macaroni and Cheese, add about 1 cup canned luncheon meat, diced, or ¼ lb. ready-to-eat sausage, diced, along with cheese.

MACARONI SAUTÉ
See picture on p. 74.

2 cups elbow macaroni
(8-oz. pkg.), uncooked
½ cup chopped onion
½ cup chopped green pepper
1 clove garlic, minced
½ cup cooking (salad) oil
3 cups tomato juice
1 tsp. salt
¼ tsp. pepper
2 tsp. Worcestershire sauce

Sauté macaroni, onion, green pepper and garlic in hot oil till macaroni turns slightly yellow. Add tomato juice and seasonings; bring to boiling. Cover and simmer 20 min. *6 servings.*

MACARONI CUPS
A lift to leftover ham.

2 cups cooked macaroni
(1 cup uncooked)
½ cup leftover bits of
baked ham
1 cup cubed cheese
1 tsp. prepared mustard
1 tsp. horse-radish
1 cup Medium Cream Sauce
(p. 122)

Heat oven to 400° (mod. hot). Combine all ingredients; place in greased individual casseroles or 1-qt. baking dish. Top with buttered crumbs or crushed Wheaties. Bake 20 to 25 min. *4 servings.*

LEFTOVERS

Leftover noodles, macaroni, spaghetti and rice can be reheated. Rinse first with cold water to remove excess starch. Drop into boiling water, heat 5 min., drain.

TOMATO SAUCE FOR MACARONI OR SPAGHETTI
Can be made ahead of time, with or without meat.

2 medium onions, diced
1 clove garlic, minced
2 tbsp. cooking (salad) oil
no. 2 can tomato juice
6-oz. can tomato paste
1 tbsp. chili sauce

1 tsp. basil
½ tsp. sugar
½ tsp. salt
¼ tsp. pepper
dash cayenne

Brown onion and garlic in hot oil. Add remaining ingredients; bring to boiling and simmer 30 min., stirring occasionally. Serve hot over cooked macaroni or spaghetti; sprinkle with Parmesan cheese. *4 servings.*

Meaty Tomato Sauce: Brown ½ lb. ground beef with the onions in making the sauce.

MACARONI SUPPER CASSEROLE

4 cups cooked macaroni (8-oz. pkg.)
½ cup mayonnaise
¼ cup diced green pepper
¼ cup chopped pimiento
1 small onion, chopped
½ tsp. salt
10½-oz. can cream of mushroom soup blended with ½ cup milk
1 cup grated cheese (¼ lb.)

Heat oven to 425° (hot). Combine all ingredients, using only half the cheese. Pour into greased 1½-qt. casserole. Sprinkle with remaining cheese. Bake 20 min. *6 servings.*

Tuna-roni Casserole: Use 6½-oz. can tuna in place of mayonnaise in Macaroni Supper Casserole (above).

NOODLES CANTONESE

½ lb. lean pork
1 tbsp. fat or oil
salt and pepper
½ cup water
2 cups cooked noodles (4-oz. pkg.)
1 cup sliced celery
1 cup thinly sliced fresh or frozen French green beans
1½ tbsp. grated onion
2 tbsp. soy sauce

Cut pork in very thin slivers; brown in hot fat. Add seasoning and water; cook 20 min. While meat is cooking, cook noodles in 2 qt. boiling salted water (2 tsp. salt). Combine all ingredients; cook 5 min. *4 servings.*

Tuna-noodle Bake: Follow recipe for Tuna-roni Casserole but use 4 cups cooked noodles (8-oz. pkg.) in place of macaroni.

CORNED BEEF AND CORN

Fry 2 medium onions, chopped, in 2 tbsp. hot fat. Add 12-oz. can corned beef (cut in small pieces) and no. 2 can cream-style corn. Stir to mix. Heat and serve. *4 to 6 servings.*

QUICK DRIED BEEF ON TOAST

Thin 10½-oz. can condensed cream of mushroom soup with ½ soup can milk. Cut in pieces and add 4-oz. can dried beef (¼ lb.). Serve on toast. *4 servings.*

EGGS AND CHIPS

Heat oven to 400° (mod. hot). Place 1 cup crushed potato chips in 1-qt. greased casserole. Add 6 hard-cooked eggs, sliced. Blend together 10½-oz. can cream of mushroom soup, ½ cup milk and 2 tbsp. finely chopped onion. Season with salt and pepper. Pour over eggs. Sprinkle with another cup crushed potato chips. Bake 25 min., until bubbly. *6 servings.*

ASPARAGUS ON DEVILED HAM TOAST

Spread toast with deviled ham. Top each slice with 5 or 6 stalks cooked asparagus. Pour hot Cheese Sauce (p. 122) over it.

CHILI-ETTI

Combine one can chili and one can spaghetti; mix gently to avoid mashing. Heat and eat. *4 servings.*

POACHED EGGS ON DEVILED HAM TOAST

Spread toast with deviled ham. Top each slice with a poached egg. Add Cheese Sauce (p. 122), if desired.

HASH HATS

Heat oven to 350° (mod.). Break apart with a fork 1-lb. can corned beef hash; blend in ¼ cup finely chopped sweet pickle or pickle relish. Place four ¼″ slices Bermuda onion in baking dish. Season with salt and pepper; top with butter. Mold hash in rounds on onion slices. Bake 20 min. Serve with hot chili sauce. *4 servings.*

HASH ROUNDS

Chill a can of corned beef hash. Open both ends and push out. Cut in 4 rounds. Broil 3″ from heat for about 7 min. Turn; spread thinly with horse-radish; top with tomato slice. Sprinkle with seasoning and grated cheese. Broil 5 min., until cheese is bubbly. *4 servings.*

BAKED RICE, CHEESE AND TOMATO

1 cup boiling water
5-oz. pkg. precooked rice
2 cups grated American
   cheese (½ lb.)
1½ tsp. salt
pepper
¼ tsp. Worcestershire sauce
2 cups Medium Cream Sauce
   (p. 122)
3 tomatoes, sliced

Heat oven to 400° (mod. hot). Pour water over rice; let stand. Add cheese and seasonings to Cream Sauce. Alternate rice, cheese sauce and tomato slices in greased 2-qt. baking dish. Bake 20 to 25 min., until golden brown. *6 servings.*

CHINESE PORK AND RICE

⅔ cup uncooked rice
2 tbsp. cooking (salad) oil
1 tsp. salt
1½ cups boiling water
1 bouillon cube
2 tsp. soy sauce
1 medium onion, chopped
2 stalks celery, chopped
1 green pepper, chopped
1 cup diced cooked pork

Cook rice in hot oil until golden brown. Add salt, water, bouillon cube, soy sauce. Cover; cook 20 min. Add rest of ingredients and ¼ cup more water, if necessary. Cover tightly, cook 10 min. more. *4 servings.*

SPANISH RICE

4 slices bacon, cut up
¼ cup finely chopped onion
¼ cup chopped green pepper
3 cups cooked rice (1 cup
   uncooked)
2 cups canned tomatoes
1½ tsp. salt
⅛ tsp. pepper
¼ cup grated cheese

Heat oven to 400° (mod. hot). Fry bacon until crisp; remove to 1½-qt. casserole and whisk bacon around to grease casserole. Add onion and green pepper to bacon fat; cook until onion is yellow. Combine all ingredients in casserole. Sprinkle cheese over top. Bake 25 to 30 min. *4 to 6 servings.*

CHICKEN-RICE BAKE

Especially nice for entertaining.

3 cups cooked rice (1 cup
   uncooked)
2-oz. jar pimiento
¼ cup or 4-oz. can
   mushrooms
½ cup blanched almonds
1½ cups cooked chicken
½ cup sliced celery
1½ cups chicken broth
salt and pepper
1½ tbsp. flour

Heat oven to 350° (mod.). Sauté mushrooms and almonds in butter. Combine rice and pimiento; place ⅓ in greased casserole; alternate chicken, celery, mushroom-almond mixture with remaining rice. Pour over this the chicken broth, seasoned with salt and pepper and blended with flour. Bake 1 hr. *6 to 8 servings.*

CREAMED EGGS ON TOAST

4 hard-cooked eggs
1 cup well seasoned Medium
Cream Sauce (p. 122)

Cut eggs in quarters; add to Cream Sauce. Serve on hot buttered toast or in Toast Cups (p. 55). Sprinkle with paprika. *4 servings.*

Goldenrod Eggs: Make Creamed Eggs (above), reserving 2 egg yolks. Serve on toast; press yolks through sieve or tea strainer to decorate tops.

Creamed Tuna or Salmon and Eggs: Add 1 cup flaked tuna or salmon to Creamed Eggs.

Creamed Dried Beef and Eggs: Frizzle 1 cup dried beef in butter; add to eggs.

Creamed Ham and Eggs: Add 1 cup diced cooked ham and ¼ cup mushrooms (browned in butter used in making Cream Sauce) to eggs.

CONTENTS OF CANS

Of the different sizes of cans used by commercial canners, the most common are:

Size	Average Contents
8-oz.	1 cup
picnic	1¼ cups
no. 300	1¾ cups
no. 1 tall	2 cups
no. 303	2 cups
no. 2	2½ cups
no. 2½	3½ cups
no. 3	4 cups
no. 10	12 to 13 cups

WELSH RAREBIT

2 cups grated sharp
    American cheese (½ lb.)
⅔ cup milk
¼ tsp. dry mustard
¼ tsp. Worcestershire sauce
⅛ tsp. salt
dash of pepper

Melt cheese over hot water; gradually add milk and stir until smooth. Blend in seasonings. Serve on crisp crackers or toast. *4 servings.*

Welsh Rarebit Sandwich: Make Welsh Rarebit and serve over toasted Bacon-and-Tomato Sandwiches (p. 45).

½ lb. cheese = 2 cups grated

PINK BUNNY

¼ cup minced onion
¼ cup minced green pepper,
    if desired
2 tbsp. butter
3 tbsp. flour
1 cup cooked tomatoes
1½ cups grated sharp cheese
½ tsp. salt
¼ tsp. dry mustard
¼ tsp. Worcestershire sauce

Cook onion and green pepper in butter until soft. Stir in flour; let bubble. Add tomato, cheese and seasonings. Cook over hot water 15 min. Serve over toast or crackers. *4 servings.*

Brer Rabbit: Make Pink Bunny, adding 1 cup whole kernel corn with tomato and cheese.

EASY CHEESE FONDUE

4 slices bread, cut in half
   and buttered
1 cup cheese, cut in small
   pieces or grated (¼ lb.)
½ tsp. dry mustard

2 eggs, well beaten
2 cups milk
½ tsp. salt
⅛ tsp. pepper

Heat oven to 350° (mod.). Place bread in shallow oblong baking dish 8 x 12". Spread cheese over bread; sprinkle with mustard. Mix egg, milk, and seasoning; pour over bread. Bake 30 min., until puffy and brown. If desired, dish can stand ready for the oven up to 1 hr. before baking. *4 servings.*

Ham-Cheese Fondue: Scatter 1 cup diced leftover ham over bread before adding cheese.

Shrimp-Cheese Fondue: Scatter 1 cup cut-up cooked shrimp over bread before adding cheese.

Tuna-Cheese Fondue: Scatter 6½-oz. can tuna, flaked, over bread before cheese.

CHEESE SOUFFLÉ

1 cup grated sharp cheese
1 cup Thick Cream Sauce
   (p. 122)

3 egg yolks, well beaten
¼ tsp. cream of tartar
3 egg whites

Heat oven to 350° (mod.). Blend cheese into Cream Sauce; add egg yolks. Add cream of tartar to egg whites; beat until stiff. Fold in cheese mixture. Pour into ungreased 1½-qt. baking dish; make groove with spoon 1" from edge. Bake in pan of hot water (1" deep) 50 to 60 min., until puffed and golden brown. *4 servings.*

Tomato Cheese Soufflé: Use tomato juice in place of milk.

SPEEDY TUNA SOUFFLÉ

10½-oz. can cream of
   celery soup
6½-oz. can tuna, flaked

4 egg yolks, beaten thick
   and lemon-colored
4 egg whites, beaten stiff

Heat oven to 300° (slow). Heat half of soup in saucepan; stir in tuna. Remove from heat. Blend into egg yolks. Fold into egg whites.

Pour into ungreased 1½-qt. baking dish. Bake 50 to 60 min. Dilute remaining soup with ¼ can water. Heat and serve as sauce. *4 to 5 servings.*

QUICK CORNED BEEF AND CABBAGE

½ cup chopped onion
2 tbsp. hot fat
3 cups finely shredded
   cabbage
½ 12-oz. can corned beef
½ tsp. salt
¼ tsp. pepper
½ cup water

Sauté onion in hot fat; stir in remaining ingredients. Cover and cook 6 to 8 min. *4 servings.*

RUTH'S HASH

2 cups ground cooked meat
3 cups finely ground raw
   potatoes
½ cup ground onion
1 cup milk
1 tsp. salt
¼ tsp. pepper
2 tbsp. butter

Heat oven to 350° (mod.). Mix meat, potatoes and onion; add milk and seasoning. Place in greased 1½-qt. casserole. Dot with butter. Bake about 1 hr.

Serving Suggestion: Serve with heated catsup or chili sauce.

QUICK BAKED BEANS

See picture, p. 235.

few pieces crisply fried bacon
   or small leftover ham bone
   or fried salt pork
19-oz. can baked beans
1 tbsp. vinegar
1 tbsp. catsup
¼ tsp. dry mustard
1 medium onion, sliced

Heat oven to 350° (mod.). Mix all ingredients in 1-qt. casserole. Bake about 1 hr. *4 servings.*

Variations: Brown sugar, molasses or fruit juices may be added. With fruit juices, omit catsup.

POTATO-EGG SCRAMBLE

A good and easy treat for lunch in a hurry, when you have some boiled potatoes on hand. Dice 4 or 5 medium potatoes, boiled. Dice 6 slices bacon and fry until crisp; pour off half the fat. Add potatoes and onions (1 bunch green or 1 dry finely chopped); fry until lightly browned. Add 4 eggs and seasonings. Stir gently until eggs are lightly set.

KEEPING CASSEROLES

You can bake your casserole ahead, all but the last 20 min. Cool and store in refrigerator, covered—with self-sealing plastic if your baking dish has no cover. Allow 10 min. extra baking time for rewarming.

ESPECIALLY FOR THE GIRLS

QUICK CHICKEN À LA KING

10½-oz. can cream of
   mushroom soup
5-oz. can boned chicken, diced
2-oz. jar pimiento, cut up
½ cup cut-up celery (raw or
   cooked)

Heat soup; stir in remaining ingredients. Heat thoroughly and
season to taste. Serve in Patty
Shells (p. 193) or Toast Cups.

Toast Cups: Heat oven to 350°
(mod.). Cut crusts from bread;
brush lightly with melted butter.
Press into muffin pan or custard
cups. Toast in oven 15 to 20 min.

FOURSOME LUNCH

One of the Recipes on This Page
Melba Toast or Toasted Rolls
Citrus Fruit Salad
Cookies
Beverage

ASPARAGUS HAM ROLLS

16 stalks cooked asparagus
4 thin slices boiled ham
1 cup Cheese Sauce (p. 122)

Roll 4 stalks asparagus in each
ham slice. Secure with toothpicks. Place in broiler, 3″ from
heat; broil 5 min., turn and broil
on other side. Serve with Cheese
Sauce.

SCALLOP CASSEROLE

1 pt. scallops
½ to ¾ cup cream
½ cup butter (¼ lb.), melted
1 tsp. salt
¼ tsp. pepper
3 cups soft bread crumbs
1 tbsp. celery seed

Heat oven to 375° (quick mod.).
Arrange scallops in greased 7½ x
11½ x 1½″ baking dish. Over
them pour thin layer of cream.
Toss together remaining ingredients; sprinkle over scallops.
Over this pour more cream; it
should come three-fourths of the
way up on scallops. Sprinkle with
paprika. Bake 30 to 40 min. Serve
in shells, if you have them.

SHRIMP 'N' RICE CASSEROLE

1 tbsp. butter
1½ cups cream
5-oz. can shrimp
2 cups cooked rice (⅔ cup
   if uncooked)
¼ cup catsup
¼ tsp. Tabasco sauce
1 tsp. Worcestershire sauce

Melt butter in saucepan; add remaining ingredients. Bring to
boil and simmer 5 min.

Note: Can be prepared ahead
and allowed to mellow. To reheat in casserole, bake in mod.
oven (350°) about 15 min.

The good old days are fun to recall. Don't "forget to remember" these lunchtime stand-bys of years ago. They are every bit as good and easy today.

Cereal Fruit Milk or Cream	Chili Con Carne (canned) Crisp Crackers Dill Pickles
Fried Corn Meal Mush Maple Syrup	Milk Apple Hot Gingerbread
Asparagus on Toast Cheese Sauce Crisp Bacon	Eggnog Grapes Salty Crackers
Corned Beef Hash Poached Eggs	Hot Cereal Brown Sugar and Cream
Potato Soup Hot Buttered Toast	Creamed Chipped Beef over Asparagus on Toast
Strawberries and Cream over Hot Buttered Toast	Fruit Milk Popcorn
Milk Toast	Chipped Beef on Baked Potato
Waffles Butter and Syrup	Scrambled Eggs with Onion and Tomato

PICTURE PLATE SALAD LUNCHEONS

For entertaining at lunch or supper in summertime.

SUNBURST FRUIT PLATE

See picture on p. 75.

Red apple slices
Orange slices
Sliced banana
Green seedless grapes
Melon slices
Cheese-stuffed prunes

Arranged on garden lettuce, centered with orange sherbet and accompanied by thin nut bread sandwiches and iced tea. Pass a sweet fruit dressing or combination of French and mayonnaise.

THREE-IN-ONE

Small tomato stuffed with
    cottage cheese and chives
Chicken salad
Ripe olives, celery, pimiento
Grapefruit sections, orange
    and avocado slices
Watercress garnish

Arranged in lettuce cups, accompanied by toasted English Muffins and coffee. Pass double dish of mayonnaise for chicken and tomato, sweet fruit dressing for fruit.

GARDEN PATCH QUILT

See picture on p. 75.

Tomato sections
Notched cucumber slices
Oval carrot slices
    (cut diagonally)
Green beans
Cauliflowerets marinated in
    French dressing

Arranged in lettuce cups, accompanied by toasted cheese-topped wiener buns and milk. Creamy mayonnaise in glass cup in center. You make your own combinations as you eat. Any selection of cooked or raw vegetables may be used.

MAKING A LETTUCE CUP
Slit leaf part way and overlap.

VEGETABLE COMBINATIONS

Tomato and cottage cheese with French dressing.

Grated raw carrots with raisins or peanuts, salad dressing.

Shredded cabbage, grated carrot, chopped green pepper and onion with mayonnaise.

Shredded cabbage, tart red apple and diced cheese with salad dressing.

Frozen mixed vegetables (cooked and chilled) or mixed canned vegetables (chilled) with crumbled Roquefort cheese and French dressing.

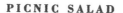

PICNIC SALAD

Add ½ cup each of sliced radishes, chopped green onions, diced unpared cucumber to 1 pt. creamy cottage cheese. Season with salt and pepper. For special meals, add ¼ to ½ cup sour cream. *6 servings.*

KIDNEY BEAN SALAD

Mix together 2 cups drained chilled kidney beans (no. 2 can), 1 tbsp. minced onion, ¼ cup each chopped celery and sweet pickle. Add 2 chopped hard-cooked eggs, salt and pepper, and enough mayonnaise to moisten. *4 servings.*

GREEN AND GOLD SALAD

Combine 1½ cups cooked peas, ¼ cup diced American cheese, 2 tbsp. minced onion. Toss together with ¼ cup cooked dressing and 1 tbsp. prepared mustard. Chill. *4 servings.*

MEXICAN GREEN BEAN SALAD

Marinate 2 cups cooked thinly sliced fresh or frozen French green beans in 2 or 3 tbsp. French dressing with ¼ cup minced onion several hours or overnight. Add 3 to 4 tbsp. grated sharp cheese. Garnish with red or white onion rings. *4 servings.*

CHEF'S SALAD

1 head lettuce
½ bunch romaine or endive
½ cup chopped green onion
½ cup sliced celery
1 cup match-like sticks of
  Swiss cheese
1 cup match-like strips of cold
  cooked meat (beef, ham,
  tongue, bologna)
2-oz. can flat fillets of
  anchovy, if desired

Rub bowl with cut clove of garlic. Toss greens, onion and celery in bowl. Arrange mixed greens over top of the cheese and meat. Just before serving, toss with ½ cup mayonnaise blended with ¼ cup French dressing. *4 servings.*

MACARONI-SALMON SALAD

2 cups cooked and cooled
  macaroni (1 cup broken,
  uncooked)
1 cup diced cucumber
8-oz. can salmon, flaked
1 tbsp. grated onion
1 tbsp. minced parsley
¾ cup mayonnaise
½ tsp. salt
¼ tsp. pepper

Combine all ingredients; toss together until blended. Serve hot or cold. *4 to 6 servings.*

Variations: Tuna or leftover cooked meat, chicken or veal (1½ cups) may be used in place of salmon.

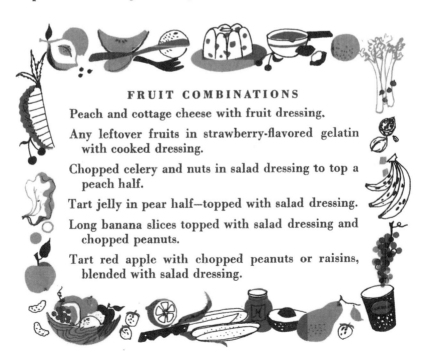

FRUIT COMBINATIONS

Peach and cottage cheese with fruit dressing.

Any leftover fruits in strawberry-flavored gelatin with cooked dressing.

Chopped celery and nuts in salad dressing to top a peach half.

Tart jelly in pear half—topped with salad dressing.

Long banana slices topped with salad dressing and chopped peanuts.

Tart red apple with chopped peanuts or raisins, blended with salad dressing.

PRETTY PARTY LUNCH
Hot Chicken Salad
Assorted Relishes   Hot Rolls
Chiffon Cake with
Orange Sauce or Cocoa Fluff
(pp. 163, 168, 170)

CHIP-CHICKEN SALAD

1½ cups cut-up chicken
   (5-oz. can, boned)
½ cup sliced celery
½ cup chopped green pepper
2 tsp. minced green onion
⅓ cup mayonnaise
1 cup crushed potato or corn
   chips

Toss together all ingredients except chips; chill. Toss in chips;
serve on crisp lettuce. Garnish
with slices of honeydew melon
and strawberries. *4 servings.*

CHICKEN-FRUIT SALAD

2 cups cut-up cooked chicken
1 cup sliced celery
1 cup green seedless grapes
1 tbsp. lemon juice
½ cup mayonnaise

Combine chicken, celery, grapes
and lemon juice. Chill. Before
serving, fold in mayonnaise.
Serve on lettuce. *6 servings.*

Holiday Chicken Salad: Make
Chicken Fruit Salad, using ½
cup toasted almonds in place of
grapes. Serve on thick slices of
canned cranberry sauce on lettuce.

HOT CHICKEN SALAD

2 cups cut-up cooked chicken
   (crabmeat may be used
   instead)
2 cups thinly sliced celery
½ cup chopped toasted
   almonds or peanuts
½ tsp. salt
2 tsp. grated onion
1 cup mayonnaise
2 tbsp. lemon juice
½ cup grated cheese
1 cup crushed potato chips

Heat oven to 450° (hot). Combine ingredients, except cheese
and potato chips. Pile lightly in
sea shells or individual baking
dishes. Sprinkle with cheese and
potato chips. Bake 10 to 15 min.
6 servings.

SHRIMP SALAD

5-oz. can shrimp (¾ lb. fresh
   shrimp, cooked)
1 cup sliced celery
2 hard-cooked eggs, cut up
1 tbsp. lemon juice
½ cup mayonnaise

Combine cleaned and cooked
shrimp, celery, egg and lemon
juice. Chill. Before serving, fold
in mayonnaise. Serve on lettuce.
2 servings.

Variation: Crabmeat, tuna, salmon or lobster may be used in
place of shrimp.

**LUNCH OR
SUMMER SUPPER**
Shrimp Salad
Toasted Bacon-and-Tomato
Sandwiches (p. 45)
Fruit   Beverage

PACIFIC LIME MOLD

1 cup boiling water
1 pkg. lime-flavored gelatin
9-oz. can crushed pineapple
1 cup creamy cottage cheese
1 tsp. horse-radish
½ cup mayonnaise or ½ cup
　heavy cream, whipped
¼ cup chopped nuts

Dissolve gelatin in water. Add juice from pineapple; chill until slightly thickened. Beat until frothy. Fold in remaining ingredients. Chill until set. *6 servings.*

Variation: 1 cup mashed banana and 2 tbsp. lemon juice may be used in place of cottage cheese and horse-radish.

FROZEN FRUIT SALAD

1 tbsp. or 1 envelope
　unflavored gelatin
¼ cup cold water
⅓ cup mild mayonnaise or
　salad dressing
1 cup heavy cream, whipped
1 cup canned pineapple
　chunks
1 cup sliced bananas
1 cup cut-up oranges
½ cup halved maraschino
　cherries, dates and nuts
2 tbsp. lemon juice

Soften gelatin in cold water; dissolve over hot water. Blend into mayonnaise and whipped cream. Fold in fruits and juice. Pour into refrigerator tray; freeze until firm. Serve on lettuce. *8 servings.*

POTATO SALAD

See pictures, pp. 77, 234.

4 cups cubed cooked
　potatoes
¼ cup clear French
　dressing (or ¼ cup
　salad oil and
　2 tbsp. vinegar)
3 hard-cooked eggs,
　cut up
1 cup diced celery
2 to 3 tbsp. chopped
　onion
½ cup salad dressing,
　mayonnaise or Sour
　Cream Dressing
　(p. 153)

Marinate potatoes in French dressing for 1 to 2 hr. Add remaining ingredients; season with salt and pepper. Serve in lettuce-lined bowl; garnish with 1 hard-cooked egg, parsley and pimiento. *6 servings.*

Variations: Add 3 tbsp. chopped green pepper, pimiento or sweet pickle.

Add ¼ cup grated carrots, sliced radishes or diced cucumber.

Add ½ cup diced cooked ham or luncheon meat.

Potato Salad Tips: Potatoes have better flavor if cooked in skins or baked.

Cut potatoes while warm, not cold.

Marinating potatoes improves flavor.

TO SERVE WITH SOUPS AND SALADS

TOASTED CHEESE ROLLS

Cut rolls in half lengthwise. Butter lightly; sprinkle with grated
cheese. Toast cheese side up under broiler until golden brown.

MELBA RYE WAFERS

Slice small-loaf salty rye bread
thin. Spread with soft butter.
Toast buttered side up under
broiler.

CHEESE PUFFS

Made in a jiffy from Brown 'n
Serve Rolls. The cheese topping
melts and puffs up while baking.

**Brown 'n Serve pan rolls or
tea biscuits
2 cups grated sharp cheese
(½ lb.)
2 tbsp. soft butter
½ tsp. dry mustard
¼ tsp. salt
⅛ tsp. pepper**

Split Brown 'n Serve Rolls in two
crosswise. Combine remaining
ingredients. Place a tablespoon
of the cheese mixture on each
half roll. Bake as directed on pkg.

Recipes for Refrigerator Rolls,
Hot Buttered Bread, Brown 'n
Serve variations and other quick
and novel breads are on pp. 154
and 155.

Recipes for other breads are on
pp. 156 and 157.

TOASTED ENGLISH MUFFINS

Split the muffins crosswise with a
knife or pull them apart with a
fork. Spread cut sides with butter. Toast buttered side up under
broiler.

LIGHTNING-QUICK HERB BISCUITS

Follow recipe for Biscuits on Bisquick pkg., first mixing ¼ tsp.
nutmeg, ½ tsp. crumbled dry
sage and 1¼ tsp. caraway seeds
with the Bisquick.

CHEESE ROLLS

Heat oven to 350° (mod.). Remove crusts from thin slices of
fresh bread. Spread with softened butter and sprinkle with
grated cheese. Roll up; fasten
each with toothpicks. Toast in
oven until lightly browned.

HOT BUTTERED BREAD STICKS

Heat oven to 350° (mod.). Butter slices of bread on one side. Cut each slice into 6 equal strips and place buttered side down on baking sheet; then butter top side of each. Bake until crisp, turning to brown each stick on both sides.

Celery-seed Sticks: Sprinkle Buttered Bread Sticks with celery seeds before toasting.

Sesame-seed Sticks: Sprinkle Buttered Bread Sticks with sesame seeds before toasting.

Poppy-seed Sticks: Sprinkle Buttered Bread Sticks with poppy seeds before toasting.

BUTTER-CRISP BREAD

Melted butter drips down over slices as they brown.

½ loaf sliced bread
6 tbsp. soft butter

Heat oven to 400° (mod. hot). Cut stacks of slices in halves crosswise; stand, cut edges up, in loaf pan. Spread butter over top of bread. Bake until golden brown and crisp, about 20 min. *6 servings.*

Recipes for Muffins, Coffee Cakes, Coffee Breads, Biscuits, Yeast Rolls, toast variations and Pancakes and Waffles that are just as appropriate for lunch as for breakfast are on pp. 10 through 29.

LIGHTNING-QUICK NUT BREAD

You can't tell it from old-fashioned nut bread. It has the same rich flavor, the same lasting freshness you've always liked in the nut bread you've made the long way.

½ cup sugar
1 egg
1¼ cups milk
1½ cups chopped nuts
3 cups Bisquick

Heat oven to 350° (mod.). Mix sugar, egg, milk and nuts. Stir in Bisquick. Beat hard 30 sec. Pour into well greased loaf pan, 9 x 5 x 2½". Bake until toothpick thrust into center comes out clean, 45 to 50 min. A slight crack in top is characteristic. Cool slightly before cutting with a bread knife.

Fruit-Nut Bread: Apricot, Raisin, Date or Fig. Follow directions for Nut Bread above, except—use ¾ cup sugar, and use orange juice instead of milk. Use only ¾ cup chopped nuts and add 1 cup raisins or other chopped dried fruit. Bake 55 to 60 min.

63

HOT COCOA

Follow directions for cocoa you are using.

Extra Richness: In place of plain milk, use evaporated milk diluted according to directions on the can.

Interesting Flavor: Just before serving, add dash of either cinnamon or vanilla.

Cocoa Continental: Pour hot cocoa over a marshmallow in each cup; or top with whipped cream.

Ready-to-serve Cocoa: In powdered form, it has sweetening, powdered milk, and flavoring already mixed in. You need only add hot or cold water or milk, mix well and serve.

Note: To avoid "skin" forming on top of cocoa, beat until frothy with rotary beater as soon as cocoa is made.

HOT CHOCOLATE

1 cup water
2 sq. unsweetened chocolate
  (2 oz.)
pinch of salt
3 to 4 tbsp. sugar
3 cups milk

Heat water and chocolate together over low heat, stirring until chocolate melts. Stir in salt and sugar. Boil 4 min., stirring. Then slowly stir in milk. Heat until scalded. Do not boil. Just before serving, beat with rotary beater until smooth. Serve hot, topped with whipped cream. *6 servings.*

CHOCOLATE SYRUP

Excellent to keep on hand for making a variety of chocolate drinks. Buy it ready-prepared. Or make it yourself from the following recipe.

1 cup cocoa or 4 sq.
  unsweetened chocolate
  (4 oz.)
2 cups sugar
¼ tsp. salt
2 cups cold water
1 tbsp. vanilla

Combine cocoa or chocolate, sugar and salt in saucepan. Stir in water. Simmer until smooth and thick, stirring or beating with rotary beater. Cool. Stir in vanilla. Pour into jar, cover well and store in refrigerator.

ICED CHOCOLATE

Cool Hot Chocolate. Pour over cracked ice. Top with whipped cream.

MILK SHAKES

1 cup thoroughly chilled
milk
fruit, chocolate or other
flavoring (see below)

Shake or beat milk with fruit or other flavoring (and ice cream, if desired) until well blended. Serve cold, topped with whipped cream and sprinkled with nutmeg.

Banana Milk Shake: Use ½ banana, mashed.

Orange Blossom Milk Shake: Use 1 cup orange juice, ⅛ tsp. almond flavoring and sugar to taste.

Prune Milk Shake: Use ½ cup prune juice.

Strawberry Milk Shake: Use ¼ cup crushed sweetened berries.

Chocolate Milk Shake: Use 1½ to 2 tbsp. Chocolate Syrup (p. 64).

Frosted Chocolate: Beat a small spoonful of ice cream into each Chocolate Milk Shake.

Chocolate Malted Milk: Beat 1 tbsp. malted milk powder into each Chocolate Milk Shake.

INSTANT MALTED MILK DRINKS

Make malted milks in a hurry from either of the malted milk powders on the market: (1) plain unflavored malted milk powder and (2) sweetened milk powder to which malt extracts and chocolate or cocoa have been added. Just add hot or cold water or milk, mix and serve.

EGGNOGS

1 egg, well beaten
2 tbsp. sugar
1 cup chilled rich milk
¼ tsp. vanilla (or 1½ tbsp.
sherry flavoring and 1 tbsp.
brandy or rum flavoring)
dash of nutmeg

Beat together egg and sugar. Then beat in milk and flavoring of your choice. Serve cold, sprinkled lightly with nutmeg.

Fruit Eggnog: Use 2 tbsp. fruit or 1 tbsp. fruit juice (grape, orange or cherry, etc.) instead of vanilla and nutmeg.

Chocolate Eggnog: Omit sugar and beat 2 tbsp. Chocolate Syrup (p. 64) with the egg.

Ready-to-serve Eggnog: Many dealers sell it. You add flavoring.

FRUIT FOR DESSERT

Fruit makes an easy finish to a meal, and almost everyone's favorite finish, too. Enjoy fresh fruits in season, quick-frozen and canned fruits the year around. Serve them plain, with crispy crackers and your favorite cheese, whole or cut up, with plain or whipped cream, whipped ice cream, fruit sherbet or soft custard. Fruit is fine any way!

Choose the canned or frozen fruit that is specially suited to your need. Apples, for example, come sliced for cakes and pies, cubed for compotes, in applesauce sweetened or unsweetened, and baked all ready to serve.

FRUIT AMBROSIA
See picture on p. 79.

Make it with almost any fruit you have on hand.

Sprinkle the fruit (such as cut-up orange slices, bananas and apples, or pineapple) with confectioners' sugar. Chill. To dress up, top with plain or toasted shredded coconut, salted peanuts or maraschino cherries just before serving.

FRUIT...WITH FRUIT SHERBET

One of many delectable combinations to serve when company comes.

Sprinkle cubes of pineapple or other fresh fruit with a little confectioners' sugar. Chill. When ready to serve, place scoop of lime sherbet in each individual serving dish and surround with the sweetened fruit.

BERRIES OR GRAPES WITH BROWN SUGAR

Cover washed berries or seedless green grapes with brown sugar. Serve cold with thick sweet or sour cream, or with cream cheese beaten smooth with cream.

PINEAPPLE ZIP

2 cups diced pineapple
½ cup orange juice
2 tbsp. maraschino cherry syrup
¼ cup confectioners' sugar
dash of cinnamon

Combine ingredients. Cover and chill thoroughly. *4 servings.*

MINTED GRAPEFRUIT

2 cups grapefruit sections and
    juice (fresh or canned)
about 20 crushed after-dinner
    mints or peppermints

Mix. Cover. Chill thoroughly to
blend flavors. *4 servings.*

FRUIT-MARSHMALLOW CREAM

about 14 marshmallows,
    quartered
¼ cup milk
¼ cup heavy cream, whipped
sweetened sliced strawberries,
    bananas or maraschino
    cherries

Let marshmallows soak in milk
½ hr., then fold into stiffly whipped cream. Chill thoroughly.
Serve garnished with the sliced
fruit. *4 to 6 servings.*

FRUIT WHIP

1 cup slightly sweetened,
    sieved, drained cooked
    fruit (dried apricots,
    prunes or applesauce may
    be prepared ahead and
    chilled, or puréed fruits
    for infants may be used)
¼ to ⅓ cup sugar
1 tsp. lemon juice
dash of salt
2 egg whites, stiffly beaten

Into mixture of fruit, sugar, lemon juice and salt, fold stiffly beat-
en egg whites. Chill. *4 servings.*

Extra Touches: Soft Custard
(p. 172), chilled, makes a tasty
topping, using two egg yolks and
1 whole egg.

A spoonful of whipped cream
gives each serving a touch of elegance.

FANCY FRUITS FOR THE FAMILY

STRAWBERRIES AU NATUREL:
Serve circle of washed unhulled
strawberries around mound of
confectioners' sugar on each
plate. Eat with fingers.

BROILED GRAPEFRUIT: Sprinkle with a bit of brown or maple
sugar. Broil slowly until heated
(15 to 20 min.). Add a little
maraschino cherry juice or sherry flavoring. Serve hot.

STEWED FRESH FRUIT
(Apples, Peaches, Pears,
Plums, Rhubarb)

1 cup boiling water
4 cups prepared fruit
   (washed, peeled and cut
   up as desired)
½ to 1 cup sugar
dash of salt
1 tsp. lemon juice
⅛ tsp. grated lemon rind
⅛ tsp. cinnamon, cloves or
   nutmeg

Prepare and cut up fresh fruit as desired. Add to boiling water in saucepan and simmer until nearly tender. Stir in ½ cup sugar and salt—also, if desired, lemon juice, grated lemon rind and choice of spices. Cook until fruit is tender.

Taste; add more sugar, if desired. Cook 1 min. more. Serve cold.

STEWED DRIED FRUIT

Packaged Variety: Apples, apricots, figs, peaches, pears, prunes and other modern packaged dried fruits are so tender that they do not need soaking. Just follow the cooking directions on each pkg.

Bulk Variety: Dried fruits sold in bulk usually need washing, then soaking in cold water to cover until plump (1 hr. or overnight). Simmer, tightly covered, in same water until tender (30 to 45 min.), then sweeten to taste.

FRUIT COOKING FACTS

FRESH FRUIT Approximate Cooking Time	DRIED FRUIT Sugar or Honey per Cup
Apples .... 15-20 min.	Apricots .... ¼ cup
Peaches .... about 10 min.	Figs .... 1 tbsp.
Pears .... about 15 min.	Peaches .... ¼ cup
Plums .... 20-25 min.	Prunes .... 2 tbsp.
Rhubarb .... 10-15 min.	Apples .... ¼ cup

POACHED FRESH FRUIT

Peaches, pears, apricots and cherries are especially delicious prepared this way.

Wash and peel fruit, then cook it gently (a single layer) just until tender in a syrup.

Thin Sugar-and-Water Syrup: Use ¾ cup water to 1½ cups sugar. Do not stir. Dip syrup over fruit to glaze.

CHERRIES JUBILEE

Bing cherries (canned or fresh)
grated orange rind or brandy flavoring
vanilla ice cream

Poach (see above) canned cherries in their own juice; or fresh cherries in Thin Sugar-and-Water Syrup, adding flavoring to taste. Serve hot over ice cream.

RED JELLY PEACHES OR PEARS

canned peaches or pears (no. 2 can)
juice of 1 lemon
⅓ cup red jelly or jam

To ⅓ cup syrup from fruit, add lemon juice and jelly or jam. Bring to boil, stirring until blended. Pour over the canned fruit. Chill before serving.

BAKED CANNED PEACHES, APRICOTS, PEARS

Heat oven to 425° (hot). Place drained fruit halves hollow side up in baking dish with bit of butter in each. Sprinkle with mace and grated lemon rind. Pour a little fruit juice around. Bake 12 min. Serve cold with cream or ice cream.

MAGIC APPLES

cored apples (about 1″ of peel removed from around middle)
for each apple:
  1 to 2 tbsp. brown or granulated sugar
  ¼ tsp. butter
  dash of cinnamon

Place apples in saucepan. Fill center of each with sugar, butter and cinnamon. Pour in water to depth of ½″. Cover. Cook until almost tender, about 8 min.; then remove cover and cook until tender, turning apples once in the syrup to glaze.

OVEN-BAKED PEARS OR APPLES

Same as Magic Apples, except place apples or pears in baking dish.

Heat oven to 350° (mod.). Pour in water just to cover bottom of dish. Cover. Bake until tender, 45 to 60 min. Cool. Serve with plain or whipped cream.

Variation: After taking baked apples from oven, poke a marshmallow into center of each. Cover dish again and let stand out of oven. Sprinkle with dash of nutmeg before serving.

BERRY, CHERRY PUFFS

See picture on p. 79.

¾ cup fresh or frozen berries
  or pie cherries
6 tbsp. sugar
1 cup Bisquick
½ cup more sugar
1 egg, beaten
⅓ cup milk

Clean or thaw and drain berries. Into each of 6 greased custard cups, put 2 tbsp. berries and 1 tbsp. sugar. Mix Bisquick and the ½ cup sugar; stir in mixture of beaten egg and milk; pour over berries in cups, filling each ⅔ full. Tie waxed paper over top of each cup. Steam ½ hr. Serve warm with cream. *6 servings.*

EASY FRUIT
UPSIDE-DOWN CAKE

Take 9-oz. can of well drained pineapple slices, chunks, or crushed pineapple, *or* peach or apricot slices (fresh may be used) *or* pitted cooking prunes and follow Velvet-Crumb Upside-Down Cake recipe on Bisquick pkg. See picture, p. 78.

PEACH OR APPLE PUD-
DING, COBBLER-TYPE

8 medium peaches or apples,
  peeled and sliced
¾ cup granulated or brown
  sugar
1 cup Bisquick
½ tsp. nutmeg or cinnamon

Heat oven to 425° (hot). Place sliced fruit in bowl, sprinkle with sugar and let stand 10 min. Toss together lightly with Bisquick and spice. Pour into well greased square pan, 9 x 9 x 1¾". Bake 30 to 35 min. Serve warm with cream. *6 servings.*

SPEEDY
DESSERT DUMPLINGS

3 tbsp. flour
3 tbsp. sugar
¼ tsp. salt
1½ cups juice from canned
  fruit (or syrup made by
  boiling ½ cup sugar with
  1 cup water)
1 cup canned, frozen or cut-
  up fresh fruit
2 to 3 tsp. lemon juice
½ tsp. grated lemon or
  orange rind
dash of nutmeg or cinnamon
batter for Dumplings (½
  recipe on Bisquick pkg.)

Mix in saucepan flour, sugar and salt. Gradually stir in fruit juice (or syrup). Boil gently 2 min., stirring constantly. Stir in fruit, lemon juice, grated rind, spice. Drop Dumpling batter by spoonfuls into hot sauce and proceed as directed in recipe on Bisquick pkg. Serve at once. *6 servings.*

STIR-N-ROLL FRUIT SHORTCAKE

See pictures, pp. 22, 79.

Make Stir-N-Roll Biscuits (p. 28), adding 2 tbsp. sugar to dry ingredients. Cut rolled-out dough with unfloured 3″ biscuit cutter. Split each baked shortcake in half and spoon sweetened sliced berries or peaches (not chilled) between and on top. Serve warm with plain or whipped cream. *6 to 8 servings.*

TOP-SIDE PEACH COBBLER

Shortcake dough (see Bisquick pkg.)
fresh peach slices (about 4 medium peaches)
mixture of ½ cup sugar, ½ tsp. cinnamon, ½ tsp. nutmeg
1 tbsp. butter

Heat oven to 375° (quick mod.). Pat Shortcake dough into well greased 8″ sq. pan. Press peach slices into the dough in rows. Sprinkle with sugar mixture. Dot with butter. Bake about 30 min. Serve warm, cut in squares, with cream. *8 servings.*

DOUBLE-BERRY SHORTCAKE

Drop Biscuit dough (p. 28 or Bisquick pkg.)
2 tbsp. sugar
sweetened raspberries, blackberries or strawberries

To Drop Biscuit dough add sugar. Fold in berries carefully. After baking, split biscuits while hot. Put additional sweetened berries between halves and on top. Serve warm with cream.

FRUIT OR BERRY BUTTERCAKE

1 cup sifted Gold Medal Flour
½ cup butter
3 tbsp. confectioners' sugar
sweetened sliced fruit or berries

Heat oven to 350° (mod.). Mix flour, butter and sugar with hands until smooth. Divide into 6 equal parts. Shape into flat rounds about 3″ in diameter. Place on baking sheet. Bake until very lightly browned, 15 to 20 min. Serve each round topped with sweetened fruit or berries and whipped cream. *6 servings.*

LIGHTNING-QUICK FRUIT SHORTCAKE

See pictures, pp. 22, 79.

Just follow easy directions on Bisquick pkg.

TAPIOCA CREAM
See picture on p. 79.

2 egg yolks, slightly beaten ,
2 cups milk
2 tbsp. sugar
2 tbsp. quick-cooking tapioca
¼ tsp. salt
1 tsp. vanilla
2 egg whites
4 more tbsp. sugar

Cook egg yolks, milk, 2 tbsp. sugar, tapioca and salt together over low heat, stirring constantly, until mixture boils. Cool. Stir in vanilla. Beat egg whites until frothy, then beat in 4 tbsp. sugar, a little at a time, continuing until stiff and glossy. Fold into tapioca custard mixture. Serve with or without cream. Refreshing with fruit juices or sauces. *6 servings.*

Orange: Add 1 tbsp. grated orange rind to the 2 tbsp. sugar. In place of vanilla, use 1 tbsp. lemon juice. Garnish with orange sections.

Chocolate: Fold in semisweet chocolate pieces.

Fruit: Fold in drained fresh, frozen or canned fruit or berries.

Nut: Top with chopped nuts.

RICE CUSTARD CREAM
¼ cup uncooked rice, washed
2 cups milk
2 egg yolks, well beaten
3 tbsp. sugar
¼ tsp. salt
1 tsp. vanilla
2 egg whites
3 more tbsp. sugar

Cook rice and milk together over boiling water until tender (about 1 hr.). Into beaten egg yolks stir 3 tbsp. sugar, salt; then stir in some of the hot rice mixture. Return to double boiler and cook 2 min. more, stirring constantly. Cool partially. Stir in vanilla. Beat egg whites until frothy; then beat in 3 tbsp. sugar a little at a time, continuing until stiff and glossy. Fold into rice custard mixture. Chill. Serve with or without cream. *6 servings.*

To save time use instant tapioca and rice and prepared pudding mixes.

CREAMY RICE PUDDING
2½ cups milk
½ cup uncooked rice, washed
½ tsp. salt
¼ cup sugar
¼ tsp. nutmeg or cinnamon
½ cup seedless raisins

Scald milk in top of double boiler. Add other ingredients slowly, stirring constantly. Cook covered over hot water until rice has absorbed the milk, about 1¼ hr., stirring frequently. Serve warm with cream. *6 servings.*

People can make their own sandwiches in this easy soup-salad-sandwich lunch.

73

Macaroni Sauté

The unusual flavor of this dish is developed
by first browning the uncooked macaroni in hot fat (p. 48).

Picture Plate Salads

These salads (p. 57) are as good as they are pretty.

Memorable Picnics

Nothing is more refreshing than eating out-of-doors...
on the porch, in the garden, by the roadside, in the woods
or on the beach. The most satisfying food for any picnic
is that which is easy to prepare and simple to serve.

Fresh-caught fish fries golden brown over open fire (p. 119).

Improvise a portable barbecue with a wheelbarrow (see p. 117).

A fitted hamper for a roadside lunch (p. 85).

Easy Fruit Desserts

1. Pineapple Upside-down Cake (p. 70). 2. Apricots and Cookies.
3. Fruit Ambrosia (p. 66). 4. Tapioca Cream with Peaches (p. 72).
5. Cherry Puffs (p. 70). 6. Strawberry Shortcake (p. 71).

1

2

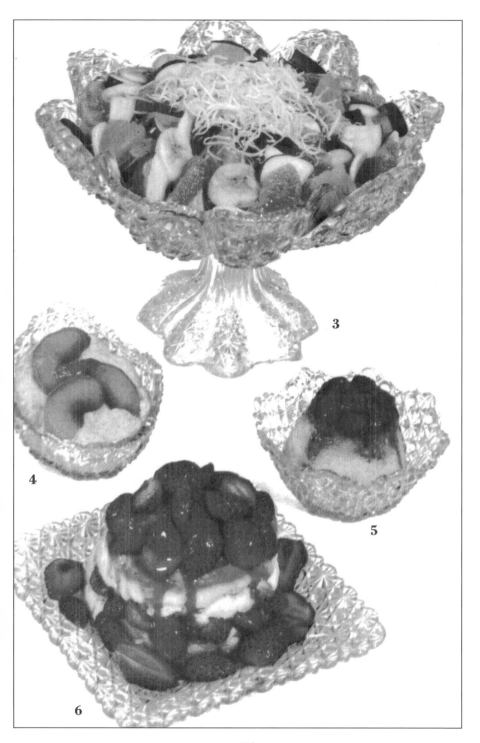

3

4

5

6

Packing the Lunch Box

Variety makes lunch boxes interesting.

SPICY, COZY GINGERBREAD DESSERTS

Make Gingerbread in just a jiffy from directions on pkg. of Betty Crocker Gingerbread Mix. Serve warm squares of it with applesauce, whipped cream, your favorite orange, lemon or chocolate sauce or any of the following:

Berry Cream Topping: Just before serving, fold crushed sweetened strawberries or raspberries into stiffly whipped cream.

Apricot Surprise Topping: Mix 1 cup apricot preserves with 1 tbsp. grated lemon rind and 2 tbsp. lemon juice.

Lacy Sugar Topping: Sift confectioners' sugar through paper doily placed on top of cooled gingerbread. Carefully lift off doily. A lacy design remains.

Peppermint Treat Topping: Fold crushed peppermint stick candy into stiffly whipped cream.

CAKE TREATS

Delicious fresh and warm from the oven . . . or the next day.

SQUARES OR WEDGES OF ANY OF THESE:

Yellow Cake (p. 159)
White Cake (p. 158)
Honey Spice Cake (p. 161)
Chocolate Devils Food Cake (p. 160)

TOPPED WITH:

Lemon Sauce (p. 170)
Vanilla Sauce (p. 170)
Whipped Cream (p. 168)
Butterscotch Sauce (p. 170)
Chocolate Sauce (p. 170)
Ice Cream
Sweetened sliced fruit

SLICES OF THESE:

Angel Food (p. 162)
Sponge Cake (p. 165)
Chiffon Cake (p. 163)

DELICIOUS WITH ANY OF THESE:

Strawberry Fluff (p. 168)
Lemon Sauce (p. 170)
Caramel Sauce (p. 170)
Banana Whip (p. 168)
Whipped Cream (p. 168)
Chocolate Fluff (p. 168)
Orange Sauce (p. 170)
Choco-Mint Cream (p. 168)
Pineapple Cream (p. 168)

DROP COOKIES... OR CRINKLES

1 pkg. Betty Crocker White, Yellow, Honey Spice or Chocolate Devils Food Cake Mix
¼ cup soft shortening
1 medium egg
2 tbsp. water

Mix all ingredients thoroughly with hands. Chill dough. Heat oven to 375° (quick mod.). Roll into balls the size of walnuts. Place 2″ apart on ungreased baking sheet. Or drop by teaspoonfuls on ungreased baking sheet. Bake about 10 min., until delicately browned. (Do not overbake. Cookies will be soft when removed from oven but will be crisp when cool.) *About 3½ doz. cookies.*

Choco-Nut Crinkles: Mix one 6-oz. pkg. semisweet chocolate pieces and ½ cup chopped nuts into the dough.

Coconut Crinkles: Mix 1 cup shredded coconut into the dough.

Fruit Crinkles: Mix ½ cup mixed candied fruit into the dough.

Peanut Crinkles: Mix 1 cup chopped salted peanuts into the dough.

REFRIGERATOR COOKIES

1 pkg. Betty Crocker White, Yellow, Honey Spice or Chocolate Devils Food Cake Mix
¼ cup soft shortening
1 medium egg
1 tbsp. water

Mix all ingredients thoroughly with hands, adding ½ cup each cut-up dates and nuts, if desired. Press and mold into a long smooth roll about 2″ in diameter. Wrap in waxed paper and chill until stiff (several hr.). Heat oven to 375° (quick mod.). With a thin sharp knife, cut cooky dough into thin slices (⅛″). Place a little apart on ungreased baking sheet. Bake about 6 min., until delicately browned. *About 6½ doz. cookies.*

ROLLED COOKIES

Use same ingredients and mix as for Refrigerator Cookies above. Heat oven to 375° (quick mod.). Roll out very thin (1/16″), cut into desired shapes and place on ungreased baking sheet. Sprinkle with sugar. Or roll into balls, place on ungreased baking sheet and flatten with greased glass dipped in sugar (see picture on p. 182). Bake 5 to 7 min. *About 7 doz. cookies.*

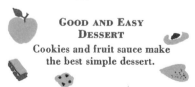

GOOD AND EASY DESSERT
Cookies and fruit sauce make the best simple dessert.

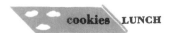

CHOCOLATE CHIP COOKIES

¼ cup soft butter
¾ cup brown sugar (packed)
1 egg
1⅓ cups Bisquick
½ cup chopped nuts
6-oz. pkg. semisweet
   chocolate pieces

Heat oven to 375° (quick mod.). Mix thoroughly butter, brown sugar and egg. Stir in remaining ingredients. Drop with teaspoon 2″ apart on ungreased baking sheet. Bake about 10 min., until lightly browned. *About 3 doz.*

Chocolate Drop Cookies: Use granulated sugar in place of brown, omit chocolate pieces, and blend in 2 sq. unsweetened chocolate (2 oz.), melted. Do not overbake.

Coconut Orange Drops: Omit chocolate; blend in 1 cup shredded coconut and 1 tbsp. grated orange rind. Do not overbake.

PEANUT BUTTER COOKIES

1 cup peanut butter
¼ cup soft butter or other
   shortening
1 cup granulated sugar or
   1 cup brown sugar
   (packed)
½ cup boiling water
2 cups Bisquick

Heat oven to 400° (mod. hot). Mix peanut butter, butter, sugar and boiling water. Blend with rotary beater or spoon until smooth. Stir in Bisquick. Drop with teaspoon on lightly greased baking sheet; flatten with greased glass, or press with fork dipped in flour. Bake 8 to 10 min., until set but not hard. *About 6½ doz.*

Double Peanut Cookies: Add 1 cup halved salted peanuts to peanut butter mixture before stirring in Bisquick. Flatten by pressing with floured fingers. *8 doz. cookies.*

BROWNIES AND GINGER COOKIES

Jiffy-quick directions are right on the packages of Betty Crocker Gingerbread Mix and Betty Crocker Brownie Mix.

QUICK PICK-UP LUNCH

Through-the-Garden Salad
Sliced Cold Roast
Buttered Rolls   Crisp Pickles
Fresh Fruit   Chocolate Cookies

BUY-IT-ON-THE-WAY LUNCH

Assorted Cold Meats
Potato Chips   Whole Tomatoes
Bottle of Olives
Crackers and Cheese, or
Bread and Butter
Fruit   Bottled Beverage
Cookies

GYPSY CAMP PICNIC FOR CHILDREN

Vegetable Soup
(heated in kettle over the fire)
Wieners   Sandwich Buns
Grapes   Oranges
Soft Molasses or Ginger Cookies
Marshmallows
Chocolate or Plain Milk

CAMPFIRE LUNCH

Cheeseburgers (p. 85), or
Toasted Cheese Sandwiches
Cabbage Salad
Brownies   Peaches   Coffee

THROUGH-THE-GARDEN SALAD

Assemble any salad vegetables you find in your garden or refrigerator: radishes, carrots, lettuce, cucumbers, tomatoes, tender young spinach, little green onions. Have them ready to toss together with desired dressing for a vegetable salad bowl and serve at once.

SOUTHERN BURGERS

1 lb. ground beef
1 medium onion, diced
3 tbsp. catsup
3 tbsp. prepared mustard
10½-oz. can chicken gumbo soup

Brown beef and onion in a little hot fat. Stir in catsup, mustard and soup. Simmer until mixture has thickened a little, about 15 min. Spoon over toasted split buns. (May be made early, refrigerated and reheated.) *6 servings.*

POPULAR OUTDOORS OR IN

Southern Burgers
Fresh Vegetable Relishes
Dill Pickles
Honey Spice Cake with Easy
Penuche Icing (pp. 161, 167)

CHEESEBURGERS

Pan-fry hamburgers in skillet over campfire; slip them while hot into the made-at-home Cheese Sandwiches. Toast in folding wire toaster over campfire until browned and cheese is melted.

Serve with chilled crisp shredded cabbage brought in vacuum jar or plastic bag. Carry mayonnaise in separate jar. Toss salad together just before serving.

MIROTON OF SEA FOOD

2 cups cubed cold boiled
    potatoes
2 tbsp. French dressing
2 cups flaked tuna, salmon,
    crabmeat, shrimp or
    lobster
3 tbsp. chopped crisp pickles
mayonnaise to moisten

Marinate potatoes by tossing with French dressing. Chill potatoes and sea food thoroughly. Mix together lightly with pickles and mayonnaise. Heap in high mound on serving platter. Sprinkle with paprika and finely minced parsley. Surround with lettuce cups, each containing wedges of tomatoes and shiny black olives for one serving. *6 to 8 servings.*

DEVILED EGGS

6 hard-cooked eggs
½ tsp. salt
¼ tsp. pepper
½ tsp. dry mustard
about 3 tbsp. salad dressing
    or cream (enough to
    moisten)

Cut eggs in halves. Slip out yolks. Mash with fork or electric mixer. Add seasonings and salad dressing or cream, continuing mashing until smooth. Refill whites with egg yolk mixture, heaping it lightly.

To carry deviled eggs to picnics, wrap in waxed paper, twisting the ends.

COMPANY PORCH LUNCHEON
Miroton of Sea Food
Tomato Wedges
Cucumber Sticks
Buttered Peas   Potato Chips
Crusty Enriched Bread
Strawberry Shortcake (p. 71)

HAMPER PICNIC FOR
ROADSIDE LUNCH
(See picture on p. 77)
Coffee, Milk or Lemonade
Fried Chicken
Potato Salad
Sandwiches   Relishes
Frosted Cake in Pan
Fresh Fruit

Lunch-box meals by the millions go to school and work every day. They can be dull and unappetizing or attractive. It's up to you, the packer. Here are some points to check.

A 4-STAR LUNCH IS:

*Nourishing. Remember it is a meal, not just a snack. Have a hot dish or main dish.

*Appetizing. Not hard-cooked eggs and peanut butter sandwiches every day, when so much variety is available.

*Tasty. Keep hot things hot, cold things cold; include small salts and peppers.

*Planned for Carrying. Guard against sandwiches that dry out or leak juices, against cut fruits that discolor, etc.

A 4-STAR LUNCH BOX IS:

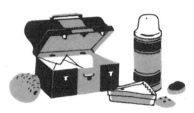

FOR THE MAN

FOR THE YOUNG LADY

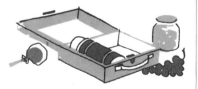

FOR THE SCHOOL CHILD

*Easy to Clean. Metal boxes can be scalded frequently.

*Supplied with Vacuum Bottle. To allow for a greater variety of nourishing hot or cold foods.

*Attractive. So carrying it doesn't seem a burden.

*Durable. For long economical service.

PACKING THE LUNCH...
THE LUNCH-BOX CORNER

Keep one drawer or part of a cupboard for lunch-box supplies to make your job easier. Be sure you have on hand:

1. Small jars with wide mouths, screw tops.	**2.** Heavy paper cups with lids.	**3.** Small salt and pepper shakers of the "no-spill" variety.
 **4.** String, rubber bands and cellulose tape.	 **5.** Waxed paper (colored adds variety) and sandwich bags.	**6.** Plastic sandwich boxes (which also come wedge-shaped for pie).
 **7.** Paper or wooden spoons and forks.	 **8.** Paper napkins (vary these).	 **9.** Aluminum foil to hold food flavors in (foil can be re-used).

FILLING SUGGESTIONS

Use the vacuum bottle for hot soups (warm the bottle with warm water first) or cold eggnogs, milk shakes, etc. (chill the bottle first).

If you have a wide-mouthed bottle, pack hot spaghetti, baked beans, chili.

Use small jars and cups for potato and macaroni salads, puddings, cooked fruits.

Use plastic and waxed paper bags for sandwiches, potato chips, crackers, cookies, nuts, pickles, radishes, carrot sticks, celery. Save wrappings from bread loaves and other food.

FOODS THAT CARRY WELL

SOUP: Choose a soup from pages 34 to 37. (Cream soups are better served at home). Have soup good and hot when it goes into the hot vacuum bottle. Tuck in some crackers.

SANDWICHES: Meat and cheese, cream cheese in nut bread, any variation of peanut butter. Omit lettuce or other greens—they wilt. Keep containers of fillings on hand so the same sandwich doesn't appear two days in a row.

SALADS: Pack in covered glass or plastic cup or paper cup with tight cover. Try potato (p. 61), pea and cheese, kidney bean (p. 58), macaroni, apple and celery.

HOT MAIN DISHES: Spaghetti, macaroni, chili and baked beans give heartiness to the lunch.

RELISHES: Pickles, sweet and sour, celery, carrot sticks, radishes, cottage cheese, olives, American cheese.

DESSERTS: Dried fruits such as dates, prunes, apricots. Fresh fruits such as apples, pears, peaches, bananas, oranges, grapes, cherries. Fruit gelatin carries well, and so do tapioca and rice pudding and baked custards.

BEVERAGES: Milk, buttermilk, Hot Chocolate (p. 64), tomato juice, coffee, lemonade, tea, orangeade.

COOKIES OR CAKE: Bake cupcakes in paper lined cups to keep moist longer. Place toothpicks in top of icing to keep waxed paper from sticking. Wrap cookies, bottoms together, two in a package for a good fit. Put graham crackers together with chocolate butter icing. Make gingerbread boy from Betty Crocker Gingerbread Mix to tuck in top of box.

A TREAT: Candy or nuts, Sugar-coated Jets, stuffed dates, Cheese Kix, popcorn ball, chewing gum, small package of raisins.

Dinner...
Easy and Good

"Meat, potatoes and vegetable" used to be the dinner pattern, unless we were being very formal with "soup and fish and roast." Nowadays we tend to branch out for more variety. Hearty, tasty meat-and-potatoes dinners are still the general favorite, but "casserole, green salad and dessert" combinations are gaining in popularity. Casseroles offer wide variety, are as tasty and good as they are easy, and represent a real economy too.

Here you will find basic ideas for all kinds of meat, fish and poultry, and for potatoes to go with them. You will find some good and easy tricks with vegetables and salads. And there are many suggestions for delicious cakes and icings, puddings, pies and cookies which make the meal for so many people. There are good and easy dress-up touches too, such as appetizers and before-dinner snacks. Try all the ideas on these pages and you will keep your family well fed and happy for many a dinner to come!

For a "party start" to dinner, serve an appetizer course, either in the living room or at the table.

In the living room: Serve juice cocktails or other beverages in small glasses from a tray. Have a small napkin or plate for each person. Pass plates of canapés or hors d'oeuvres (or-durv). Or let guests and family make their own canapés from bowls of spreads arranged with crackers, toast rounds or potato chips on a table in the living room.

At the dining table: Serve fruit, sea-food or juice cocktail in sherbet cups or small glasses. Just before everyone is seated, place cocktail cup or glass on small plate on top of the dinner or service plate at each place.

READY-TO-USE JUICE COCKTAILS

Try mixed vegetable, tomato, clam and fruit juices frozen, canned or bottled. Garnish with mint, parsley, slice of lemon, orange or lime, or grated lemon or orange rind.

Fruit Juice - Ginger Ale: To chilled grape, grapefruit or orange juice, add an equal amount of ginger ale and a small ball of lemon or lime sherbet for each serving.

Tart and Tasty: To equal parts of cranberry and pineapple juice, add a small ball of pineapple or lemon sherbet for each serving.

COCKTAIL SNACKS

Crackers of many flavors and shapes
Olives, green or ripe
Pretzel sticks and balls

Popcorn, salted nuts
Toasted pumpkin or sunflower seeds
Chips—potato, corn, cheese, coconut

CRABMEAT, TUNA OR LOBSTER COCKTAIL

For each serving, use:
⅓ cup chilled flaked canned
   or cooked crabmeat, tuna
   or lobster
about 1 tbsp. minced celery

Combine and chill. Arrange in lettuce-lined cocktail or sherbet glasses. Pour 1 to 2 tbsp. Cocktail Sauce over each. Garnish with parsley or watercress and lemon wedge.

COCKTAIL SAUCE

½ cup chili sauce
⅓ cup catsup
2 to 4 tbsp. prepared
   horse-radish
1½ tsp. Worcestershire
   sauce
1 tbsp. lemon juice

Mix well. Chill thoroughly. Serve with sea-food cocktails.

Note: For a sharper sauce, add ¼ tsp. salt, 1 tbsp. lemon juice, dash of pepper and a few drops of Tabasco sauce.

To Save Time: Use one of the ready-made cocktail sauces.

SHRIMP, OYSTER OR CLAM COCKTAIL

For each serving, use:
6 chilled cleaned canned or
   cooked shrimp or fresh or
   quick-frozen raw oysters
   or hard-shell raw clams

Place in lettuce-lined cocktail or sherbet glasses. Pour 1 to 2 tbsp. Cocktail Sauce over each. Garnish with parsley or watercress sprig and lemon wedge.

FRUIT COCKTAILS

Use fresh, frozen or canned fruits, whole or cut up, for fruit cups to begin dinner.

Garnish with berries, cherries, fresh mint or small scoop of fruit sherbet or ice.

Citrus Cup: Combine sliced grapefruit and orange sections with diced pineapple or banana slices. Add Thin Sugar Syrup (below) and a little lime juice. Chill. Garnish.

Melon Ball Cocktail: Use chilled watermelon, cantaloupe and honeydew balls, alone or in combination, covered (1) with chilled ginger ale or (2) with chilled Thin Sugar Syrup and lime juice. Garnish.

Fresh and Canned Fruit Cocktail: Add interest to canned fruit cocktail by adding a little colorful fresh fruit: sliced banana, cut-up orange, melon balls, sliced strawberries or sweet seedless grapes. Garnish.

Thin Sugar Syrup: Boil together equal parts of sugar and water and a little lemon or lime juice 5 min. without stirring.

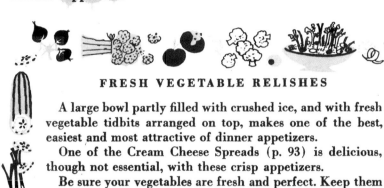

FRESH VEGETABLE RELISHES

A large bowl partly filled with crushed ice, and with fresh vegetable tidbits arranged on top, makes one of the best, easiest and most attractive of dinner appetizers.

One of the Cream Cheese Spreads (p. 93) is delicious, though not essential, with these crisp appetizers.

Be sure your vegetables are fresh and perfect. Keep them crisp in ice water or in your refrigerator until serving time.

FOR YOUR RELISH BOWL

Radishes: Scrub and serve, leaving a couple of green leaves attached to each.

Celery Hearts: Save coarse outer stalks for soup; peel root end. Then quarter and slice the quarters lengthwise, leaving some heart with each piece.

Cucumber Petals: Run a sharp tined fork down the length of an unpeeled cucumber. Cut thin slices crosswise; chill in ice water. Sprinkle with minced parsley.

Carrot Sticks: Cut carrots in narrow, lengthwise strips. Chill in damp cloth.

Carrot Cheese Sticks: Dip ends of carrot sticks into softened cream cheese. Sprinkle with minced parsley.

Cauliflowerets: Break head of raw cauliflower into bite-size flowerets. Chill, crisp and serve.

Lake Louise Poppies: Slice carrots lengthwise paper thin. Chill in ice water until crisp and curled. Draw sprig of parsley or watercress through curl, or place ripe olive in center.

Spring or Green Onions: Trim off green stalks (save for soup), leaving about 2". Cut off root ends and remove loose skin. Wrap in damp cloth; chill.

Turnip Sticks in Olive Rings: Cut sticks from peeled white turnips. Chill in ice water. Draw through ready pitted ripe olives.

Broccoli Buds: Break head of raw broccoli into bite-size flowerets. Serve chilled and crisp.

Stuffed Cherry Tomatoes: Remove centers from tiny cherry tomatoes. Fill with softened cream cheese. Top with parsley.

GOOD-AND-EASY CANAPÉS

For canapés, you need bite-size bases of cracker or toast, and a variety of spreads. You can make them up in advance and arrange them on trays, or let guests spread or dip their own, from trays of "makings." Since many spreads tend to soak into the base or to dry, we favor the latter—most people find it more fun, too.

CANAPÉ BASES

Bread: Cut thin slices into fingers, rounds or any small shape you like. Toast or quickly brown in butter on one side only. Spread topping on untoasted side.

Crisp, unsweetened crackers.
Potato chips or pretzel sticks.
Toasted English muffin wedges.
Tiny cream puff shells.
Melba toast.

CANAPÉ SPREADS, DIPS

CREAM CHEESE SPREAD

Soften 3-oz. pkg. cream cheese with just enough rich milk to spread. Season to taste with salt, freshly ground pepper, paprika, lemon juice and onion juice or minced chives.

Sardine or Anchovy: Blend into Cream Cheese Spread minced clams, sardines or anchovies (may be bought as a paste), Worcestershire sauce and lemon juice.

Savory: Blend into Cream Cheese Spread ½ tsp. Worcestershire sauce and 2 tbsp. chili sauce or catsup or chopped pimiento-stuffed olives.

MUSHROOM CANAPÉ

Sauté chopped mushrooms in butter. Season with salt, Worcestershire sauce and onion salt. Spread on untoasted side of grilled bread fingers. Heat under broiler just before serving.

SEA FOOD

Mash canned or cooked crabmeat, shrimp, lobster, salmon or tuna; moisten with mayonnaise; add a few drops lemon juice, minced parsley.

CHICKEN OR TURKEY

Chop cooked chicken or turkey finely, add mayonnaise to moisten; season to taste with salt and pepper; add a little finely chopped celery or almonds.

For tempting Hors d'Oeuvres Quickies and Appetizers on Picks for entertaining, see p. 223.

 MEAT

Meat is the mainstay of most well rounded dinners, not only for its valuable proteins but for its rich, juicy flavors as well.

There are many good and easy ways to cook your dinner meat, but all methods fall into one of two classes—dry cooking or moist cooking. Each method is preferable for some types and cuts. Check the chart below:

DRY HEAT METHODS

ROASTING	1. Season with salt and pepper. 2. Place fat side up, on rack in roasting pan. 3. Do not add water, do not cover. 4. Roast at 325° (except fresh pork—350°) until done.
BROILING	1. Set oven for broiling. 2. Broil 2 to 3″ from heat until top is brown. 3. Season with salt and pepper. 4. Turn and broil until done. 5. Season and serve at once.
PAN-BROILING	1. Place meat in heavy frying pan. 2. Do not add fat or water, do not cover. 3. Cook slowly, turning occasionally. 4. Pour off fat as it accumulates. 5. Cook until done, season and serve.
PAN-FRYING	1. Brown on both sides in small amount of hot fat. 2. Season with salt and pepper. 3. Do not cover. 4. Cook over medium heat until done, turning occasionally.

MOIST HEAT METHODS

BRAISING	1. Brown on all sides in fat in heavy utensil. 2. Season with salt and pepper. 3. Add small amount of liquid, if necessary. 4. Cover tightly and cook at low temperature until tender.
COOKING IN LIQUID (Stew and Soup)	1. Brown on all sides in own fat or other fat. 2. Season with salt and pepper. 3. Add liquid; cover kettle and cook below boiling until tender. 4. Add vegetables just long enough before serving to be cooked.

BEEF	PORK	LAMB	VEAL
Ribs, Meat loaf Rump (high quality)	Loin, Leg Spareribs Ham—butt or picnic Ham loaf	Leg, Shoulder	Leg, Shoulder Loin, Meat loaf
Steaks—rib, loin, top round Ground	Smoked ham Bacon	Chops—shoulder, rib, loin Ground, Kidney Leg steaks	Liver
Same as for Broiling	Same as for Broiling	Same as for Broiling	Same as for Broiling
Same steaks as for broiling, only cut thinner Ground	Thin chops Tenderloin Smoked ham slice Bacon	Chops—shoulder, rib, loin Ground	Chops, Liver Steaks or cutlets Ground

BEEF	PORK	LAMB	VEAL
Pot roasts Short ribs, Heart Steak—round or flank	Shoulder steaks Chops, Spareribs	Shoulder chops Neck slices Shanks, Heart	Breast, Heart Shoulder, Chops Steaks or cutlets Liver
"Boiling beef" Stew meat, Tongue Corned beef	Ham—butt, picnic, hocks	Stew meat, Shanks	Stew meat Tongue

95

ROAST BEEF

Choose: **Standing rib roast
Rolled rib roast
Rump (high quality)**

Heat oven to 325° (slow mod.). Season meat with salt and pepper. Place fat side up, in open pan. Do not add water; do not cover; do not baste. Roast:

Rare: 22 to 26 min. per lb.
Medium: 26 to 30 min. per lb.
Well done: 33 to 35 min. per lb.
Add 10 min. per lb. for rolled roast.

BROILED STEAK

Choose: **Rib, Club, T-bone
Tenderloin (filet
mignon)
Porterhouse, Sirloin
Top round, Ground**

Oven-broiled: Broil 1" thick steaks 2" from heat until brown; turn and broil on other side. Season and serve.

Rare: 15 to 20 min.
Medium: 20 to 25 min.

Thicker steaks: increase distance from heat and time of broiling.
Pan-broiled: Place meat in heavy frying pan. Do not add fat or water; do not cover. Cook slowly, turning as meat browns. Pour off fat as it accumulates. Time: about the same as for oven-broiled. Season and serve.

EVERYDAY POT ROAST
See picture, p. 178.

**3- to 4-lb. beef chuck
⅓ cup horse-radish
salt and pepper
6 to 8 small onions
6 to 8 carrots
6 to 8 pieces celery
3 potatoes, cut in half**

Roll meat in flour; brown well on all sides in hot fat. Spread with horse-radish. Season with salt and pepper. Add a little water; cover and cook slowly 2 to 2½ hr. Add vegetables and continue cooking 1 hr. *6 servings.*

SICILIAN POT ROAST

**4-lb. beef rump roast
8 ripe olives, cut up
8 stuffed olives, cut up
⅓ cup raisins
1 clove garlic, minced
strips of salt pork or
     bacon (2 oz.)
1 large onion, sliced
no. 2½ can tomatoes
salt and pepper**

Heat oven to 325° (slow mod.). Roll meat in flour; brown well on all sides in hot fat. Cut gashes in top and sides of meat; stuff with mixture of olives, raisins and garlic. Place in roaster or Dutch oven. Lay salt pork over top; put onion around meat and pour tomatoes over. Season; cover and roast 2½ hr. *6 to 8 servings.*

Note: In pressure cooker, cook pot roasts 45 min. at 10 lb.

SWISS STEAK ROYAL

6 tbsp. Gold Medal Flour
1 tsp. dry mustard
1½ tsp. salt
¼ tsp. pepper
1½-lb. round steak,
    cut 1″ thick
1 cup onion slices
3 tbsp. fat
1 clove garlic, grated
½ cup water
½ cup chili sauce or
    drained tomatoes

Mix flour and seasonings; rub into both sides of steak. Cook onion in hot fat until yellow; remove. Brown meat thoroughly on both sides. Return onions to top of steak. Add garlic, water and chili sauce. Cover tightly and cook over low heat or in slow mod. oven (325°) 2 hr. *6 servings.*

Note: Cook Swiss steaks in pressure cooker at 10 lb. for 45 min. Reduce liquid about half.

SIMPLE SWISS STEAK

Rub flour thoroughly into 1½-lb. round steak (1½″ thick). Brown in hot fat in heavy skillet or Dutch oven. Pour on half of 12-oz. can mixed vegetable juice. Cover tightly; cook slowly 2 hr.

SWISS STEAK DINNER

Swiss Steak   Gravy
Mashed Potatoes   Relishes
Buttered Carrots
Cabbage Slaw
Fruit Dessert

ROUND STEAK ROUNDUP

The secret of tender, flavorsome round steak is thorough browning and long, slow cooking.

1½-to-2-lb. round steak,
    cut ½ to 1″ thick
¼ cup Gold Medal Flour
3 tbsp. fat
1½ tsp. salt
¼ tsp. pepper
½ tsp. seasoned salt or
    { ¼ tsp. celery salt
     ⅛ tsp. garlic salt
     ⅛ tsp. onion salt
½ cup water

Dredge meat with flour; brown in hot fat over medium heat. Sprinkle with seasonings. Add water and other ingredients (below); cover and simmer 1½ hr. *6 servings.*

Country Steak: Spread 1 onion, sliced, over steak after 30 min. of cooking. If desired, use a sprinkling of thyme or marjoram.

City Steak: Use 1 cup sour cream and 4-oz. can mushrooms (½ cup) instead of other liquid.

Steak and Stuff: Spread bread stuffing over steak; roll up and tie with string. Flour and brown as above. Use only ¼ cup water.

Note: Cook in pressure cooker at 10 lb. for 30 min.

GOOD BROWN STEW

Secret of a good stew is browning of meat and wise seasoning.

    2 lb. boneless beef chuck,
      cut in 1″ cubes
    2 cups hot water
    1 tsp. lemon juice
    1 tsp. Worcestershire sauce
    1 clove garlic, minced
    1 medium onion, sliced
    2 small bay leaves
    2 tsp. salt
    ½ tsp. pepper
    pinch allspice
    1 tsp. sugar
    6 carrots, halved
    8 small onions
    3 potatoes, quartered

Thoroughly brown meat on all sides in hot fat in pressure cooker; add all ingredients, except vegetables. Cook at 10 lb. for 30 min. Open cooker, add vegetables; continue cooking 10 min. at 10 lb. Remove meat and vegetables, thicken liquid. *6 servings.*

Dumplings for Stew: For light, plump dumplings, follow recipe on Bisquick pkg.

Note: In deep well or kettle, increase water to 4 cups. Cook meat 2 hr., add vegetables and continue cooking 30 min.

BRAISED SHORT RIBS

This has especially good flavor.

    2 lb. short ribs, cut in
      serving-size pieces
    flour
    salt and pepper
    ⅛ tsp. onion or garlic salt
    ⅛ tsp. each of thyme and
      rosemary
    ¼ tsp. marjoram
    ¼ cup water

Roll meat in flour; brown well on all sides in hot fat in pressure cooker. Allow at least 20 min. Drain off all but 2 or 3 tbsp. fat. Add seasonings and water. Cook at 10 lb. for 45 min. In deep well cooker, or heavy skillet, allow 2 hr. and increase water to 1 cup. *4 servings.*

Note: Vegetables (carrots, onion, celery) may be added, if desired. Open cooker; add vegetables and cook at 10 lb. for 10 min. more.

OVEN DINNER

Favorite Meat Loaf
Scalloped Potatoes Buttered Beets
Pineapple Cole Slaw
Lemon Surprise Cake (p. 174)

BEEFBURGER SPECIALS

1 lb. ground beef
3 tbsp. catsup
2 tsp. prepared mustard
1½ tsp. horse-radish
1 small onion, finely chopped
1 tsp. salt
½ cup soft bread crumbs
¼ cup rich milk
1½ tsp. Worcestershire sauce

Combine all ingredients. Shape into 4 large (½″) or 8 small (¼″) patties. Broil on pan 3″ below source of heat, about 6 min. on each side for the large patties (4 min. for smaller ones), or until browned outside and medium done inside. *4 servings.*

For Juicy Hamburgers, see p. 44.

LAZY DAISY MEAT BALLS

1 lb. ground beef
1 tsp. salt
⅛ tsp. each of pepper,
    celery salt, garlic salt
    or nutmeg, if desired
½ cup dry bread or
    cracker crumbs
½ cup water
2 tbsp. grated onion
10½-oz. can cream of
    mushroom soup
¼ soup can of water
gravy coloring, if desired

Mix meat, seasonings, bread crumbs, water and onion. Form into 24 small balls. Roll in flour; brown in hot fat. Mix soup, water, gravy coloring; pour over meat balls. Cover and simmer about 30 min. *6 servings.*

FAVORITE MEAT LOAF

3 slices soft bread
1 cup milk
1 egg
⎰1 lb. ground beef
⎱¼ lb. ground pork
⎰¼ lb. ground veal, or
    1½ lb. ground
    meat loaf mixture
¼ cup minced onion
1¼ tsp. salt
¼ tsp. each of pepper,
    mustard, sage, celery salt,
    garlic salt
1 tbsp. Worcestershire sauce

Heat oven to 350° (mod.). Tear bread into large mixing bowl; add milk and egg. Add meat and seasonings; mix thoroughly. Form lightly into loaf and place in shallow baking pan. Bake 1 hr. *6 to 8 servings.*

Frosted Meat Loaf: Spread catsup or chili sauce over top of loaf before baking.

Tuck-away Meat Loaf: Mold 3 hard-cooked eggs, 6 or 8 1″ cubes cheese or 12 stuffed olives in center of loaf. (See picture p. 178.)

Barbecued Beefies: Shape into 8 individual loaves; place in shallow baking pan. Top each with a thin slice of onion. Pour Barbecue Sauce (p. 117) over loaves; baste once during baking. (See picture p. 178.)

BEEF CRUMBLE ON MUFFIN SQUARES

2 tbsp. chopped onion
2 tbsp. fat
1 lb. ground beef
1½ tsp. salt
few grains pepper
2 tbsp. chopped green pepper
2 cups mixed vegetables
liquid from vegetables plus
    water to equal 1½ cups
2 bouillon cubes
2 tbsp. flour
¼ cup water

Sauté onion in hot fat over medium heat; add meat and brown. Add seasonings, vegetables and liquid, bouillon cubes; simmer 15 min. Mix flour and water; slowly blend into mixture, stirring constantly. Cook until thick. Serve over hot split Muffin Squares. *6 to 8 servings.*

Muffin Squares: Follow recipe for Bisquick Muffins on pkg. except — mix ¼ tsp. dry mustard, ⅛ tsp. poultry seasoning with the Bisquick. Bake in greased 8″ sq. pan in mod. hot oven (400°) 20 min. Cut in squares.

SPANISH HASH

1 lb. ground beef
no. 2 can tomatoes (2½ cups)
½ cup washed rice
1½ tsp. salt
pepper
other seasonings, if desired

Brown meat in fat in pressure cooker, stirring to break up. Add rest of ingredients; cook at 10 lb. about 15 min., or in tightly covered skillet 45 min. *4 to 6 servings.*

HAMBURGER STROGANOFF

½ cup minced onion
1 clove garlic, minced
¼ cup butter
1 lb. ground beef
2 tbsp. flour
2 tsp. salt
¼ tsp. pepper
1 lb. fresh mushrooms, or
    8-oz. can mushrooms, sliced
10½-oz. can cream of
    chicken soup, undiluted
1 cup sour cream
2 tbsp. minced parsley

Sauté onion and garlic in butter over medium heat. Add meat and brown. Add flour, salt, pepper and mushrooms. Cook 5 min. Add soup, simmer uncovered 10 min. Stir in sour cream. Heat through. Sprinkle with parsley. Serve with noodles. *4 to 6 servings.*

BUFFET DINNER
Hamburger Stroganoff
Buttered Noodles   Green Beans
Orange Slices and Dates on Endive
Chocolate Layer Cake

FLANK STEAK ROLL

Have 1½- to 2-lb. flank steak scored. Season with salt and pepper; spread with Bread Stuffing (p. 120). Roll up and tie with string. Brown in hot fat; add ½ cup water or tomato juice. Cover tightly and cook slowly over low heat or in mod. oven (350°) about 1½ hr. *4 to 6 servings.*

PEPPER STEAK
See picture, pp. 178-179.

1 lb. beef chuck, cut in very
   thin strips
¼ cup cooking (salad) oil
1 clove garlic, minced
1 tbsp. soy sauce
1 tsp. salt
¼ cup water
1 cup green pepper, cut in
   1″ pieces
1 cup chopped onion
½ cup chopped celery
1 tbsp. cornstarch
1 cup water
2 tomatoes, cut in eighths

Brown beef in hot oil; add garlic
and cook until yellow. Add soy
sauce, salt and ¼ cup water;
cook 45 min. Add vegetables;
cook 10 min. Stir in cornstarch
blended with 1 cup water; add
tomatoes and cook 5 min. Serve
over hot fluffy rice. *4 servings.*

NEW ENGLAND
BOILED DINNER

3 lb. corned beef
6 carrots, quartered
2 turnips, cubed
12 small or 6 medium onions
6 potatoes, quartered
1 head cabbage, in wedges

Cut meat in serving-size pieces;
cover with water; bring to boiling and cook slowly 3½ hr. Remove meat and keep hot; bring
broth to boiling; add carrots,
turnips, onions and potatoes.
Cook 15 min. Add cabbage, cook
another 15 min. Arrange vegetables around meat on platter.
6 servings.

CREAMED DRIED BEEF

4 oz. dried beef, shredded
¼ cup butter
¼ cup Gold Medal Flour
⅛ tsp. pepper
2 cups milk

If dried beef is too salty, cover
with hot water; bring to boiling
and then drain. Sauté in butter
until edges curl; then blend in
flour and pepper; let bubble.
Gradually add milk; bring to
boiling, stirring constantly. For
more flavor, add ½ tsp. Worcestershire sauce, ½ tsp. paprika
and ⅛ tsp. mustard. If desired,
add sliced mushrooms or ripe
olives. Serve on toast or crisp
noodles. *4 servings.*

Dried Beef Curry on Rice:
Omit other seasonings and add
¼ tsp. curry powder in sautéing
dried beef. Serve over hot fluffy
rice (directions on pkg.).

BEEF BIRDS
Have 2-lb. flank steak split to
make 2 layers. Cut in 3x6″ pieces.
Spread lightly with prepared
mustard. Place chopped onion
and 1 slice dill pickle on each
piece. Roll up and fasten with
toothpicks. Brown on all sides in
hot fat; add ½ cup water. Cover
tightly and cook over low heat
1½ hr. *6 servings.*

Pork is always cooked to the well done stage. It is never broiled unless cured as ham.

ROAST PORK

Heat oven to 350° (mod.). Have backbone of loin cut loose or removed. Season. Place, fat side up, in roasting pan. Do not add water; do not cover; do not baste. Roast 30 min. per lb. See Leftovers (pp. 200-205) for other uses.

ROAST PORK DINNER
Roast Pork   Applesauce
Browned Potatoes   Cream Gravy
Baked Whole Carrots
Assorted Vegetable Relishes
Spice Cake

PORK CHOP MEAL

4 medium thick pork chops
salt and pepper, as desired
4 slices onion
1 green pepper, cut in 4 rings
1 cup cooked rice or
⅓ cup raw rice
no. 2 can tomatoes

Brown pork chops in hot fat over medium heat. Season with salt and pepper. Place onion slice on each chop, then green pepper ring on each chop. Fill pepper ring with rice, then spoon tomatoes over rice. Cover and cook slowly 1½ hr. *4 servings.*

BROWN PORK CHOPS

Brown chops on both sides in hot fat. Season. Cook over medium heat until done, turning occa-

sionally. If desired, braise by adding small amount of liquid: cover tightly and cook until tender, 25 to 30 min.

PORK CHOPS AND APPLES

6 pork chops
3 or 4 unpeeled apples, cored and sliced
¼ cup brown sugar
½ tsp. cinnamon
2 tbsp. butter

Heat oven to 350° (mod.). Brown chops on both sides in hot fat. Place apple slices in greased baking dish. Sprinkle with sugar and cinnamon; dot with butter. Top with pork chops. Cover and bake 1½ hr. *6 servings.*

STUFFED PORK CHOPS

Have pork chops cut double-thick with a pocket on the bone side. Stuff pocket with well seasoned bread stuffing. Brown chops on both sides in hot fat. Cover closely and cook slowly on top of range or in mod. oven (350°) for 1½ hr.

PORK CHOP DINNER
Stuffed Pork Chops
Oven-creamed Potatoes
Chopped Spinach
Orange-Onion Salad (p. 150)
Gingerbread

HOME BARBECUE

Barbecued Ribs
Baked Potatoes   Green Beans
Buffet Salad (p. 150)
Cheese   Fruit   Crackers

BARBECUED RIBS

3 to 4 lb. ribs, cut in serving
    pieces
1 lemon, sliced
1 large onion, sliced
1 cup catsup
3 tbsp. Worcestershire sauce
1 tsp. chili powder
1 tsp. salt
2 dashes Tabasco sauce
1 cup water

Heat oven to 450° (hot). Place ribs in baking pan, meaty side up. On each piece place a slice each of lemon and onion. Roast 30 min. Combine remaining ingredients; pour over ribs. Reduce heat to 350° (mod.) and bake 1½ hr. more. Baste 2 or 3 times. *4 servings.*

BAKED SPARERIBS

Heat oven to 350° (mod.). Cut ribs in 2- or 3-rib portions. Brown over low heat in roasting pan; season with salt and pepper. Top with onion slices, if desired. Add small amount of water or tomato juice. Cover and bake 1½ to 2 hr. Allow ½ to ¾ lb. ribs per person.

Stuffed Spareribs: Have ribs in 2 strips; brown as above. Place Bread Stuffing or Corn Bread Stuffing (p. 120) between pieces, meaty side out. Bake as above.

SPARERIBS AND SAUERKRAUT

1½ lb. spareribs
salt and pepper
2 cups sauerkraut
¼ cup hot water

Heat oven to 350° (mod.). Season ribs with salt and pepper. Place sauerkraut in baking dish; top with ribs. Add water; cover tightly and bake 1½ hr., removing cover the last 15 min. to brown. *4 servings.*

To Vary: Add ½ tsp. caraway seed to sauerkraut or add ¼ cup brown sugar and 2 apples, cut in eighths, to sauerkraut.

CITY CHICKEN

1 lb. veal, in 1½" cubes
1 lb. lean pork, in 1½" cubes
fine dry bread crumbs
1 slightly beaten egg
    with 1 tbsp. water
salt and pepper
6 wooden skewers
¼ cup fat

Alternate veal and pork cubes on stick. Dip in crumbs, then in egg, and again in crumbs. Brown on all sides in hot fat in heavy skillet over med. heat. Season. Add a little water. Cover and cook over low heat or in mod. oven (350°) 1 hr. *6 servings.*

WEEKDAY DINNER

City Chicken
Scalloped or Creamed Potatoes
Buttered Peas or Asparagus
Crisp Relishes
Fruit Compote

BAKED HAM

Heat oven to 325° (slow mod.). Place ham, fat side up, in roasting pan. Do not add water; do not cover. When using tenderized ham, roast 15 min. per lb. for whole ham, 18 to 20 min. per lb. for half ham (or follow packer's directions). About 30 min. before done, pour off drippings; score through fat in diamond shape; stick a whole clove in fat of each diamond; sprinkle with dry mustard, then brown sugar. Pour spiced fruit juice over it. Return to oven. Baste.

BAKED HAM DINNER
Baked Ham
Horse-radish Sauce (p. 123)
Candied Sweet Potatoes
Buttered Cauliflower
Grape, Apple, Celery Salad
Pumpkin Pie

BAKED HAM SLICE

2" center-cut of ham
cloves
1 cup pineapple
    or orange juice
½ cup brown sugar

Heat oven to 325° (slow mod.) Cut slashes in fat edge every 2". Insert cloves in fat. Place in baking pan; pour fruit juice over it and sprinkle with sugar. Bake 1½ to 2 hr. Baste 2 or 3 times during baking.

BROILED HAM SLICE

Have ham slice cut 1" thick. Cut through fat on edge in several places to prevent curling. Broil 20 min. 3" from heat. Turn and broil on second side 15 min.

HAM 'N' LIMAS

1 pkg. frozen baby
    Lima beans
1 center-cut slice ham,
    ¾" thick
1 cup grated American
    cheese (¼ lb.)

Cook Lima beans until tender. Meanwhile, place ham in shallow pan; broil 5 min. on each side, 3" from heat. Arrange Lima beans over ham; sprinkle with cheese; broil until cheese melts and bubbles. Serve immediately. *4 to 6 servings.*

HAM LOAF

⅔ lb. ground smoked ham
1½ lb. ground pork
1 cup dry bread crumbs
¼ tsp. pepper
2 eggs, beaten
1 cup milk

Heat oven to 350° (mod.). Combine all ingredients; mix thoroughly. Form in oblong loaf in baking pan. Bake 1 hr. Serve with Horse-radish Sauce (p. 123).

GOOD AND EASY DINNER
Ham Loaf
Horse-radish Sauce
Candied Yams   Broccoli
Peach Salad
Your Choice of Dessert

Veal deserves careful cooking, for it is tender and delicate. It should be cooked slowly for a long time—never broiled. Adding sour cream or tomato and seasonings keeps it moist and gives more flavor.

ROAST VEAL

Choose: Rib, Loin, Leg
Breast, Rolled
shoulder or rump

If roast lacks covering of fat, cover with salt pork or fat bacon. Sprinkle with salt and pepper. Place, fat side up, in roasting pan. Do not add water, do not cover. Roast in slow mod. oven (325°) 25 to 30 min. per lb.

VEAL PARMESAN

1½ lb. veal round, cut
or pounded very thin
salt and pepper
paprika
½ cup Parmesan cheese

Season meat with salt, pepper and paprika; rub cheese into both sides. Fry quickly in hot fat until golden brown on both sides, about 5 min. Serve with Poppy-seed Noodles (below). *6 servings.*

Poppy-seed Noodles: Cook 3 cups noodles in 3 qt. boiling salted water (1 tbsp. salt). Drain. Melt 3 tbsp. butter; add 1 tbsp. poppy seeds and ¼ cup chopped blanched almonds (if you're having company). Add drained noodles and toss.

VEAL CUTLETS

Dip slices of veal round or chops in cracker or bread crumbs, then into beaten egg mixed with a little water, then again in crumbs. Brown both sides in hot fat. Add small amount of water; cover tightly; cook slowly 1 hr.

Paprika Schnitzel: Cook veal as for Veal Cutlets. Sprinkle with paprika. In place of water, add tomato juice or sour cream.

JANETTE'S VEAL AND NOODLES

2 lb. veal, cut in 1″ pieces
⅓ cup Gold Medal Flour
2 tsp. paprika
1 tbsp. salt
⅛ tsp. pepper
3 tbsp. hot fat
1 clove garlic, minced
2 cups sweet or sour cream

Heat oven to 350° (mod.). Dredge meat in flour mixed with seasonings; brown in hot fat with garlic. Add cream, cover and bake 1 hr. (Cream may curdle.) Serve in circle of Poppy-seed Noodles (left). *6 to 8 servings.*

ROAST LAMB

Choose:
Leg—full leg or short
Shoulder—bone-in or
rolled

Heat oven to 325° (slow mod.).
Place roast, fat side up, on rack
in roasting pan. Do not cover;
do not add water. Roast 30 to 35
min. per lb. Increase time 5 min.
per lb. for rolled roast.

For additional seasoning, cut
gashes in leg and stuff with dry
mustard and clove of garlic.

BROILED LAMB CHOPS AND STEAKS

Choose:
Rib or loin chops
Shoulder chops
Leg steaks
Ground lamb

Remove skin covering from fat.
Slash edges of fat. Broil chops
and steaks 1" thick 3" from heat.

CUT	BROIL EACH SIDE
Rib or loin chops	6 to 7 min.
Shoulder chops and leg steaks	8 min.
Ground 1" lamb patties	10 min.

BRAISED LAMB SHANKS

Have bones cracked in 4 lamb
shanks. Roll in flour; brown
thoroughly in hot fat over medium heat in pressure cooker. Season with salt, pepper, pinch of
thyme and rosemary, 2 pinches
marjoram. Add ½ cup water;
cook at 10 lb. for 45 min.

GROUND LAMB PATTIES

2 cups soft bread crumbs
¼ cup water
1 egg
1 lb. ground lamb
1 tbsp. soft butter
1½ tsp. salt
½ tsp. pepper
2 tbsp. chopped onion
1 small clove garlic, minced
3 tbsp. minced parsley
3 tbsp. fat

Soak crumbs in water. Mix in
rest of ingredients. Shape lightly
into 8 patties. Dip in flour. Cook
in hot fat 15 min. Turn to brown.
Serve with catsup. *8 patties.*

LAMB STEW

2 lb. lamb shoulder,
cut in 2" cubes
2 cups hot water
2 tsp. salt
¼ tsp. pepper
1 small bay leaf
3 tbsp. minced parsley
3 carrots, cut in ½" pieces
1 medium onion, sliced
1 small turnip, diced
1 cup fresh or frozen peas

Brown meat in hot fat over medium heat in pressure cooker. Add
water and seasonings; cook at
10 lb. for 45 min. Open cooker,
add vegetables and cook for 10
min. at 10 lb. Cook in deep well
or Dutch oven 2 hr. Thicken, if
desired. *6 servings.*

SAUSAGE PEACH BALLS
Unusual—and good.

1 lb. pork sausage
2 tbsp. minced onion
2 cups soft bread crumbs
¼ tsp. salt
⅛ tsp. pepper
1 egg, beaten
8 canned peach halves
24 cloves
peach syrup

Heat oven to 350° (mod.). Combine sausage, onion, bread crumbs, seasonings and egg. Form into 8 balls. Arrange peach halves, cut side up, in shallow baking dish. Stick 3 cloves around edge of each peach half, place sausage ball in center. Bake 45 min. Drain off fat and pour on heated syrup, drained from peaches. *4 servings.*

POLISH OR COUNTRY SAUSAGE

Place sausage in skillet; for sausage in casing, add small amount of water; cover and cook 10 min. Drain water and fry until well browned on all sides, about 10 min. Remove sausage and keep hot; add drained canned hominy, fry until brown.

SAUSAGE TREAT
Polish Sausage   Fried Hominy
Stewed Tomatoes with Croutons
Apple Cabbage Slaw   Dill Pickles
Dessert

FRANKFURTERS

Do not pierce with fork.

Simmered: Drop in boiling water; reduce heat, cook 5 to 8 min.

Grilled: Heat slowly in hot fat, turning to brown.

Broiled: Rub with butter or salad oil; broil 3″ from heat, turning to brown.

Serve in hot-dog bun with chili sauce or Barbecue Sauce (p. 117). Or serve with baked beans.

QUAILS
See picture, p. 235.

Split frankfurters lengthwise almost through. Place ¼″ stick of sharp cheese in each. Wrap each spirally with strip of bacon, fastening with toothpick at each end. Starting with split side down, broil until bacon is crisp.

FRANKS AND BEANS

½ lb. frankfurters
1½ tbsp. chopped onion
1 tbsp. fat
1-lb. can baked beans
1 tsp. prepared mustard
1 tsp. celery salt

Heat oven to 350° (mod.). Slice frankfurters. Lightly brown onion in hot fat; add to beans with mustard and salt. Place in 1-qt. baking dish with frankfurter slices in middle layer and on top. Cover, bake 30 min. *4 servings.*

CRISPY FRIED LIVER

Trim skin and membrane from 1 lb. baby beef liver. Leave in serving-size pieces or cut in strips ¾ x 4″. Dip in Bisquick, then in milk and again in Bisquick. Fry in hot fat over medium heat until crispy brown, about 5 min.; turn and fry on other side. Season with salt and pepper. *4 servings.*

With Bacon: Fry bacon first, remove and keep warm while frying liver.

With Onions: Fry liver, remove and keep warm. Put sliced onion rings into fat; cover and steam until soft. Uncover and cook until golden brown.

STUFFED HEART

Trim small cords and vessels from veal heart. Fill cavity with 1 cup well seasoned Bread Stuffing (p. 120). Tie with string. Brown in hot fat. Add ½ cup hot water; cover tightly and simmer 1½ hr. Or cook in pressure cooker at 10 lb. for 30 min.

BROILED LAMB KIDNEYS

Cut 8 lamb kidneys and 8 strips of bacon in half. Wrap half a strip of bacon around each kidney half and secure with toothpick. Broil 3″ from heat until bacon is crisp, 15 to 20 min. Turn once. *4 servings.*

TONGUE

Choose baby beef, veal or lamb tongues. To fresh tongue add 1 tbsp. salt, 1 small onion, few whole black peppers and 1 bay leaf. Cover tongue with cold water; bring to boiling, reduce heat and simmer until tender, about 1 hr. per lb. Or use 1 cup water and cook in pressure cooker at 10 lb. for 45 min. Remove from water; remove bones, gristle and skin. Slice.

TONGUE WITH HORSE-RADISH
Hot Tongue with Horse-radish Sauce
Spinach   Baked Potatoes
Fruit Pie

OXTAIL STEW

2 lb. oxtail, disjointed
¼ cup Gold Medal Flour
1 tsp. salt
¼ cup fat
1 cup tomato juice
½ cup water
1 cup chopped onion
1 tsp. salt
4 whole allspice
1 bay leaf, crumbled
1 clove garlic, minced
2 tbsp. lemon juice

Roll oxtail pieces in mixture of flour and salt. Brown in hot fat. Add tomato juice, water, onion and seasonings. Cover. Simmer 3 hr., or cook in pressure cooker at 10 lb. for 45 min. Remove allspice and bay leaf. Add lemon juice. Serve with hot buttered noodles. *4 to 6 servings.*

Choose chicken as you want it—roaster, fryer, broiler or stewing hen. You'll find it whole, cut up, or by the individual piece—either fresh or frozen.

ROAST CHICKEN

Select roasting chicken; remove pinfeathers and wash. Pat dry. Sprinkle ½ to 1 tsp. salt inside cavity. Stuffing may be made ahead of time but place in chicken just before roasting. Make 1 cup stuffing for each ready-to-cook lb. of chicken. Stuff body and neck cavities lightly.

Place skewers across opening and lace together with string. Fasten neck skin to back with skewer. Fold wings across back with tips touching. Tie drumsticks to tail —a skewer above tail on back helps hold string in place. If there is bridge of skin at cavity opening, push drumsticks under it—then no tying is necessary.

Rub skin with unsalted fat. Place, breast up or down, on rack in shallow roasting pan. Do not sear, do not add water, do not cover. If desired, a thin cloth moistened with melted fat may be placed over chicken; it helps to give uniform browning and makes basting unnecessary. If cloth dries, it may be moistened with fat in pan. If bird is started breast side down, turn when ¾ done. Roast at 325° until done.

READY-TO-COOK WEIGHT	ROASTING TIME
1⅓ to 2½ lb.	1¼ to 2 hr.
2½ to 3½ lb.	2 to 3 hr.
3½ to 4¾ lb.	3 to 3½ hr.
4¾ to 6 lb.	3½ to 4 hr.

FRIED CHICKEN

Any size of tender chicken may be fried—in shallow fat on top of range, in oven or in deep fat. Coating with flour (or batter, if deep-fat fried) prevents drying, gives crispness and a nice brown. Dip pieces in flour or Bisquick, seasoned with salt, pepper and paprika. Brown meaty pieces first in ½" hot fat over mod. heat; turn to brown evenly. When lightly browned (15 to 20 min.) reduce heat; cover and

cook slowly 30 to 40 min. If pan cannot be covered tightly, add 1 to 2 tbsp. water. Uncover last 5 to 10 min. to recrisp skin. Keep warm while making gravy.

Oven Finish: Final cooking may be done in a slow mod. oven (325°)—less attention is required. For oven finishing, it is best to add a little liquid. Turn once or twice. Cook 45 to 60 min., until tender.

OVEN-FRIED CHICKEN AND BISCUITS

See picture on p. 179.

1 fryer chicken
1 cup Bisquick
2 tsp. salt
¼ tsp. pepper
2 tsp. paprika
¼ cup each of shortening and butter

Heat oven to 425° (hot). Mix Bisquick, salt, pepper and paprika in a paper sack. Melt shortening in a shallow baking pan (13x9½x2″) in oven. Shake 3 or 4 pieces of chicken in the sack at a time to coat thoroughly. Remove baking pan from oven and place chicken, skin side down, in a single layer. Bake 45 min., turn. In the meantime make Rolled Biscuit dough — see Bisquick pkg. Roll dough ½″ thick; cut 2″ biscuits. Place on bottom of pan, being sure both biscuits and chicken remain in a single layer. Bake another 15 min. or until biscuits are lightly browned and chicken is tender. *4 servings.*

Gravy: Add 2 tbsp. Bisquick (saved from dredging) to drippings in pan; bring to boiling. Add about 1½ cups hot water. Boil 1 min.

BRAISED OR FRICASSEED CHICKEN

This method is good for the less tender chicken or stewing chicken. Use a heavy skillet or kettle or a pressure cooker.

Coat pieces of chicken as for frying. Brown slowly in thin layer of fat, allowing 30 min. for a 4-lb. chicken; turn to brown evenly. Slowly add ½ to ⅓ cup liquid (water, milk, sweet or sour cream—even tomato, chili, barbecue sauce). Cover tightly and cook over low heat or in slow mod. oven (325°) 2½ to 3½ hr. Other seasonings may be added, such as allspice, bay leaf, ginger, nutmeg, onion or garlic. In pressure cooker, allow 45 min. at 10 lb.

BROILED CHICKEN

Select broilers 1½ to 2½ lb.; have split lengthwise. Brush with melted butter; season with salt and pepper. Broil slowly, skin side down, 6 to 8″ from heat. Turn every 15 min., brushing each time with butter. Broil until tender, nicely browned and crisp on outside (45 to 60 min.). Lemon juice brushed over chicken during broiling browns skin and makes it tender.

Barbecued Broilers: See p. 118 for recipe. Baste with Barbecue Sauce (p. 117) during broiling. Or marinate in Barbecue Sauce before broiling.

STEWED CHICKEN

Stewing is for the older chicken. The cooked meat is used for salads, hot dishes or sandwiches; the broth for soup or sauce.

Place chicken in kettle with tight-fitting cover, deep well or pressure cooker. Add ½ cup water and ½ tsp. salt for each pound of ready-to-cook weight. For more flavor, add 1 carrot, 1 small onion, 2 pieces celery, a clove and 3 peppercorns. Bring to boiling; reduce heat and cook slowly until fork tender, 2½ to 4 hr. (40 min. at 10 lb. in pressure cooker). Remove chicken; serve chicken and broth promptly. Or cover and refrigerate if meat and broth are to be kept.

CHICKEN À LA KING

2-oz. can mushrooms
¼ cup chopped green pepper
¼ cup butter
¼ cup Gold Medal Flour
1 tsp. salt
⅛ tsp. pepper
1 cup chicken broth
1 cup cream or rich milk
1 cup diced cooked chicken
¼ cup chopped pimiento

Sauté mushrooms and green pepper in butter; blend in flour, salt and pepper; let bubble. Slowly stir in chicken broth and cream; bring to boiling over low heat, stirring constantly. Boil 1 min. Add chicken and pimiento; heat through. Serve in Toast Cups (p. 55), timbale cases or Pastry Shells (p. 193). *6 servings.*

CHICKEN PIE

1 recipe Stir-N-Roll Pastry (p. 176)
6 tbsp. butter or chicken fat
6 tbsp. Gold Medal Flour
½ tsp. salt
¼ tsp. pepper
1¾ cups chicken broth
⅔ cup cream or rich milk
2 cups cut-up cooked chicken

Heat oven to 425° (hot). Divide pastry in 2 parts, ⅔ in one part and ⅓ in other. Roll larger part 10x14″ between waxed papers. Peel off top paper. Place, paper side up, in 10x6x1½″ baking pan. Peel off paper; ease pastry into pan. Melt butter, add flour and seasoning; let bubble. Add liquid and cook slowly until thickened. Add chicken; pour into pastry-lined pan; top with rest of pastry rolled to fit top. Pinch edges together. Bake about 35 min. *6 servings.*

CHICKEN 'N' DUMPLINGS

Cook Stewed Chicken. Drop Bisquick Dumplings by tablespoonfuls onto boiling chicken and broth. Cook uncovered 10 min.; cover and continue cooking 10 min.

Bisquick Dumplings: Add ¾ cup milk to 2 cups Bisquick; mix thoroughly with fork. *10 to 12 dumplings.*

ROAST TURKEY

Young turkeys of any size may be roasted. Remove pinfeathers and wash. Pat dry. Rub cavity with salt. Stuff just before roasting. Make ¾ to 1 cup stuffing for each ready-to-cook lb. of bird. Stuff body and neck cavities lightly. Place skewers across opening and lace together with string. Skewer neck skin to back. Fold wings across back with tips touching. Tie drumsticks to tail.

Rub skin with unsalted fat. Place on rack in shallow roasting pan. Heat oven to 325° (slow mod.). Start breast down unless bird is too heavy to turn during roasting. Place thin cloth dipped in fat over bird. If started breast down, turn breast up last hour. Roast until done (leg joint should move readily or break).

READY-TO-COOK WEIGHT	COOKING TIME
4 to 8 lb.	3 to 4½ hr.
8 to 12 lb.	4 to 5 hr.
12 to 16 lb.	5 to 6 hr.
16 to 20 lb.	6 to 7½ hr.
20 to 24 lb.	7½ to 9 hr.

In figuring time, plan to finish bird 30 to 40 min. ahead of dinnertime to make gravy, remove string and arrange on platter.

ROAST TURKEY HALF

Rub cavity side with salt. Skewer skin to meat along cut edges. Tie leg to tail and tie breast and wing together. Stuff cavity, then cover open side of bird with aluminum foil. Put roasting rack on top of foil and turn bird over quickly onto roasting pan. Rub with fat and cover with fat-moistened cloth. Roast as for whole turkey.

ROAST DUCK

Heat oven to 325° (slow mod.). Clean duck — see directions for Roast Chicken (p. 109). Sprinkle inside with salt; stuff with Wild Rice or Orange Stuffing (p. 120). Or place a quartered apple and 1 small whole onion in cavity. Place breast side up in shallow roasting pan. Lay bacon slices over breast of wild duck. Roast young wild ducks 15 min. per lb., older wild ducks 20 min. per lb., tame ducks 20 to 25 min. per lb. If tame duck is fat, baste with hot water.

ROAST PHEASANT

Heat oven to 325° (slow mod.). Only young pheasants are suitable for roasting. Clean, following directions for Roast Chicken (p. 109). Sprinkle salt inside; stuff with Sausage-Apple Stuffing (p. 120). Place bacon slices over breast. Roast about 1½ hr.

FISH DINNER
Crispy Fried Pike
or
Oven-broiled Fish
Parsley Potatoes   Buttered Peas
Beets-in-Cream Salad (p. 150)
Lemon Meringue Pie

CRISPY FRIED PIKE

6 serving-size pike fillets
  (other fillets may be used)
sour milk
1 tsp. salt for each lb. fish
Bisquick
4 tbsp. fat (part butter)

Place fillets in shallow pan; add salt and sour milk to cover. Let stand 30 min. At mealtime, dip each fillet in Bisquick; fry in hot fat over low heat. Fry until golden brown and crisp, turn and fry on second side. Do not overcook. *6 servings.*

TASTY BAKED SALMON

1-lb. can salmon
1 cup sour cream
½ tsp. salt
few grains pepper

Heat oven to 450° (hot). Drain salmon; place in 9" pie plate; pour sour cream over it; sprinkle with salt and pepper. Bake 20 to 30 min. or until cream becomes thick and has a few brown patches. Serve with lemon. *4 to 6 servings.*

OVEN-BROILED FISH

4 to 6 pieces fresh fillet of
  walleyed pike or trout
salt as desired
paprika
2 to 4 tbsp. chicken broth or
  bouillon cube dissolved
  in water
1 tsp. lemon juice
¼ cup butter, melted

Coat shallow baking pan with oil; sprinkle with salt; place in oven heated to about 500°. Dip fish in oil, place skin side down on very hot pan. Sprinkle with salt and paprika; place 2 to 3" from heat in broiler for 3 min. Remove. Pour broth around fish. Place in very hot oven 10 to 15 min. Pour hot lemon juice-butter mixture over fish just before serving. *4 to 6 servings.*

QUICK SALMON BAKE

1-lb. can red salmon
½ tsp. salt
¼ tsp. pepper
2 tbsp. butter
1 lemon, sliced thin

Heat oven to 400° (mod. hot). Place flaked salmon and liquid in 1-qt. baking dish. Sprinkle with salt and pepper, dot with butter and lay lemon slices over top. Cover and bake 20 min. *4 to 6 servings.*

STUFFED BAKED FISH

3- to 4-lb. fish, dressed
1½ tsp. salt
Bread Stuffing (p. 120)
4 tbsp. butter or other fat,
 melted

Heat oven to 400° (mod. hot).
Wash and dry fish; sprinkle inside and out with salt. Cut 3 or 4
gashes through skin on each side
to keep from breaking. Stuff fish
loosely with the Bread Stuffing;
close with skewers. Place fish in
greased baking pan. Brush with
melted fat. Bake 45 to 60 min.
(15 min. per lb.) or until fish
flakes when tested with a fork.
If fish seems dry, baste occasionally with fat or lay bacon slices
over fish the last 15 min. Serve
with lemon wedges or Tartar
Sauce (p. 123). *6 servings.*

Serving Help: For easy removal
after baking, lay about 3 strips
aluminum foil in pan and up
over sides.
Pull up on ends of strips to lift
to platter, pull out strips.

FRESH COOKED SHRIMP

To use in salads and cooked
dishes. Plunge 2 lb. fresh shrimp
into boiling water seasoned with
1 tbsp. salt, 1 bay leaf, 1 tsp.
pickling spice and 1 tbsp. vinegar. Cook until shell just turns
pink, about 10 min. Drain, cover
with cold water, drain again. Remove shells. With pointed knife,
remove black line down back.

SALMON LOAF

1-lb. can salmon
milk
1 egg
1½ cups soft bread cubes
2 tsp. lemon juice
1 tsp. chopped onion,
 if desired
¼ tsp. salt
⅛ tsp. pepper

Heat oven to 350° (mod.). Drain
liquid from salmon into measuring cup. Add milk to make ¾
cup. Flake salmon, removing
bones and skin. Blend in egg; stir
in rest of ingredients. Spoon
lightly into greased loaf pan, 9x
5x2½", or 1-qt. baking dish.
Bake 45 min. Serve with lemon
wedges. *4 servings.*

FRENCH FRIED SHRIMP

1 cup sifted Gold Medal Flour
½ tsp. sugar
½ tsp. salt
1 egg
1 cup cold water
2 tbsp. melted fat or salad oil
2 lb. fresh shrimp

Combine ingredients, except
shrimp; beat well. Peel shell
from shrimp, leaving last section
and tail intact. Cut slit through
center back without severing
either end; remove black line.
Dry shrimp thoroughly; dip into batter; fry in deep hot fat
(375°) until golden brown. Drain
shrimp on absorbent paper.
Serve immediately with Tartar
Sauce (p. 123) or with soy sauce.
6 servings.

FILLET STUFFED TOMATOES

6 large tomatoes
salt and pepper
1½ lb. fish fillets
1½ cups soft bread crumbs
2 tbsp. chopped onion
6 tbsp. minced parsley
6 tbsp. butter, melted
2 tbsp. lemon juice
1 tsp. salt
¼ tsp. pepper
½ tsp. each of thyme and savory

Heat oven to 425° (hot). Scoop out centers of tomatoes (save for salad); sprinkle with salt and pepper. Cut fillets in 6 pieces. Mix rest of ingredients; spread on fillets. Roll up and place one in each tomato. Place in shallow baking dish. Bake 30 min. *6 servings.*

Note: Select thin fillets; if thick, split in half.

BAKED FISH FILLETS

1 lb. fresh or frozen fish fillets
1 tbsp. chopped green onion
2 cups Cheese Sauce (p. 122)
8 thick slices tomato
1 cup soft bread crumbs
2 tbsp. soft butter
¼ tsp. each of salt and pepper

Heat oven to 350° (mod.). Place fish in greased 7½x11½x1½" baking dish. Add onion to Cheese Sauce and pour over fish. Arrange tomato slices over top. Mix crumbs, butter and seasonings; sprinkle over tomato slices. Bake 30 to 35 min. *6 to 8 servings.*

SHRIMP DE JONGHE

3 lb. uncooked shrimp
salt and pepper
½ cup consommé
4 or 5 cloves garlic, sliced
1 cup butter
2 cups dry bread crumbs
6 tbsp. minced parsley

Heat oven to 400° (mod. hot). Shell and remove black vein from shrimp; place 6 to 8 in each of 6 individual baking dishes. Season with salt and pepper. Pour consommé over shrimp. Cook garlic in butter until butter browns; remove garlic. Add crumbs and parsley; sprinkle over shrimp. Bake 15 min. Don't overcook. *6 servings.*

HALIBUT FISH MOLD

4 cups soft bread crumbs, in 1 cup cream
1 lb. uncooked halibut, cut into small pieces
1 tsp. soft butter
1 tsp. salt
¼ tsp. celery salt
4 egg whites, stiffly beaten

Heat oven to 350° (mod.). Combine all ingredients, folding egg whites in lightly. Pour into greased 2-qt. casserole. Set in pan of hot water and bake 40 to 50 min. Serve with Almond Sauce (p. 123). *6 to 10 servings.*

Outdoor eating is fast growing in popularity, especially where the climate is mild. If you haven't an outdoor fireplace, get a portable barbecue and find out how wonderful simple foods taste cooked in the out-of-doors. Here are some pointers to help you start.

BARBECUE SAUCE TIPS

(Recipe on page 117)

Keep Sauce warm or hot for basting meat, fish or chicken.
Let Sauce stand several hours or overnight to blend flavors.
Make an herb swab for brushing on Sauce. Cut stalks of fresh mint, rosemary, thyme or other herbs; tie firmly to a willow stick. Dip in Sauce and baste meat. Toss on fire to burn when meat is barbecued—smells wonderful!
For smoky flavor, add liquid smoke to Barbecue Sauce.

FOOD TIPS

Meat and poultry should be at room or outdoor temperature before barbecuing, for flavor and moist tenderness. Keep them dry, too, as more natural juices escape from wet flesh. Chicken: Start with inside of cuts next to heat (bones will hold heat while outside is browning).

FIRE TIPS

Coals without flame are needed for even heat. Use plenty of fuel for a thick bed of coals.
Charcoal: Start fire 1 hour ahead.
Wood: Start fire 1½ to 2 hours ahead. Arrange grate so food is 8 to 10″ from coals.

BARBECUED SPARERIBS

Cover ribs with hot water; add a little fresh or dried thyme and simmer until partially tender. Drain. When ready, barbecue until crisp and meat is done, about 10 to 15 min.—using Barbecue Sauce (p. 117).

BARBECUE BUTTERS

Spread on meat as it comes from the grill, in place of sauce.
Or spread on toasted split rolls for hot dogs, hamburgers or steak sandwiches.

Use: ½ cup butter, 2 tsp. dry or powdered mustard, 3 tsp. Worcestershire sauce and ¼ tsp. minced garlic.

Or: Blend mustard or chili sauce with butter.

BARBECUED FRANKFURTERS

Plunge frankfurters into boiling water for 1 min. Remove, drain. Barbecue for 8 to 10 min.

BURGER 'N' BEAN BARBECUE
Barbecued Beefburgers
Lazy Man's Chili Beans
Toasted Burger Rolls
Tossed Greens
Relishes
Fresh Fruit-Melon-Berry Platter
Coffee

BEEFBURGERS

2 lb. ground beef
2 tsp. salt
1 tsp. pepper
¼ cup grated onion
1 tsp. flavor extender (p. 124)
herbs, grated cheese or
   chopped pickle, if desired
¼ cup water, broth or milk
   for extra juicy ones

Mix ingredients together lightly.
Form lightly into 8 thick patties.
Place on grill over bed of coals
and barbecue until done, about
15 to 20 min.

BARBECUE SAUCE

½ cup tomato catsup
1 can bouillon (or 1 bouillon
   cube dissolved in 1 cup
   hot water)
2 tbsp. Worcestershire sauce
½ tsp. onion juice
dash of cayenne
1 tsp. mustard (dry or
   prepared)
1 clove garlic, minced
1 tbsp. minced parsley

Measure all ingredients into a
small saucepan; bring to boiling.
Use to baste meat while cooking.

LAZY MAN'S CHILI BEANS

4 cloves garlic
2 tsp. salt
¼ cup sugar
10-oz. can Spanish chili
4 slices bacon, diced
2 large onions, sliced
   ⅛″ thick
2 no. 2 cans red kidney beans
1 cup water

Mash garlic, salt and sugar to a
paste; blend into chili. Fry bacon until golden; add onion and
cook until soft and transparent.
Stir in kidney beans, water and
chili mixture; simmer 20 to 30
min. May be made day or so before and reheated. *8 servings.*

FRESH FRUIT PLATTER

Arrange narrow slices cantaloupe or honeydew in "spoke"
fashion from center of plate. Between "spokes," place halves of
peaches, apricots, plums, Bing
cherries and strawberries.

HOME-MADE PORTABLE GRILL

Materials needed: metal
wheelbarrow, wire mesh
for fire basket and grill,
wire for hooks.

See picture,
p. 77.

CHICKEN 'N' CORN BARBECUE
Barbecued Chicken Halves
Grilled Young Corn-on-the-Cob
Toasted French Bread
Parsley Tomatoes
Pickled Peaches   Pickled Figs
Butterscotch Swirl Ice Cream
Coffee

BARBECUED CHICKEN HALVES

Have young chickens (no heavier than 2½ lb.) split. Lay flat in pan; pour on Marinade (below) and let stand several hours before barbecuing. Use drained Marinade to baste chickens while on the grill. Place on grill over bed of coals and barbecue until done, about 30 to 45 min.

MARINADE

1 cup cooking sherry
½ cup cooking (salad) oil
1 large onion, minced
1 tbsp. Worcestershire sauce
1 tbsp. mustard (dry or
    prepared)
1 tbsp. mixed herbs (such as
    thyme, marjoram,
    rosemary, oregano)
½ tsp. coarse black pepper
1 tsp. garlic salt
1 tsp. soy sauce

Measure all ingredients into large jar. Shake well to blend. *Enough for 2½-lb. chicken.*

TOASTED FRENCH BREAD

Split loaves in half, lengthwise; spread both halves liberally with Garlic Butter (p. 155); then sprinkle with parsley (minced and wrung out in cloth until dry and fluffy). Toast in oven or on grill until hot. If toasted on grill, wrap loosely in foil to keep from burning.

GRILLED CORN

Strip husks, roll ears in butter. Place on grill to barbecue about 5 min. Brush with same sauce as used on chicken. Turn, of course, and be careful not to overcook.

PARSLEY TOMATOES

Slice in generous circles; chill and marinate in good French Dressing. Sprinkle liberally with minced parsley, chives or mint.

BUTTERSCOTCH SWIRL ICE CREAM

¼ cup butter
6 tbsp. brown sugar
2 cups Wheaties
½ cup chopped nuts
1 qt. vanilla ice cream

Cook butter and brown sugar until thick and smooth, stirring constantly. Blend in Wheaties and nuts. Spread in thin layer on baking sheet. When cool, crumble. Stir into softened ice cream; chill until firm in tray of refrigerator. *6 servings.*

FISH 'N' DIP BARBECUE
Barbecued Trout
(or other fish)
Cole Slaw or Summer Potato Salad
Fish Dips   Hot Crusty Rolls
Finger Relishes (p. 92)
Lemon Meringue Tarts or Pie
Coffee

BARBECUED TROUT
See picture p. 76

Brush trout inside and out with lemon or lime juice before refrigerating—this keeps fish fresh in appearance and aroma. Place fish in shallow pan; pour on Marinade (below) and let stand an hour before barbecuing. Use drained Marinade for basting during barbecuing. Tuck a sprig or two of fresh herbs in cavity. Place on grill over bed of coals and barbecue until done, about 10 to 15 min.

MARINADE FOR FISH

½ cup soy sauce
½ cup cooking sherry
1 tbsp. lime or lemon juice
1 clove garlic, crushed
¼ cup cooking (salad) oil

Measure all ingredients into large jar. Shake well to blend.

SUMMER POTATO SALAD

3 cups diced cooked potatoes
1 cup diced cucumber
1 tbsp. minced parsley
1 tbsp. grated onion
½ cup thinly sliced radishes
¼ cup sliced sweet pickle
salt to taste
¼ cup French dressing

Measure all ingredients except dressing into chilled bowl; toss together with French dressing. Chill 2 hr. or more. Add cooked salad dressing or mayonnaise, if you like. Serve on lettuce leaves. *Serves 8.*

SPICY BARBECUE DIP

¼ cup chili sauce
¾ cup catsup
1 tbsp. grated onion
1 tbsp. horse-radish
2 tbsp. lime or lemon juice
1 tsp. soy sauce
2 tbsp. chopped celery
salt to taste

Mix all ingredients together.

CREAMY BARBECUE DIP

1 cup mayonnaise
2 tbsp. finely chopped green
  pepper or pickle relish
1 tbsp. chili sauce
lemon juice to taste
salt to taste

Mix all ingredients together.

BREAD STUFFING

¼ cup minced onion
¼ cup butter or other fat
4 cups very dry bread cubes
or crumbs
½ cup chopped celery
1 tsp. salt
¼ tsp. pepper
sage or poultry seasoning
to taste
1 tsp. crumbled herbs to suit
taste: thyme, marjoram,
rosemary
hot water or stock

Cook onion in butter until soft and yellow; stir in some of the crumbs and heat until light brown. Mix lightly into remaining crumbs and seasonings. For dry stuffing, add little or no liquid. For moist stuffing, add just enough liquid to moisten. *4½ cups stuffing.*

To Vary: Add 1 cup mushrooms sautéed in butter, 2 tbsp. minced parsley; or the cooked giblets.

Corn Bread Stuffing: Use crumbled corn bread or corn muffins for half the bread.

Prune Stuffing: Add ½ to ¾ cup cut-up cooked prunes with seasoning. Use prune juice as part of liquid.

Apple Stuffing: Add ½ cup chopped apples and ½ cup diced celery with seasonings.

Orange Stuffing: Add 1 cup diced orange and 2 tsp. grated orange rind with seasonings.

Sausage Stuffing: Brown and crumble ⅓ lb. pork sausage over medium heat. Add to Bread Stuffing, using sausage fat for part of fat and reducing herbs and poultry seasoning by half.

Sausage-Apple Stuffing: Add 1 cup chopped tart apple to Sausage Stuffing.

WILD RICE STUFFING

½ lb. sliced mushrooms or
4-oz. can mushrooms
¼ cup butter
¼ cup minced onions
¼ cup minced parsley
½ cup chopped celery
⅓ cup water
2 cups cooked wild rice
(directions on pkg.)
¾ tsp. salt
few grains pepper

Cook mushrooms in butter 5 min. Remove mushrooms; add onion, parsley and celery; cook until onions are yellow. Add rest of ingredients and mushrooms; simmer 15 min. Enough for 4 lb. chicken.

STUFFING TIPS

1-lb. loaf bread makes 8 cups crumbs.
Use 1 cup stuffing for each lb. ready-to-cook bird.
Pack stuffing loosely—it swells.
Stuffing may be made ahead of time but should be stuffed in poultry just before roasting.
For dry, crusty stuffing (a favorite with some), spread an extra amount in shallow pan and bake the last 30 min. of roasting.

PAN GRAVY

Pan Gravy is rich with the natural meat fats left in the pan after cooking roasts, steaks, chops, roasted and fried chicken.

For each cup of medium gravy:

2 tbsp. fat
2 tbsp. flour
1 cup liquid (water, meat stock or bouillon)

Remove meat or poultry to warm place. Pour off fat; measure amount needed back into pan. Add level tablespoons of flour. Use equal amounts of flour and fat. Stir fat and flour together until smooth, then cook over low heat, stirring steadily until it's bubbly and brown. Take from heat, stir in liquid slowly. Always measure liquid—too much weakens flavor. Return pan to heat, stirring and scraping in the rich drippings. Boil 1 min., season and serve.

KETTLE GRAVY

Kettle Gravy is made from the liquid in which pot roasts and stews have been simmered. Remember, the less liquid you use, the richer the flavor of the broth will be.

For each cup of medium gravy:

1 cup meat broth
¼ cup cold water
2 tbsp. flour

Remove meat to platter. Keep warm. Skim excess fat from meat broth and store for future use. Pour off broth, measure amount needed and return to kettle. Shake water and flour together in covered jar. Remember, always put the water in first and the flour on top, for a smooth mixture. Stir flour and water slowly into hot broth. Bring to boil. Cook 1 min., until thickened. Season and serve.

HINTS ON MAKING GRAVY

PAN GRAVY

For improved flavor, cook meat with some of these: bay leaf, peppercorns, onion, garlic, celery salt or any favorite seasoning.

For thin gravy, use 1 tbsp. each flour and fat for each cup liquid.

For thick gravy, use 3 tbsp. each flour and fat for each cup liquid.

To make cream gravy for chicken or chops, use milk for part of liquid.

KETTLE GRAVY

The broth will be tastier if you flour meat and brown slowly on all sides—for about 30 min. before simmering.

To make cream gravy for chicken, pork or ham, use milk instead of water.

For thick gravy, use 3 tbsp. flour.

For thin gravy, use 1 tbsp. flour.

When short of drippings, add butter and brown with drippings.

CREAM SAUCE

THIN	MEDIUM	THICK
For creamed vegetables, scalloped potatoes, base for soup.	For creamed vegetables, scalloped dishes, creamed chicken and sea food.	For croquettes.
1 tbsp. butter 1 tbsp. flour ¼ tsp. salt 1 cup milk	2 to 3 tbsp. butter 2 to 3 tbsp. flour ¼ tsp. salt 1 cup milk	3 to 4 tbsp. butter 4 tbsp. flour ¼ tsp. salt 1 cup milk

Melt butter in saucepan; blend in flour and salt and let bubble up together. Take off heat, add milk all at once; cook over low to medium heat, stirring constantly until thickened.

Cheese Sauce: Add ½ cup grated American cheese to 1 cup hot Medium Cream Sauce.

Quick Mustard Sauce: Add 1 tbsp. prepared mustard.

Curry Sauce: Add ½ tsp. curry powder and a little minced onion to the butter.

Egg Sauce: Add 2 cut-up hard-cooked eggs. Season.

MUSTARD SAUCE

Blend in saucepan 1 egg yolk slightly beaten, ⅓ cup each of sugar, prepared mustard, canned tomato soup, butter and 3 tbsp. vinegar. Boil 1 min., stirring constantly. *1¼ cups sauce.*

CREAMY HOLLANDAISE SAUCE

Place 3-oz. pkg. cream cheese in saucepan; soften with spoon. Blend in 2 egg yolks, one at a time. Slowly stir in 2 tbsp. lemon juice and a dash of salt. Let thicken over low heat, stirring constantly. *⅔ cup sauce.*

EASY HOLLANDAISE SAUCE

Place 2 slightly beaten egg yolks, 2 to 3 tbsp. lemon juice and 1 stick cold butter (¼ lb.) in saucepan. Cook over low heat, stirring constantly, until butter melts and sauce is slightly thick. Season to taste with salt. *1 cup sauce.*

DOUBLE-QUICK HOLLANDAISE

Blend 2 tbsp. hot water into ½ cup mayonnaise; set in hot water to heat, stirring occasionally. *½ cup sauce.*

LEMON BUTTER SAUCE
Nice with vegetables.

Heat ¼ cup butter; add 2 tbsp. lemon juice. Keep hot.

TARTAR SAUCE
Nice with fish and shrimp.

Combine 1 cup real mayonnaise, 1 tsp. grated onion, 2 tbsp. minced dill pickle, 1 tbsp. minced parsley and 2 tsp. cut-up pimiento. *1 cup sauce.*

HORSE-RADISH SAUCE
Nice with ham.

Fold 3 tbsp. well drained horse-radish and ½ tsp. salt into ½ cup heavy cream, whipped. *1 cup sauce.*

RAISIN SAUCE
Nice with baked ham.

Mix ½ cup brown sugar, 1 tsp. dry mustard, 2 tbsp. cornstarch; slowly add 2 tbsp. each of vinegar and lemon juice, ¼ tsp. grated lemon rind, 1½ cups water, ½ cup seedless raisins. Stir over low heat until thick. *1½ cups sauce.*

ALMOND SAUCE
Nice with fish.

In making 1 cup Medium Cream Sauce, brown ½ cup chopped almonds in the butter before adding flour. For extra richness, stir some of sauce into 2 slightly beaten egg yolks, then back into remaining sauce. *1½ cups sauce.*

CUCUMBER SAUCE
Nice with ham.

Add 1 cup diced and drained cucumber and ½ tsp. minced onion to ½ cup mayonnaise. Season with salt, pepper and paprika. *1¼ cups sauce.*

MUSHROOM SAUCE
Nice with meats and main dishes.

2-oz. can mushrooms or
½ cup fresh, sliced
2 tbsp. butter
2 tbsp. flour
1 cup water
1 bouillon cube or 1 cup stock
dash of nutmeg
salt and pepper to taste
1 slightly beaten egg yolk

Brown mushrooms in butter; blend in flour. Add water, bouillon cube and seasonings; cook until thick, stirring constantly. For extra richness, add egg yolk. Stir some of sauce into yolk, then back into remaining sauce. *1¾ cups sauce.*

TOMATO SAUCE
Nice with meats and main dishes.

Brown 2 tsp. grated onion in 2 tbsp. butter; blend in 2 tbsp. flour and let bubble up. Add 1 cup tomato purée or tomato juice, dash of celery salt, ¼ tsp. Worcestershire sauce, salt and pepper to taste; cook until thick, stirring constantly. *1 cup sauce.*

DOUBLE-QUICK SAUCES

Thin condensed cream of mushroom or tomato soup with milk.

SPECIAL SEASONINGS

Herbs, spices and special seasonings can make the difference between ordinary and delicious food. Use imagination, taste as you go and keep on hand a variety of seasonings.

Lemon: Always keep a lemon or bottled lemon juice on hand. Lemon juice points up the flavor of many foods.

Vinegar: There are many kinds of vinegar, cider being best known. But try tarragon, shallot and wine vinegars.

Sour Cream: Use natural sour cream (pasteurized sour cream has an "off" flavor), or cultured sour cream (available in many stores). Sweet cream may be soured by adding a tbsp. of lemon juice or vinegar to a cup of cream.

SOUR CREAM RECIPES

Hamburger Stroganoff (p. 100)
Farmers' Pork Chops (p. 129)
Lasagna (p. 135)
Sour Cream Dressing (p. 153)
Quick Russian Borsch (p. 36)
Crumbled Hamburger (p. 45)

ONION FAMILY

Onions come as young green (scallions), dry, dried flakes, onion salt or liquid onion.

Chives are slender young shoots with mild onion flavor usually sold growing in pots.

Garlic comes fresh, dried, as garlic salt, powdered garlic, or liquid garlic.

Leeks are large green onions, mild in flavor; they come fresh or powdered.

SAUCES

Worcestershire Sauce: Made of soy, anchovies, shallots, onions, garlic, vinegar and seasonings. Use to season soups, sea foods, steaks, chops and gravies.

Tabasco Sauce: Made of red pepper, vinegar and salt—only a few drops are needed to flavor sea foods, gravy, eggs, French dressing.

Soy Sauce: Use not only in Chinese-type dishes but in other casseroles and stews. It is very salty, so cut down on salt in these recipes.

FLAVOR EXTENDER

Monosodium Glutamate (MSG): A white crystalline substance made from vegetable proteins. Brings out natural flavor of foods. Comes in small shaker-top packages under various brands. Ask your grocer.

FOR EXTRA MEAT FLAVOR

Meat Extract: Liquid and paste concentrates; increase meat flavor and color in gravies and sauces.

Bouillon Cubes: Beef and chicken bouillon cubes also give depth of flavor to stocks, casserole dishes and soups.

GARNISHES

Parsley: Fresh parsley is not only a pretty garnish, but adds flavor to soups, stews, Tartar Sauce (p. 123). Dried parsley is easy to keep on hand and more economical for use in cooking.

Mint: Use fresh leaves in beverages and vegetables, and to make sauce for lamb.

KEEP THESE EVERYDAY SEASONINGS ON YOUR SHELF:

mustard	cinnamon	allspice	cloves
paprika	sage	nutmeg	ginger

poultry seasoning

SELECT SOME SPECIAL SEASONINGS FROM THESE:

Use herbs with a light hand, to enhance, not disguise. You may have fresh herbs from your garden or buy them in dry powdered form.

Bay Leaf: For soups, stews, meats, poultry, herb bread. Use sparingly, either crumbled or whole, and remove before serving.

Marjoram: For soups, stews, sauces, meats, stuffings and fish.

Thyme: For soups, stews, sauces, meats, poultry, fish, cheese dishes, tomato dishes, herb bread. Use sparingly, then taste.

Rosemary: A fragrant herb for meat, poultry, stews, stuffings, sauces —gives a subtle flavor.

Basil: Unusual flavor for soups, sauces, meats, especially good for tomato dishes, salads and herb bread.

Savory: For stuffings, pork, green beans.

Curry Powder (a powdered combination of herbs and spices): Livens up lamb, veal, pork, chicken and seasoned butters.

Caraway Seed (an aromatic seed): Used in cookies, bread, sauerkraut, other vegetables, cheese, roast pork.

Peppercorn: Used in soups, stews and meat dishes.

Chili Powder (made from mild red pepper): Used in meats and vegetables.

Poppy Seed (seed of the poppy plant without opium): For buttered noodles, breads.

Tarragon: Delicate pungent herb, slightly acid, for salads, salad dressings, soups, fish sauces, meats, stews and herb bread.

Oregano (wild marjoram): Used in all Spanish and Mexican dishes, excellent with lamb, tomatoes.

Celery Seed: For potato salad, salad dressings. Celery Salt (celery seed mashed and mixed with salt): For meats, stews, egg dishes, soups.

QUICK PICKLED BEETS

no. 2 can sliced beets
¼ cup vinegar
1 tsp. salt
¼ tsp. cinnamon
⅛ tsp. cloves
dash of pepper

Drain juice from beets; add remaining ingredients to juice and bring to boiling. Pour over beets and set in refrigerator to chill and season overnight.

CURRIED FRUIT BAKE

no. 1 can pear halves
6 maraschino cherries
no. 1 can cling peach or
apricot halves
no. 2 can pineapple slices or
chunks
⅓ cup butter, melted
¾ cup brown sugar (packed)
4 tsp. curry powder

Heat oven to 325° (slow mod.). Drain fruit and arrange in 13x 9½x2″ pan. Pour over a mixture of remaining ingredients. Bake 15 min. Baste with drippings in pan; bake 15 min. more. Serve hot as meat accompaniment.

SPICED PRUNES

½ lb. prunes (about 1 cup)
1 stick cinnamon
½ tsp. whole cloves
¼ cup brown sugar
2 tbsp. vinegar

Cover prunes with water; simmer 30 min. Add remaining ingredients; simmer 30 min. more, until tender. Serve hot as a garnish with meat. *6 servings.*

QUICK FROZEN PRESERVES

16-oz. pkg. frozen fruit
(strawberries, other
berries, peaches)
2 tbsp. powdered pectin
(such as Sure-Jell, Certo)
¾ cup sugar

Place frozen fruit in tightly covered saucepan; cook over high heat about 2 min., stirring occasionally to break up fruit. Stir in pectin; bring to a rapid boil and boil 1 min. Add sugar and bring to full rolling boil; boil 1 min. while stirring constantly. Pour mixture into jelly glasses and chill until it sets.

MINUTE CHUTNEY

½ cup canned mincemeat
¼ cup chopped pear or
apple
1 tbsp. chopped green
pepper
1 tbsp. vinegar
1 tsp. grated onion
dash of cayenne pepper

Combine all ingredients. ⅔ *cup relish.*

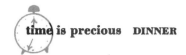

You can save many minutes—sometimes hours—by using some ready-to-serve foods when getting a meal. You will eat well, but the cost will be slightly higher. It is up to you to decide whether the saving in time or in money is of greater importance to you.

Examples of time-saving foods are given all through this book. Here is a whole menu you might like to prepare —in three ways—to prove to yourself the difference in time and money involved in using home-prepared, partially prepared and ready-to-serve foods.

 A BAKED HAM DINNER FOR SIX
(with approximate times for preparation)

HOME-PREPARED	PARTIALLY PREPARED	READY-TO-SERVE
4-lb. baked ham (tenderized) 2½ hr.	Baked ham (canned) 1½ hr.	Baked ham (purchased) no time
Candied sweet potatoes (homemade) 1¼ hr.	Candied sweet potatoes (canned sweet potatoes; canned caramel syrup) ½ hr.	Candied sweet potatoes (canned) ½ hr.
Green beans, cut (fresh) 20 min.	Green beans, cut (frozen) 10 min.	Green beans, cut (canned) 5 min.
Rolls (homemade) 2½ hr.	Rolls (partially baked) 10 min.	Rolls (purchased) no time
Cabbage and pineapple salad (fresh cabbage; canned pineapple) with homemade dressing ½ hr.	Cabbage and pineapple salad (prepackaged cabbage; canned pineapple) with commercial dressing 5 min.	Cabbage and pineapple salad (purchased) no time
Angel food cake (homemade) with whipped cream (fresh) and strawberries (fresh) 1¼ hr.	Angel food cake (prepared mix) with whipped cream (fresh) and strawberries (frozen) 1 hr.	Angel food cake (purchased) with whipped cream (commercial) and strawberries (frozen) no time

CHILI CON CARNE

1 large onion, chopped
1 lb. ground beef
½ lb. bulk pork sausage
no. 2 can tomatoes
no. 2 can kidney beans
   (use 2 cans, if desired)
1 to 2 tbsp. chili powder
½ to 1 tsp. salt

Brown meat; crumble with fork.
Add rest of ingredients. Simmer
1 hr. *4 servings.*

CHILI WITH CORN CHIPS

Heat oven to 350° (mod.). Place
in alternate layers in greased 1-
qt. baking dish, a no. 2 can chili
with meat and half of a 4-oz. bag
corn chips. Sprinkle grated
cheese over top. Cover and bake
30 to 45 min. *4 servings.*

PORK CHOP DINNER

4 pork chops, 1″ thick
½ cup seasoned
   Gold Medal Flour
2 tbsp. hot fat
4 medium potatoes
4 medium onions
4 medium carrots
1 tsp. salt
¼ tsp. pepper

Dredge chops in flour; brown
slowly in hot fat in pressure
cooker. Turn chops; place vegetables on top of chops. Season.
Cook at 10 lb. 30 min. *4 servings.*

CABBAGE PATCH STEW

½ lb. ground beef
2 tbsp. fat
2 medium onions,
   sliced thin
1 cup shredded cabbage
½ cup diced celery
no. 1 can red kidney beans
1 cup cooked tomatoes
salt and pepper
1 tsp. chili powder
hot mashed potato

Brown ground beef in hot fat
over med. heat; add onions, cabbage and celery; cook until yellow. Add water to cover (about
2 cups); simmer 15 min. Add
beans, tomatoes and seasonings;
cook 15 to 25 min. Serve in bowls
topped with spoonfuls of mashed
potato. *6 servings.*

FULL O' BOLONEY

2 cups cubed raw potatoes
1½ cups cut-up bologna
2 tbsp. minced green pepper
6 tbsp. Gold Medal Flour
¼ tsp. salt
¼ tsp. pepper
3 tbsp. butter
2 cups milk

Heat oven to 350° (mod.). Arrange potatoes, bologna, green
pepper, flour and seasonings in
layers in 1½-qt. baking dish, dot-
ting each layer with butter. Pour
milk over and bake 1 hr. 15 min.
4 to 6 servings.

FARMERS' PORK CHOPS

See picture, p. 178.

4 loin or shoulder
  pork chops
1 clove garlic, chopped
salt and pepper
4 potatoes, sliced
2 large onions, sliced
1½ cups sour cream
1½ tsp. salt
½ tsp. dry mustard

Heat oven to 350° (mod.). Trim excess fat from chops and roll in flour. Brown chops and garlic in hot fat over medium heat. Season with salt and pepper. Place potatoes in 11½x7½x1½" baking pan; top with browned chops. Separate onion slices into rings and lay over chops. Blend sour cream, salt, mustard; pour over potatoes, chops and onions. Bake 1½ hr. *4 servings.*

PORK CHOP CASSEROLE

6 large ½" thick slices
  sweet potato (cooked or
  uncooked)
6 thin slices unpeeled orange
6 pork chops
1 tsp. salt
¼ tsp. pepper
⅓ cup brown sugar

Heat oven to 350° (mod.). Place potato slices in greased oblong baking dish; top with orange slices, then pork chops. Season with salt and pepper; sprinkle with brown sugar. Cover and bake 1½ hr., uncovering last half hr. *6 servings.*

BEEF ROLL DINNER

4 medium minute steaks
salt and pepper
2 cups Bread Stuffing (p. 120)
8-oz. can tomato sauce
1 tsp. sugar
4 small white onions,
  peeled
1 pkg. frozen French-style
  green beans, thawed
  (½ lb. fresh)

Sprinkle salt, pepper lightly over steaks. Cover with Bread Stuffing. Roll, fasten with toothpicks. Brown in hot fat. Add tomato sauce, sugar, onions. Cover. Simmer in skillet until tender, 30 to 45 min. Add green beans during last 10 to 15 min. of cooking. *4 servings.*

CALIFORNIA PILAU

1 lb. ground beef
2 to 3 tbsp. fat
4½-oz. can chopped
  ripe olives (½ cup)
⅓ cup finely chopped
  green pepper
⅓ cup finely chopped onion
1 small clove garlic, minced
½ cup rice (uncooked)
2 cups hot water
6-oz. can tomato paste
  (¾ cup)
1½ tsp. salt
¼ tsp. pepper

Heat oven to 350° (mod.). Brown meat in hot fat over medium heat; crumble with fork. Add rest of ingredients. Stir to get all brown from pan. Pour into 2-qt. baking dish. Bake 1 hr. *6 servings.*

CREOLE PIE
IN SCONE SHELL

½ lb. bulk pork sausage
¼ cup chopped green pepper
¼ cup chopped onion
¼ cup Gold Medal Flour
1 tsp. salt
⅛ tsp. pepper
1 cup cooked tomatoes
2 cups cooked vegetables
(such as corn,
green beans, peas)

Brown sausage in large skillet; add green pepper and onion; cook until soft. Stir in flour, salt and pepper. Blend in tomatoes; cook until smooth and thick, stirring occasionally. Add vegetables and heat through. Pour into hot baked Scone Shell (below); cut in wedges to serve. *6 servings.*

SCONE SHELL

1½ cups sifted
Gold Medal Flour
2 tsp. baking powder
1 tsp. salt
⅓ cup shortening
1 large egg, beaten
⅓ cup milk

Heat oven to 425° (hot). Sift together flour, baking powder and salt; cut in shortening. Stir in egg and milk. Round up and roll out larger than inverted 9″ pie pan. Place loosely in pie pan. Press from center out so there are no air pockets; build up fluted edge; prick sides and bottom well with fork to prevent puffing. Bake 15 min.

MEXICAN DINNER

1 cup chopped onion
2 tbsp. fat
1 lb. ground beef
1 tsp. salt
½ tsp. chili powder
1 tbsp. Worcestershire sauce
10½-oz. can tomato soup
1 cup water
Quick Corn Bread batter
(p. 25)

Heat oven to 450° (hot). Brown onion in hot fat; add meat and brown until crumbly. Add seasonings, soup and water; bring just to boiling, stirring occasionally. Pour Quick Corn Bread batter over meat in skillet. Bake 20 min. *6 to 8 servings.*

HASH SKILLET PIE

1 recipe Stir-N-Roll
Pastry (p. 176)
1-lb. can corned beef hash,
broken up
¼ cup milk or tomato juice
2 tbsp. chopped onion

Heat oven to 425° (hot). Roll pastry to 12″ sq.; ease into heavy 10″ skillet, let pastry hang over edge. Mix remaining ingredients; place in pastry-lined skillet. Fold pastry over filling; bake 30 to 40 min. Cut in wedges and serve with hot chili sauce or catsup. *4 to 6 servings.*

CHICKEN VEGETABLE PIE

2 cups mixed cooked
  vegetables (canned,
  frozen or leftover),
  drained
1-lb. can chicken fricassee
½ cup liquid from
  vegetables
½ tsp. salt
¼ tsp. pepper
½ recipe Stir-N-Roll
  Biscuits (p. 28)

Heat oven to 425° (hot). Place vegetables in 1-qt. baking dish or 10 x 6 x 1½″ oblong pan. Remove bones from chicken; spread chicken over vegetables. Combine vegetable liquid, salt and pepper; pour over chicken and vegetables. Place in oven while making biscuit dough. Drop biscuit dough on hot mixture. Bake 15 to 20 min. *4 to 6 servings.*

CORN-FRANK ROUND-UP

Quick Corn Bread batter
  (p. 25)
8 frankfurters or
  browned sausages
1 tbsp. prepared mustard
1 tbsp. cooking oil

Heat oven to 375° (quick mod.). Spread corn bread batter in greased 11½x7½x1½″ baking pan. Cut frankfurters in 1″ pieces; sprinkle over batter. Bake 20 min. Brush top with mixture of mustard and oil, continue baking 15 to 20 min. Serve with catsup or chili sauce. *6 to 8 servings.*

YANKEE CHICKEN HASH

½ lb. bulk pork sausage
½ cup chopped green pepper
½ cup chopped onion
2 cups cut-up cooked chicken
2 tbsp. minced parsley
2 tbsp. minced chives
½ cup dry bread crumbs
½ cup rich milk
1 cup chicken stock
½ tsp. salt
½ recipe Stir-N-Roll
  Biscuits (p. 28)

Heat oven to 475° (very hot). Brown sausage in hot skillet; add green pepper and onion and cook until soft. Drain excess fat. Stir in remaining ingredients; pour into 1½-qt. baking dish. Place in oven to heat while making biscuits. Drop biscuit dough on hot mixture. Bake 12 to 15 min. *6 servings.*

HAMBURGER PIE

1 small onion, chopped
1 lb. ground beef
½ tsp. salt
¼ tsp. pepper
½ tsp. flavor extender
  (p. 124)
no. 2 can green beans
10½-oz. can tomato soup
about 2 cups mashed potato

Heat oven to 350° (mod.). Cook onion in hot fat until yellow; add meat and cook until brown. Add seasonings, drained beans and soup; pour into 1½-qt. baking dish. Spoon mashed potato over mixture. Bake 30 min. *6 servings.*

GOLDEN FISH CASSEROLE

1 small green pepper,
    thinly sliced
2 medium onions,
    thinly sliced
3 tbsp. butter
¼ cup Gold Medal Flour
¾ tsp. salt
2 cups milk
1-lb. can salmon, flaked
1 tbsp. lemon juice
Pimiento-Cheese
    Pinwheels (below)

Heat oven to 425° (hot). Sauté green pepper and onions in butter; blend in flour and salt; cook until bubbly. Add milk slowly, heat for 5 min., stirring constantly. Add salmon and lemon juice; pour into greased 1½-qt. baking dish; set in oven while making Pinwheels (below). Place 8 Pinwheels on hot mixture. Bake 25 to 30 min. *8 servings.*

Pimiento-Cheese Pinwheels: Make ½ recipe Rolled Biscuits (p. 28 or Bisquick pkg.). Roll dough into 8x12″ rectangle; spread 2 tbsp. cut-up pimiento and ½ cup grated sharp cheese over top. Roll up, beginning at narrow side. Cut in ½″ slices. Bake extra Pinwheels on baking sheet the last 12 to 15 min. the casserole is in the oven.

BAKED TUNA OR SALMON PIE

Stir-N-Roll Pastry for
    2-crust Pie (p. 176)
2 cups diced cooked potato
¼ cup chopped green or
    dry onion
2 tbsp. chopped green
    pepper or pimiento
½ cup milk
1 tsp. salt
¼ tsp. pepper
6½-oz. can tuna or
    7-oz. can salmon, flaked
¼ lb. American cheese,
    sliced

Heat oven to 425° (hot). Mix potato, onion, green pepper, milk, salt and pepper; spread in pastry-lined 9″ pie pan. Place tuna, then cheese over mixture. Cover with top crust; make slits; bake 35 to 40 min. Cut in wedges and serve with Cheese Sauce (p. 122) or partially thinned cream of tomato or mushroom soup. *6 servings.*

TUNA–BROCCOLI CASSEROLE

1 pkg. frozen broccoli
7-oz. can tuna, flaked
10½-oz. can cream of
    mushroom soup
½ soup can milk
½ cup crushed potato
    chips (1 small bag)

Heat oven to 450° (hot). Split broccoli stalks; cook 3 min.; drain. Place in 1½-qt. baking dish. Cover with tuna. Mix soup and milk, pour over tuna. Sprinkle potato chips over top. Bake 15 min. *4 servings.*

TUNA TARTS

2-oz. can mushrooms
  (¼ cup), drained
1 tbsp. finely chopped onion
1½ tbsp. fat
1½ tbsp. flour
¼ tsp. salt
1½ cups milk or
  mushroom liquid
2 tbsp. finely chopped
  pimiento
7-oz. can tuna,
  broken in large pieces

Brown mushrooms and onion in hot fat; blend in flour and salt. Remove from heat. Gradually add milk or liquid; cook over low heat until thickened, stirring constantly. Add pimiento and tuna; heat. Serve in Perfect Patty Shells (p. 193). *6 servings.*

SALMON RAREBIT PIE

See picture, p. 179.

1-lb. can salmon,
  drained and flaked
1 cup cooked peas, drained
2 tbsp. finely chopped
  green pepper
1 cup grated cheese (¼ lb.)
½ cup milk
2 tbsp. mayonnaise
⅓ cup milk
1 cup Bisquick

Heat oven to 450° (hot). Mix salmon, peas and green pepper; place in greased 10x6x1½" baking pan. Blend cheese and milk; pour over salmon mixture. Add mayonnaise and milk to Bisquick; mix with fork. Drop dough by spoonfuls on salmon mixture. Bake 10 to 15 min., until browned. *6 servings.*

TUNA SWIRLS

Stir-N-Roll Biscuit Dough
  (below)
7-oz. can flaked tuna
  (or cooked chicken,
  ham or veal)
½ cup diced celery
¼ cup mayonnaise
1 tbsp. finely chopped onion
1 tsp. lemon juice
¼ tsp. salt

Heat oven to 450° (hot). Roll Stir-N-Roll Biscuit dough into oblong, ¼" thick, between sheets of waxed paper. Mix rest of ingredients. Spread on dough. Roll up, beginning at wide side; seal by pinching edge of dough into roll. Place sealed edge under on baking sheet. Bake 15 to 20 min. Slice and serve with Mushroom Sauce (p. 123). *4 servings.*

Stir-N-Roll Biscuit Dough: Take 1⅓ cups sifted Gold Medal Flour, 2 tsp. baking powder, ½ tsp. salt, ¼ cup cooking (salad) oil, ½ cup milk. Sift dry ingredients together into bowl. Pour oil and milk into measuring cup (don't stir). Then pour all at once into flour. Stir with fork until mixture cleans sides of bowl.

VEAL CASSEROLE

1 lb. cubed veal
2 tbsp. fat
1½ cups sliced celery
2 small onions, chopped
10½-oz. can cream of
  chicken soup
10½-oz. can cream of
  mushroom soup
1 to 1½ soup cans water
2 to 3 tbsp. soy sauce
½ cup uncooked rice

Heat oven to 325° (slow mod.).
Roll meat in flour; brown in
hot fat over medium heat; stir
in rest of ingredients. Pour into
2-qt. baking dish. Bake covered
1½ hr. *6 servings.*

LAMB AND SPINACH

1 clove garlic, minced
¼ cup diced onion
2 tbsp. fat or cooking
  (salad) oil
1 lb. lean lamb, cut in 1″
  strips
½ tsp. salt
¼ tsp. pepper
¼ cup water
1 lb. fresh spinach
¼ cup water
2 tbsp. soy sauce
2 tbsp. cornstarch

Sauté garlic and onion in hot fat
until yellow; add meat and
brown. Add seasoning and ¼ cup
water; cover and cook over low
heat 1 hr. Add spinach; cover
and cook 5 min., stirring once or
twice. Stir in mixture of ¼ cup
water, soy sauce and cornstarch.
Cook, stirring constantly, until
thickened. Serve with hot fluffy
rice. *4 servings.*

VEAL SCALLOPINI

1 clove garlic
1½ lb. veal, cut thin and
  in serving pieces
¼ cup cooking (salad) oil
¾ cup sliced onion
¼ lb. mushrooms, sliced or
  4-oz. can, drained
2 tbsp. flour
½ tsp. salt
⅛ tsp. pepper
½ cup water
1 cup tomato sauce

Cook garlic and meat in hot oil
until meat is brown. Remove
meat and discard garlic. Cook
onions and mushrooms in oil until tender. Blend in flour, salt and
pepper; let bubble. Gradually
stir in water and tomato sauce;
cook until thickened, stirring
constantly. Add browned meat
and cook 10 min. Serve with spaghetti. *4 to 6 servings.*
For Oven Cookery: Brown ingredients in hot oil; place in 1½-
qt. baking dish. Make the gravy
and pour over. Bake in mod.
oven (400°) for 15 min.

CHICKEN-WILD RICE CASSEROLE

2 cups cut-up cooked chicken
1½ to 2 cups cooked wild
  rice (directions on pkg.)
¼ cup chopped green pepper
10½-oz. can cream of
  mushroom soup
½ soup can milk
salt and pepper

Heat oven to 350° (mod.). Mix
ingredients together; place in
greased 2-qt. baking dish. Bake
30 min. *6 servings.*

CURRY OF LAMB

2 lb. lamb shoulder,
    cut in ½" sq.
1 tbsp. fat
3 tbsp. chopped onion
1 tbsp. curry powder
1 tbsp. flour
2 bouillon cubes
2 cups boiling water
¼ cup catsup
½ tsp. salt
½ cup chopped apple
1 cup diced celery

Brown meat in hot fat over medium heat; add onion and cook until yellow. Add curry mixed with flour; allow to bubble. Add bouillon cubes dissolved in water, catsup, salt, apple and celery; simmer 1¼ hr. Serve with hot fluffy rice. *4 servings.*

Serving Note: Serve with chutney; buy at the store or make Minute Chutney (p. 126).

AMERICAN PIZZA PIE

2 cups Bisquick
½ cup water
½ cup grated Parmesan
    cheese
1½ to 2 cups well drained
    cooked tomatoes, cut in
    small pieces
½ lb. nippy cheese,
    cut in small pieces
2-oz. can anchovies,
    chopped, or 1 can
    sardines or 1 cup
    chopped salami
pepper
2 tbsp. cooking (salad) oil
½ medium onion, grated

Heat oven to 425° (hot). Mix Bisquick and water; knead about 1 min. on lightly floured surface.

Roll out ¼" thick into a circle. Place on baking sheet. Pinch edge of dough to make a slight rim. Place other ingredients on dough in order listed above. Bake 20 to 25 min. *6 meal servings, 8 snack servings.*

LASAGNA

1 medium onion, chopped
1 clove garlic, minced
3 tbsp. olive or cooking
    (salad) oil
no. 2 can tomatoes or
    tomato juice
8-oz. can tomato sauce
1 tbsp. minced parsley
1 tbsp. sugar
2 tsp. salt
1 tsp. ground basil
2 5-oz. pkg. noodles, 2" wide
½ lb. American cheese,
    sliced
1 cup sour cream
⅓ cup grated Parmesan
    cheese

Heat oven to 350° (mod.). Brown onion and garlic in hot oil. Add tomato, parsley, sugar and seasonings; simmer 1 hr. Cook noodles in 3 qt. boiling water and 1 tbsp. oil. Alternate noodles, sliced cheese, sour cream, sauce and grated cheese in 9" sq. pan, ending with sauce and grated cheese. Bake 30 min. Cut in squares to serve. *8 servings.*

ITALIAN DINNER
Italian Spaghetti
with Meat Balls
Tossed Green Salad
Crusty Chive Bread
Spumoni Ice Cream

FIESTA TAMALE PIE

1 small onion, minced
1 clove garlic, minced
3 tbsp. butter
3 tbsp. olive oil
1 lb. ground beef
½ lb. pork sausage
no. 2½ can tomatoes
no. 2 can whole-kernel corn
2 tsp. salt
2 tsp. chili powder
20 to 24 pitted ripe olives
1 cup corn meal
1 cup milk
2 eggs, well beaten
1½ cups grated American
   cheese

Heat oven to 350° (mod.). Sauté onion and garlic in butter and oil until yellow. Add ground beef and sausage; cook until brown. Simmer tomatoes, corn, salt and chili powder in saucepan 20 min.; add to meat mixture. Pour into 11½x7½x1½" pan. Press olives into mixture. Mix corn meal, milk and eggs; spread over filling. Sprinkle with grated cheese. Bake 1 hr. *8 to 10 servings.*

ITALIAN SPAGHETTI

1 lb. ground beef
2 tbsp. minced parsley
2 medium onions, chopped
2 cloves garlic, minced
¼ cup olive oil or cooking
   (salad) oil
2 8-oz. cans tomato purée
2 6-oz. cans tomato paste
2 tsp. Worcestershire sauce
salt and pepper to taste
8-oz. pkg. long spaghetti

Brown meat in hot oil; add parsley, onions and garlic; cook until yellow. Add rest of ingredients except spaghetti; simmer over low heat 2 hr. Serve over hot drained spaghetti; top with Meat Balls (below). Pass Parmesan cheese. *6 servings.*

Note: Spaghetti doubles bulk in cooking. Follow directions for cooking on pkg. Cook *just* until tender, not soft.

MEAT BALLS

¾ lb. ground beef
¼ lb. ground pork
1 cup fine dry bread crumbs
½ cup grated Parmesan
   cheese
1 tbsp. minced parsley
1 clove garlic, minced
½ cup milk
2 beaten eggs
salt and pepper to taste

Mix together all ingredients; form in balls the size of large walnuts. Brown on all sides in hot fat; continue cooking 30 min. in all.

Note: Meat Balls can be made ahead of time, then reheated in covered pan in slow oven (325°).

Vegetable cookery has become ever so easy today, with the new methods of vegetable harvesting and shipping. You may buy field-fresh vegetables the year around, often cleaned and packaged in clear cellophane bags that help retain the foods' freshness. Or you may buy vegetables quick-frozen, or canned in new, improved ways. Choose the kind that best fits your time and purpose.

COOKING FRESH VEGETABLES

Boil them for the shortest time possible, to retain color, flavor and health-giving elements. Use ½ to 1" water in a covered saucepan (smaller amount for heavy pan with tight cover). Use high heat until steam appears, then low heat until just tender crisp.

Braise in pan or skillet with about 2 tbsp. butter and 1 to 2 tbsp. water.

Steam on a rack or in a perforated pan over a small amount of boiling water.

Simmer in milk or cream seasoned with salt, pepper and butter.

Bake or steam bake in covered casserole with small amount of water. Baking requires 2 to 3 times longer cooking than boiling.

COOKING CANNED VEGETABLES

Merely heat—do not boil. Season and serve immediately. Canned cream soups make quick, easy sauces to serve with vegetables. Use the juices from the canned vegetables themselves for soups, gravies, sauces or serve with vegetables.

PRESSURE COOKING

A pressure cooker not only saves time but preserves minerals, vitamins and flavor. Follow manufacturer's directions.

COOKING FROZEN VEGETABLES

Follow directions on each package. Do not overcook.

SERVING VEGETABLES

Vegetables may be served in many ways—raw in salads, creamed, fried, scalloped, au gratin, and just plain buttered. The next few pages bring some suggestions.

ASPARAGUS

Snap off tough ends. Wash thoroughly; remove scales if sandy. Cook covered in about 1″ boiling salted water; cook whole stalks upright in narrow deep pan or coffee pot 10 to 20 min., 1″ lengths 10 to 15 min.

WAYS TO SERVE

Add butter, salt, pepper.

Top with melted butter to which has been added a few drops of lemon juice, minced chives, grated nutmeg or prepared mustard.

Top with Creamed Eggs or Goldenrod Eggs (p. 52).

Serve on toast; top with creamed dried beef, ham or chicken.

Top with Hollandaise Sauce (p. 122); sometimes add a tsp. dry mustard.

Top with Mushroom, Cheese, Almond, Egg or Lemon Butter Sauce (pp. 122, 123).

Sprinkle with grated cheese and broil until cheese melts.

Sprinkle with buttered toast crumbs or chopped almonds or peanuts or pimiento strips.

Garnish with sieved or sliced hard-cooked egg or with lemon wedges.

LIMA BEANS

Wash. Cut off outer rim of pods. Shell like peas. Cook covered in ½ to 1″ boiling salted water, 20 to 25 min.

WAYS TO SERVE

Add butter, salt, pepper.

Combine with corn, whole-kernel or cream style, and garnish with pimiento.

Add sautéed mushrooms.

Combine with cream, salt, pepper. Bake, covered, 1 hr. at 350°.

Mix with sour cream, salt, pepper, chives and put in hollow of baked squash.

GREEN OR WAX BEANS

Wash, snip off ends. Cook covered in about ½ to 1″ boiling salted water; cook whole beans 15 to 20 min., 1″ lengths 15 to 20 min., thin lengthwise strips (French style) 10 min.

WAYS TO SERVE

Add butter, salt, pepper.

Top with Hollandaise, Mushroom, Cheese, Almond, Egg or Lemon Butter Sauce (pp. 122, 123).

Top with browned onion rings in cream, seasoned with salt and nutmeg.

Add cooked tiny green onions.

Sprinkle with grated cheese or sautéed mushrooms.

Sprinkle with toasted chopped almonds, peanuts or bacon bits or buttered toast crumbs.

BEETS

Cut off all but about 2″ of tops. Wash. Cook whole, covered, in boiling salted water to cover, until tender, 30 to 45 min. Drain. Pour cold water over; rub off skins. Serve whole or sliced or diced. Reheat with seasonings.

WAYS TO SERVE

Add butter, salt, pepper; and basil, savory or caraway.

Combine with cream, dash of horse-radish.

Combine with equal amounts of vinegar and sugar boiled until syrupy; may add a clove.

Slice and combine with onion and hard-cooked egg chopped together, mix with cream, dash of prepared mustard, horse-radish, salt and pepper.

Sprinkle with minced chives or parsley.

Cook shredded raw beets, covered, in water just covering bottom of pan. Season with salt, pepper, sugar, butter, lemon or orange juice.

BROCCOLI

Wash. Trim tips of stems. Make 3 to 4 gashes through stems.
Cook upright in pan, covered, in about 1″ boiling salted water, 10 to 15 min.
For Italian style, partially cook; then sauté in butter or oil; sprinkle with Parmesan cheese.

WAYS TO SERVE
See Asparagus, p. 138.

BRUSSELS SPROUTS

Remove loose and discolored leaves. Trim tips of stems. Wash. Cook, covered, in about ½ to 1″ boiling salted water 8 to 10 min.

WAYS TO SERVE

Add butter, salt and pepper, a little lemon juice.

Top with sautéed mushrooms.

Sprinkle with crisp bacon bits, minced parsley or chives.

CABBAGE

Wash. Cut into wedges, remove core; or shred. Cook, covered, in about ½ to 1″ boiling salted water, 10 to 15 min.
For red cabbage, add a little lemon juice or vinegar to keep color bright.
May simmer in cream or milk in place of water, but do not boil milk.

WAYS TO SERVE
Add butter, salt, pepper.

Blend with well seasoned cream, Cream or Cheese Sauce (p. 122).

Mix with corn; sprinkle with crisp bacon bits.

Sprinkle with buttered toast crumbs or caraway seeds.

Add 1 beaten egg, 1 tbsp. lemon juice, 2 tbsp. butter to hot cooked shredded head of cabbage, well drained.

CARROTS

Remove tops. Scrape or pare thinly or scrub with brush. Cook, covered, in about ½ to 1″ boiling salted water. If whole, cook 15 to 20 min.; if sliced or diced, 10 to 20 min.; or shredded, 5 min. Dash of sugar, orange rind or apple slice may be added to cooking water.

WAYS TO SERVE

Add butter, salt, pepper; dash of lemon or thyme, if desired.

Cream with celery; garnish with ripe olives.

Top with cooked little green onions and Lemon Butter Sauce (p. 123).

Top with a little Hard Sauce (p. 170) and sprinkling of grated orange rind.

Sprinkle with parsley or mint leaves or sautéed onions.

Simmer 2 cups cooked carrot strips with ¼ cup each butter and sugar until soft and glazed. Add 1 tbsp. mint sauce, fresh or bought ready-prepared.

Steam with bit of water in covered baking pan in oven. Serve with sprig of mint or parsley stuck in end of each carrot.

CAULIFLOWER

Wash well. Remove green stalks. Cook, covered, in about ½ to 1″ unsalted water. If whole, cook 20 to 30 min.; broken into flowerets, 8 to 15 min., just until tender. Add salt after cooking to keep color white; also add a little lemon juice or vinegar to the cooking water.

WAYS TO SERVE

Add butter, salt and pepper.

Top with Mushroom, Cheese, Almond, Lemon Butter, Egg or Curry Sauce (pp. 122, 123).

Top with Cream Sauce (p. 122) to which cut-up dried beef frizzled in butter has been added.

Sprinkle with grated cheese and broil until cheese melts.

Stick salted almonds or peanuts into whole cooked head. Serve with Cream Sauce (p. 122).

Stick cubes of cheese into whole cooked head. Place in casserole with small amount of cream; top with buttered crumbs and crisp bacon bits and brown in oven.

CELERY

Remove leaves; trim roots. Wash thoroughly. Reserve inner stalks to serve raw. Dice outer stalks; cook, covered, in about 1″ boiling salted water 10 to 20 min.

(See next page for Ways to Serve.)

WAYS TO SERVE CELERY
Add butter, salt and pepper.

Top with Cream, Hollandaise, Egg or Cheese Sauce (p. 122).

Combine with cooked cauliflowerets or peas.

Sprinkle with grated cheese, buttered toast crumbs, crisp bacon bits, toasted chopped almonds or peanuts, or minced parsley or chives.

CORN
Just before serving, remove husks and silk. Line bottom of pan with some of husks; place corn on top. Cook, covered, in about 1″ boiling unsalted (salt toughens) water, 3 to 6 min. Add a little sugar in cooking water.

WAYS TO SERVE OFF THE COB
Add butter or cream, salt, pepper.

Combine with sautéed onion and green pepper.

Combine with cooked little green onions.

Combine with baby green Limas as succotash.

Combine with meat in stuffed green peppers, or as filling in stuffed baked tomatoes.

Sprinkle with crisp bacon bits; parsley; chives or pimiento; or chopped green pepper.

Combine canned cream style and whole kernel corn. Add butter, seasonings.

SPECIAL TREAT SCALLOPED CORN
Combine no. 303 can cream style corn, ½ cup milk, ½ cup cracker or bread crumbs, ¼ cup each chopped onion and green pepper, salt, pepper, 1 tbsp. butter. Bake 30 min. in mod. oven (350°). *4 servings.*

EGGPLANT
Wash; do not soak. Paring not necessary unless skin is tough. Slice, cube or cut in strips. Cook, covered, in about ½″ boiling salted water 10 to 15 min. Or, season with salt, pepper; dip in flour or dry bread or cracker crumbs, egg, crumbs. Sauté in small amount of hot fat or French fry in hot fat (375°) to cover, 2 to 4 min. Or brush with butter and broil 5 to 10 min.

WAYS TO SERVE
Use boiled eggplant in scalloped and au gratin dishes combined with tomatoes, cheese.

Serve with Tomato Sauce (p. 123), catsup or chili sauce.

Combine with sautéed tomatoes (p. 145), or onions or green pepper.

Sprinkle with minced chives, parsley or grated Parmesan cheese.

Ham and Eggplant au Gratin (see p. 204).

ONIONS

Green: Wash; trim to about 5" lengths. Cook in about ½ to 1" boiling salted water, about 8 to 10 min.

Dry: Wash; remove loose layers of skin. Leave whole. Cook, covered, in about 1 to 2" boiling salted water—large, 30 to 35 min., small, 15 to 20 min. Or bake whole, in covered casserole, 50 to 60 min.

Canned: Heat in cream over hot water, or sauté in butter.

WAYS TO SERVE

Add butter, salt and pepper.

Top with well seasoned cream or Cream Sauce (p. 122).

Top with Cheese, Mushroom, Egg or Almond Sauce (pp. 122, 123).

Combine with sautéed tomato slices; plain, or with a sauce.

Combine with cooked carrot sticks and green beans.

Sprinkle with buttered toast crumbs; chopped toasted almonds; peanuts or crisp bacon; or paprika, parsley or pimiento.

Stuff onions by scooping out centers. Fill with bread crumbs or seasoned ground meat; bake.

Dip onion rings in milk and flour. Sauté in small amount of butter. Or French fry in hot fat (375°) to cover, until golden, 1 to 2 min.

PARSNIPS

Scrape or pare; or scrub with brush. Cook, covered, in 1" boiling salted water about 30 min.

WAYS TO SERVE

Add butter, salt and pepper.

Partially cook; slice and sauté in butter until golden.

Boil and mash; combine with whipped cream and nutmeg.

PEAS

Shell and wash just before cooking. Cook, covered, in about 1" boiling salted water 8 to 12 min. Drop in a few pods for flavor. May add a few mint leaves and a little sugar. May cook young, tender peas in milk or cream instead of water but do not boil.

WAYS TO SERVE

Add butter, salt and pepper.

Top with melted butter to which have been added a few drops lemon juice, minced chives, grated nutmeg or prepared mustard.

Top with well seasoned cream or Cream, Mushroom, Cheese, Egg or Almond Sauce (pp. 122, 123).

Combine with cooked green onions, carrots, celery or tiny new potatoes.

Combine with sautéed mushrooms or onions.

Combine with fluffy white rice, sprinkled with paprika.

Sprinkle with grated Parmesan cheese; chopped toasted almonds or peanuts; or minced parsley, mint leaves or chives.

POTATOES, IRISH AND SWEET

Wash. Pare if desired. Cook, covered, in about 1″ boiling salted water—whole, 30 to 40 min.; cut-up or whole tiny new potatoes, 15 to 30 min. Or bake in mod. to mod. hot oven (350° to 400°) about 1 hr. Or fry in small amount of hot fat (see Potatoes Anna, below) or French fry in hot fat (375°) to cover, 5 to 8 min. or until brown.

POTATOES ANNA

Melt 2 tbsp. butter in heavy skillet. Arrange thinly sliced raw potatoes in 2 or 3 layers. Sprinkle each layer with salt, pepper; dot generously with butter. Cover; steam 15 min. Uncover; cook until tender and crispy brown on the bottom. Invert on serving plate. *6 servings.*

IRENE'S SCALLOPED POTATOES

3 to 4 cups thinly sliced or coarsely grated raw potatoes
1 tbsp. minced onion
salt and pepper
2 to 4 tbsp. butter
1¼ cups milk, heated

Heat oven to 350° (mod.). Arrange potatoes in layers in 1½-qt. casserole. Sprinkle each layer with salt, pepper; dot with butter. Add hot milk. Bake uncovered about 1¼ hr. *4 servings.*

POTATOES IN THE HALF-SHELL

Cut hot baked potatoes in half, lengthwise. Scoop out potato. Mash, season, add butter and heated milk. Whip until fluffy. Refill shells; sprinkle with grated cheese or paprika. Brown in mod. hot oven (400°).

PRESSURE CREAMED POTATOES

4 cups cubed raw potatoes (1″ cubes)
1¼ cups milk
1 small onion, chopped
2 tbsp. butter
2 tbsp. flour
2 tsp. salt
¼ tsp. pepper
½ tsp. paprika

Combine ingredients in pressure saucepan. Bring pressure to 15 lb., let cool until pressure is reduced. Open, stir until blended. 1 cup grated cheese may be added. *4 to 6 servings.*

HASHED CREAMED POTATOES

Chop finely leftover boiled or baked potatoes. Add half as much cream as potatoes; season. Heat in saucepan until thick, 10 to 15 min. For company, pour into casserole, top with buttered Wheaties, brown in oven.

CANDIED SWEET POTATOES

See Yams, p. 145.

RUTABAGAS

Cook and serve like turnips (p. 145).

SPINACH

All greens may be prepared in the same way as spinach. Cut off root ends and any damaged leaves. Wash thoroughly. Cook, covered, 3 to 10 min., using only the water that clings to the leaves after washing. Season.

WAYS TO SERVE

Add butter, salt and pepper; dash of lemon juice or vinegar; or prepared horse-radish.

Top with Cream, Egg or Almond Sauce (pp. 122,123).

Sprinkle with sieved or sliced hard-cooked egg; chopped toasted almonds or peanuts; sautéed mushrooms; or crisp bacon bits.

Add partly thawed pkg. frozen chopped spinach to 1 cup Thick Cream Sauce (p. 122). Add ⅛ tsp. nutmeg. Cover and cook over boiling water 15 min., stirring occasionally. 4 *servings.*

SQUASH

Summer (the small scalloped and crook-necked ones and zucchini): Wash; do not pare. Remove stems and blossom ends. Slice or cube. Cook, covered, in about ½" boiling salted water until tender, 10 to 15 min. May add a little oil or butter during cooking for flavor.

Winter (acorn, Hubbard, etc.): Wash. Cut into individual servings. Bake, covered, or cut side down on shallow pan with about ¼" water (may season before or after baking with salt, pepper, butter), in mod. hot oven (400°) until tender, 30 to 60 min.

WAYS TO SERVE

Add butter, salt and pepper. For summer varieties add Worcestershire sauce and onion; lemon juice; minced parsley or chives.

Top summer varieties with Hollandaise Sauce, Tomato Sauce (pp. 122, 123), catsup or chili sauce.

Fill hollows of baked winter squash with cooked seasoned Lima beans mixed with sour cream and chives or cooked sausage meat sprinkled with parsley or chives.

Mashed; serve with a little whipped cream, sugar, nutmeg; or with brown sugar, butter or canned butterscotch sauce.

TOMATOES

Wash. Peel, if desired. To peel easily, first dip in hot water 30 seconds, then in cold. Or hold on fork over direct heat until skin splits. Cut into quarters. Simmer gently with no added water about 10 min. Season with salt, pepper and sugar, if desired. Or cut into slices, dip in flour, sauté slowly in butter.

WAYS TO SERVE

Add minced onion, parsley or sweet basil.

Sprinkle with toasted bread crumbs or croutons browned in lightly flavored garlic butter, just before serving.

Sauté seasoned fresh tomato halves in butter. Remove, then brown small amount cream in skillet and serve over tomatoes.

Bake layers of sliced tomatoes and onions, soft bread crumbs and parsley, seasoned and topped with cream and Wheaties, 1 hr. in mod. oven (350°).

TURNIPS

Turnips and rutabagas are cooked the same way. Scrub. Peel as thinly as possible. Cook, covered, in 1″ boiling salted water — whole, 20 to 30 min.; sliced or diced, 15 to 20 min.

WAYS TO SERVE

Dice; add butter, salt, pepper.

Mash, with a little whipped cream; add salt and nutmeg.

YAMS

For cooking method see Potatoes, Irish and Sweet (p. 143).

WAYS TO SERVE

Bake; serve with butter.

Candied: Cover cooked yam or sweet potato halves or slices with equal amounts of brown sugar and butter. Simmer or bake until browned.

To Save Time: Use canned yams or sweet potatoes and canned butterscotch sauce instead of sugar and butter.

VEGETABLE PLATE
Macaroni Cup (p. 48)
Broiled Tomato Slices
Buttered Spinach
Baby Green Limas
Green Olives   Radishes

VEGETABLE PLATE
Poached Egg on Toast
Carrot Sticks   Green Peas
Shredded Cabbage or
Cauliflowerets
Crisp Celery
Pass Lemon Butter Sauce (p. 123)
to serve over cooked vegetables.

Dinner salads are light—not filling; they may be tangy or mild, to complement the meat or main course. One of the most satisfying salads for dinner is tossed greens with a well chosen French-type basic dressing.

USE A VARIETY OF THESE GREENS:

Head lettuce   Leaf lettuce
Bibb or Boston lettuce
Romaine   Escarole   Curly endive
Watercress   Spinach

FOR EXTRA FLAVOR ADD SOME OF THESE:

Green onions   Leeks
Green peppers   Tomatoes
Radishes   Cucumbers   Celery
Cauliflowerets

(If tomatoes are used, place at side of salad after serving; never add, since they dilute the dressing.)

SOMETIMES TRY UNUSUAL ADDITIONS:

Sliced water chestnuts
Tiny croutons browned in garlic butter
Chopped tender raw asparagus stalks
Artichoke hearts   Palm hearts
Parmesan and Roquefort cheese
Crisp bacon   Sliced mushrooms
Ripe olives   Anchovies

TOSSED GREEN SALAD
See picture, pp. 180-181.

Sprinkle salt in wooden bowl; rub cut clove of garlic over salt in bowl. Be sure greens are dry. Twist and tear (never cut) selection of greens into bowl. Add other vegetables, as onion, celery (see list above). Sprinkle with salt, pepper, paprika and a little dry mustard. Just before serving, pour oil (half olive, half salad oil, if desired) over greens; toss lightly until leaves glisten. Then pour over greens half as much vinegar (mixture of different vinegars and lemon juice, if desired) as oil used. Toss again, serve immediately.

BEST TOSSED SALAD

1 large head lettuce
1 bunch leaf lettuce
½ small bunch endive (about 1 cup)
½ small bag spinach
¼ cup olive oil (or half salad oil may be used)
2 tbsp. white tarragon vinegar
1½ tsp. salt
1 small clove garlic, put through press or minced
⅛ to ¼ tsp. fresh ground pepper
⅛ to ¼ tsp. flavor extender (p. 124)

Use choice part of greens, discard stems and cores. Tear greens in bite-size pieces (do not cut). Have them dry and cold. Other greens may be used but keep about this amount. Toss together with oil until leaves glisten. Add vinegar combined with rest of ingredients. Toss again. Serve immediately. *6 to 8 servings.*

WILTED GREENS

lettuce, spinach, endive or a combination
4 slices bacon, cut up
¼ cup vinegar
2 tbsp. water
1 qt. shredded greens
2 green onions, chopped
1 tsp. salt
pepper
1 chopped hard-cooked egg

Fry bacon until crisp, add vinegar and water. Heat. Combine greens, onion and seasoning. Pour hot mixture over greens; toss until wilted. Sprinkle egg over top. *6 servings.*

GREEN AND WHITE SALAD

1 head lettuce
½ bunch endive
½ small head cauliflower
8-oz. can artichoke hearts
12 ripe olives, cut up
¼ cup olive or salad oil
2 tbsp. tarragon vinegar
1 tsp. salt
1 clove garlic, minced
12 shakes flavor extender (p. 124)

Tear greens in bite-size pieces. Break cauliflower in small pieces, cut artichoke hearts in half, olives in slices. Toss together. Add oil and toss until greens are coated. Add rest of ingredients and toss again. *4 to 6 servings.*

FRESH SPINACH SALAD

½ lb. washed spinach, torn in shreds (4 cups)
1 small Bermuda onion, sliced
¼ cup diced celery
4 hard-cooked eggs, sliced
salt and pepper to taste

Toss ingredients together lightly. Chill. Just before serving, add ¾ cup Lemon Salad Dressing (p. 153) ; toss lightly. *6 to 8 servings.*

GARLIC

Garlic clove may be sliced nearly through and allowed to stand in the oil an hour before serving. Or, the bowl may first be rubbed with salt; then with a cut garlic clove.

FRUIT SALAD COMBINATIONS

Diced apple, Tokay grapes halved and seeded, or green seedless grapes, diced celery, chopped nuts with Whipped Cream Dressing (p. 152).

Diced red apple, diced avocado, sliced celery with Sour Cream Dressing (p. 153).

Waldorf Salad (chopped apple, celery and nuts) with Whipped Cream or Fruit Dressing (p. 152) on a slice of chilled jellied cranberries.

Place slice of chilled pineapple on bed of greens. Put cream cheese ball in the center. Surround with 5 Bing cherries in which seeds have been replaced with almonds. Fruit Dressing (p. 152).

Orange and grapefruit sections, avocado slices, pomegranate seeds or sliced strawberries. Garnish with watercress, if desired. Serve with fruit dressing.

Melon wedges (cantaloupe or honeydew), Bing cherries, plum slices and/or green seedless grapes with fruit dressing.

Ambrosia Salad: Combine cut-up orange sections, diced apple, banana slices with Fruit Juice Dressing (p. 153). Top with plain or toasted coconut.

Diced fresh peaches, green seedless grapes and peanuts with Whipped Cream Dressing (p. 152).

Diced fresh pineapple and strawberries with cream cheese balls rolled in chopped nuts. Fruit Dressing (p. 152).

Chill 14-oz. can pineapple chunks and no. 300 can Bing cherries. Drain and add ¼ cup chopped pecans and ½ cup heavy cream, whipped, and 1 tbsp. mayonnaise. Serve on lettuce.

Two long slices of banana centered with cubes of cranberry or some other tart jelly and chopped nuts. Whipped Cream Dressing (p. 152).

Bananas cut in half and sliced lengthwise. Place 3 slices for each salad on lettuce, garnish with watercress. Top with Creamy Orange Dressing (p. 153).

COLE SLAW

½ medium head of cabbage
1 medium onion, chopped
2 tbsp. vinegar
¼ cup sour or heavy cream
¼ cup salad dressing
¼ tsp. salt
dash of pepper
½ tsp. dry mustard
paprika

Shred cabbage very thin; place in plastic bag in refrigerator to crisp. Combine cabbage, onion, vinegar in bowl. Mix cream, salad dressing and seasonings; toss with cabbage. Sprinkle with paprika. *6 servings.*

CABBAGE PATCH SALAD

Combine 2 cups finely shredded cabbage, ½ cup grated carrots, ¼ cup chopped green pepper, 2 tbsp. chopped green or dry onion. Season with salt and pepper; add Frenchaise dressing (p. 153). Toss lightly. *6 servings.*

VEGETABLE MEDLEY

Cook a pkg. of frozen mixed vegetables 8 min. Drain and chill. Marinate in 2 tbsp. French Dressing (p. 152) until serving time. Add 2 tbsp. mayonnaise and crumbled Roquefort cheese, if desired. Serve on lettuce. *4 or 5 servings.*

From a Can: Mixed marinated vegetables come in both 8-oz. and 15-oz. cans. Chill, drain and combine with mayonnaise. Serve on lettuce. *Large can serves 4, small can, 2.*

CABBAGE-CUCUMBER SALAD

Combine 3 parts crisp shredded cabbage with 1 part diced unpared cucumber. Add minced chives or green onions and celery seed. Season with salt and pepper; add mayonnaise to moisten.

OTHER VEGETABLE COMBINATIONS

Chilled cooked asparagus, sliced hard-cooked egg, sliced tomato, French Dressing.

Raw cauliflowerets, slivered raw carrots, blanched almonds with mayonnaise.

Overlapping slices of cooked beet, cucumber and onion. French Dressing.

Small tomatoes stuffed with cottage cheese and chives; or with chopped celery, onion, green pepper.

Cooked green beans, cooked carrot slices, diced celery, a little onion. Marinate in French Dressing. Toss with mayonnaise.

TOMATO SPECIAL

4 large tomatoes
salt and pepper
2 medium Bermuda onions,
    chopped fine
½ cup minced parsley

Slice tomatoes ½" thick; arrange half the tomato slices in a deep platter. Sprinkle with salt and pepper. Cover with second layer of tomatoes; sprinkle with salt and pepper. Spread onion (¼" thick) over tomato slices, then parsley (also ¼" thick). Dribble Special Dressing (p. 153) over top. Chill thoroughly 1 hr. or overnight. *8 servings.*

CHEESE MARINATED ONIONS

Sliced raw onions with elegant marinade of Roquefort cheese and olive oil.

3 oz. Roquefort cheese,
    crumbled
½ cup olive or salad oil
2 tbsp. lemon juice
1 tsp. salt
½ tsp. sugar
dash of pepper
dash of paprika
4 medium sweet onions,
    thinly sliced

Mix all ingredients except onion slices. Pour over onion and chill thoroughly. *6 servings.*

BUFFET SALAD

1 small head cauliflower
1 medium mild onion
3½-oz. bottle stuffed olives
¼ cup Roquefort cheese
1 small head lettuce
½ cup French dressing

Break cauliflower in small pieces, thinly slice onion and olives, crumble cheese, break lettuce in bite-size pieces. Toss together; pour French Dressing (p. 152) over all, and toss again. *6 to 8 servings.*

CAULIFLOWER-ORANGE SALAD

Mix 2 cups raw cauliflowerets, 2 cups orange wedges cut in pieces, ¼ cup finely chopped green pepper and 1 tbsp. onion juice. Serve on greens with Lemon Salad Dressing (p. 153). *6 to 8 servings.*

ORANGE-ONION SALAD

Cut through skin and membrane of 2 or 3 oranges. Cut in ¼" thick slices. Slice 1 Bermuda onion paper thin. Alternate slices of orange and onion on curly endive or lettuce. Serve with French Dressing (p. 152). *6 servings.*

BEETS-IN-CREAM SALAD

Chill no. 2 can baby beets. Drain and leave whole or slice. Add 1 cup sour cream and 1 tsp. salt. Chill thoroughly. Serve on lettuce or as relish. Especially good with fish. *6 servings.*

FRUIT GELATIN MOLD

1 pkg. lemon or strawberry-
   flavored gelatin
1 cup hot water
1 cup syrup from fruit and
   cold water
2 oranges, diced
1 cup pineapple chunks,
   drained
1 banana, sliced
1 apple, diced
½ cup broken walnuts

Dissolve gelatin in hot water. Add syrup and cold water; chill until partially set. Add fruits and nuts; chill until firm. Unmold on lettuce. Pass your choice of dressing. *6 servings.*

SEA DREAM SALAD

1 pkg. lime-flavored gelatin
1 cup hot water
1 cup cucumber juice (2
   medium cucumbers)
1 small onion, grated
½ tsp. salt
⅛ tsp. cayenne

Dissolve gelatin in hot water. Grate cucumbers and strain to get juice; reserve pulp. Add cucumber juice and remaining ingredients. Pour into 8″ ring mold; chill until firm. Unmold on lettuce or endive. Add cucumber pulp to 1 cup mayonnaise for dressing. Arrange tomato wedges around outside. *4 to 6 servings.*

TWO-SEASON PERFECTION SALAD

1 tbsp. (1 envelope)
   unflavored gelatin
¼ cup cold water
1½ cups hot water
1 tbsp. vinegar
1 tbsp. lemon juice
1 tsp. salt
1 cup finely shredded cabbage
1 cup chopped celery
2 finely chopped pimientos
6 chopped sweet pickles

Soften gelatin in cold water; dissolve in hot water. Add vinegar, lemon juice and salt; chill until partially set. Add vegetables; chill until firm. Unmold and serve on lettuce with mayonnaise.

Spring Variation: 1 cup diced cucumber, ½ cup each of sliced green onions and radishes, 1 cup chopped celery may be used.

BEET HORSE-RADISH MOLD

no. 2 can beets
3 tbsp. vinegar
1 pkg. lemon-flavored gelatin
½ tsp. salt
2 tbsp. onion juice
2 tbsp. prepared horse-radish
¾ cup diced celery

Drain liquid from beets; add water to make 1½ cups. Heat water and vinegar; add gelatin and dissolve. Add salt and onion juice; chill until partially set. Add horse-radish, celery and chopped beets. Chill until firm in large mold, 8″ ring or individual molds. Unmold and serve on lettuce with mayonnaise. *6 to 8 servings.*

FRENCH DRESSING

½ cup olive oil, salad oil or
   combination of the two
2 tbsp. vinegar
2 tbsp. lemon juice
½ tsp. salt
¼ tsp. dry mustard
¼ tsp. paprika

Put in jar and shake to blend.
¾ *cup.*

Roquefort: Add crumbled
Roquefort cheese and ⅛ tsp.
Worcestershire sauce.

Chiffonade: To ½ cup French
Dressing, add 1 tbsp. each of
chopped ripe olive, green pepper, finely cut chives; add 1 hard
cooked egg (white sieved, yolk
mashed).

Lorenzo: To ½ cup French
Dressing, add 1 tbsp. chili sauce.

Piquant: To ½ cup French
Dressing, add 2 tbsp. sugar, ½
tsp. each of celery seed and
grated onion. Let 1 clove garlic
stand in dressing 1 hr.

Note: The simplest French
Dressing is made along with the
salad as on p. 146.

RUBY RED DRESSING

½ cup currant jelly
¼ cup salad oil
2 tbsp. lemon juice
dash of salt
few drops onion juice

Beat jelly with fork until it is
smooth; add rest of ingredients;
mix thoroughly. Nice on orange,
grapefruit or pear.

COOKED DRESSING

¼ cup sugar
¼ cup Gold Medal Flour
2 tsp. salt
2 tsp. dry mustard
4 slightly beaten egg yolks
1½ cups milk
½ cup mild vinegar
1 tbsp. butter

Mix dry ingredients; add egg
yolks and milk; cook over hot
water until thick, stirring constantly. Add vinegar and butter;
mix well and cook until thick.
2 cups.

Fruit Dressing: Increase sugar
to 6 tbsp. in Cooked Dressing.
Substitute 1 cup unsweetened
pineapple juice and ½ cup orange juice for milk.

Whipped Cream Dressing:
Combine ½ cup Cooked Dressing with ½ cup heavy cream,
whipped.

MAYONNAISE

Mayonnaise is the best choice for sea food, poultry, meat and cooked vegetable salads. It can be bought ready-made and easily varied as follows:

Frenchaise: Beat ¼ cup French Dressing into ½ cup mayonnaise.

Sour Cream Dressing: Add ½ cup sour cream to 1 cup mayonnaise; season to taste.

Tomato-Cucumber Mayonnaise: To 1 cup mayonnaise, add ½ cup each of drained diced tomato and cucumber, 1 tsp. minced onion and salt.

Fruit Salad Mayonnaise: To ½ cup mayonnaise add ¼ cup heavy cream, whipped.

Thousand Island: To 1 cup mayonnaise, add 2 tbsp. chili sauce, 1 tbsp. chopped dill pickle, 1 tsp. minced onion, 1 hard-cooked egg, chopped.

Russian Dressing: To ½ cup mayonnaise, add 1½ tbsp. chili sauce and few drops onion juice.

CREAMY ORANGE DRESSING

3-oz. pkg. cream cheese
¼ tsp. salt
2 tsp. sugar
few grains paprika and cayenne
3 tbsp. orange juice
1 tbsp. lemon juice

Blend all ingredients together. Nice on fruits.

FRUIT JUICE DRESSING

1 cup strained canned fruit juice
½ cup orange juice
¼ cup lemon juice
1 tbsp. each of grated lemon and orange rind
1 egg, slightly beaten

Mix together; cook over low heat, stirring constantly until it boils. Remove from heat and chill thoroughly. *1½ cups.*

SPECIAL DRESSING

Crush 2 cloves garlic, add 1 tsp. salt, ½ tsp. pepper, 2 tsp. oregano, ½ tsp. dry mustard. Stir in ⅓ cup wine vinegar and 1 cup olive oil. Serve on vegetable salads accented with minced onion.

LEMON SALAD DRESSING

1 tbsp. salad oil
2 tbsp. flour
½ cup water
1 egg yolk
½ tsp. salt
½ tsp. dry mustard
¼ tsp. paprika
2 tbsp. lemon juice
¼ cup salad oil

Blend 1 tbsp. salad oil with flour and water. Bring to boiling, stirring constantly. Boil 1 min. Remove from heat; blend in remaining ingredients. Beat until smooth. *1¼ cups.*

NO-KNEAD REFRIGERATOR ROLLS
See color picture p.184.

- 2 pkg. active dry or 2 cakes compressed yeast
- 2 cups water (use warm water, 110°, with dry yeast; use lukewarm water, 85°, with compressed yeast)
- ½ cup sugar
- 2 tsp. salt
- 6½ to 7 cups sifted Gold Medal Flour
- 1 egg
- ¼ cup soft shortening

In mixing bowl, dissolve yeast in water. Add sugar, salt and about half the flour. Beat thoroughly 2 min. Add egg and shortening. Gradually beat in remaining flour until smooth. Cover with damp cloth; place in refrigerator. Punch down occasionally as dough rises in refrigerator. About 2 hr. before baking, cut off amount needed and return remaining dough to refrigerator. Shape (see opposite) into rolls and place on greased baking sheet. Cover. Let rise until light (1½ to 2 hr.). Heat oven to 400° (mod. hot). Bake 12 to 15 min. *4 doz. medium rolls.*

A VARIETY OF SHAPES

Use same baking temperature and time for all these rolls.

Old-fashioned Biscuits: Form dough into balls ⅓ size desired. Place close together in a greased round pan.

Parkerhouse Rolls: Roll dough ¼″ thick. Cut with biscuit cutter. Brush with melted butter. Make crease across each. Fold so top half slightly overlaps. Press edges together at crease. Place close together on pan.

Cloverleaf Rolls: Form bits of dough into balls about 1″ in diameter. Place 3 balls in each greased muffin cup. Brush with butter for flavor.

Picnic Buns: Use ½ of No-knead Refrigerator Roll dough. Divide into 2 parts. Roll each into 7½″ square (½″ thick). Cut into 2½″ squares. *1½ doz. buns.*

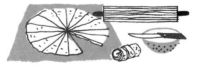

Crescents: Roll dough scarcely ¼″ thick into a 12″ circle. Spread with soft butter. Cut into 16 pie-shaped pieces. Beginning at rounded edge, roll up. Place on pan, point underneath.

QUICK DINNER ROLLS

Buy Brown 'n Serve Rolls from your neighborhood grocer or baker. Then, just before you pop them into the mod. hot oven (400°) to brown (6 to 8 min.), make variations to suit your fancy, such as the following.

Onion Rolls: Brush tops with beaten mixture of 2 tbsp. water to 1 egg yolk. Dip moistened tops into very finely chopped onion. Brown.

Herb Rolls: Brush tops with olive oil or butter. Sprinkle lightly with herbs of your choice: minced parsley or chives; or herbs such as dried or fresh thyme, sage, tarragon or basil. Brown.

Rum-flavored Rolls: After browning, brush hot Brown 'n Serve Rolls with Rum-flavored Frosting (below).

RUM-FLAVORED FROSTING

¾ cup sifted confectioners' sugar
1 to 2 tbsp. cream
½ tsp. rum flavoring

Blend together, adding just enough cream to make smooth spreading easy.

HOT BUTTERED BREAD

crusty loaf of bread
(French, rye, Vienna)
soft Herb Butter
(see below)

With sharp knife, cut uniform slices ¾ to 1" thick. Spread soft plain or Seasoned Butter generously on one side of each slice. Stand upright, close together, in loaf form in bread loaf pan (lined, if desired, with aluminum foil). Fifteen minutes before serving time, heat oven to 400° (mod. hot). Heat loaf until piping hot and crusty, about 15 min. Transfer, still in loaf shape, to oblong bread tray and serve at once.

Herb Butter: Cream the butter until soft and fluffy, then stir in seasoning of your choice (minced parsley or chives, mustard, horseradish, pepper sauce, curry or any other seasoning desired).

For Garlic Butter: Cream butter in a bowl rubbed with a cut clove of garlic.

Recipes for other quick and easy breads, such as popovers, sweet rolls, biscuits, bread sticks, nut bread, corn bread, muffins, delicious for any meal of the day, are on pp. 25-29 and 62-63.

POCKETBOOK BISCUITS

Rolled Biscuit dough
(p. 28 or Bisquick pkg.)

Heat oven to 450° (hot). Roll out biscuit dough ¼″ thick. Cut into 3″ rounds. Fold over (if desired, place about ½ tsp. red jelly in center before folding), then press edges together tightly. Bake 10 to 12 min. *12 biscuits.*

JAM GEMS

Drop Biscuit dough
(p. 28 or Bisquick pkg.)
¼ cup raspberry or
other jam
Thin White Icing (below)

Heat oven to 450° (hot). Mix dough and fill greased muffin cups ⅔ full. Make a small indentation in top of dough in each cup and fill with ½ tsp. jam. Bake 10 to 12 min. Frost while warm.

Thin White Icing: Mix sifted confectioners' sugar with cream or milk to spreading consistency. Add flavoring, if desired.

SALT-TOP BISCUITS

Drop Biscuit dough (p. 28 or
Bisquick pkg.)
milk
coarse salt
caraway seeds (or
celery salt)

Heat oven to 450° (hot). Mix dough and fill greased muffin cups ⅔ full. Slightly flatten by pressing dough with a spoon; moisten tops lightly with milk; sprinkle sparingly with coarse salt and a few caraway seeds (or celery salt). Bake 10 to 12 min.

CHEESE BISCUITS

Follow recipe for Biscuits on Bisquick pkg. or on p. 28—first mixing ½ cup grated sharp yellow American cheese with the Bisquick.

RUM-FLAVORED BISCUITS OR ROLLS

Follow recipe for Biscuits on Bisquick pkg. or on p. 28. Or follow recipe for Cinnamon Rolls on p. 29 except, in place of cinnamon and sugar, sprinkle seedless raisins over the dough (spread with butter) before rolling up. After baking, brush while hot with Rum-flavored Frosting (p. 155).

MAPLE NUT LOAF

2½ cups sifted
  Gold Medal Flour
1 cup sugar
3 tsp. baking powder
½ tsp. salt
1 egg, well beaten
1 cup milk
¾ tsp. maple flavoring
1 cup coarsely chopped nuts

Grease a loaf pan, 9x5x2½", generously and dust with flour. Sift flour, sugar, baking powder, salt together into bowl. Add egg, milk, flavoring; and mix only until dry ingredients are moistened. Stir in nuts. Pour into prepared pan. Let stand 20 min. before baking. Heat oven to 350° (mod.). Bake about 1 hr.

White Nut Loaf: Omit maple flavoring.

For thin, even slices, wrap loaf in aluminum foil or plastic wrap and store 24 hr. before cutting.

FOR VARIETY

Your baker can supply you with delicious breads and rolls in fascinating variety. For homey, informal dinners, arrange a plate of assorted rolls; choice always adds interest. For a more formal dinner, the plainer the rolls, the more style they have as a meat course accompaniment.

BUTTER STICKS

Rolled Biscuit dough
  (p. 28 or Bisquick pkg.)
⅓ cup butter

Heat oven to 450° (hot). Roll biscuit dough into rectangle 6 x10". Cut in half lengthwise. Cut each half into 12 strips (about ½x3"). Melt butter; pour half of it into oblong pan, 13x9½x2". Place strips in pan. Pour remaining butter over tops. Bake 10 to 15 min.

BOSTON BROWN BREAD

Rich and tasty with baked beans. Save time by buying it in cans at your grocer's or baker's.

Remove one end of can and loosen the loaf around top of can with a spatula; loaf will then slip out easily.

To heat, cut loaf in even slices with thin, sharp knife; then pile slices back into can. Heat in the uncovered can in same oven in which beans are baking.

Slices of Brown Bread may also be heated in top of double boiler, covered, over hot water. Or they may be toasted lightly, just enough to warm them through.

WHITE CAKE

A high, light, handsome cake, as extra good as it looks. Just follow simple directions on pkg. of Betty Crocker White Cake Mix. Finish with your favorite icing or topping (pp. 166-169) or serve uniced, warm from the oven.

VARIATIONS

White Coconut Cake: Bake in layers or in oblong. Frost with White Mountain Icing (p. 167) and sprinkle generously with shredded coconut.

Chipped Chocolate Cake: Fold into the batter 2 sq. shaved sweet, semisweet or unsweetened chocolate (2 oz. = about ½ cup). Spread Dark Chocolate Filling (p. 169) between layers, White Mountain Icing (p. 167) over top and sides. Decorate with chocolate shavings.

Peppermint Candy Cake: Fold into the batter ⅓ cup finely crushed peppermint stick candy. Frost with Pink Mountain Icing (p. 167). Sprinkle with crushed peppermint stick candy.

White Nut Cake: Fold into the batter 1 cup finely chopped nuts just before pouring into oblong pan, 13x9½x2". Frost with Glossy Chocolate Icing (p. 167), Easy Penuche Icing (p. 167) or White Butter Icing (p. 166).

Cherry-Nut Cake: Add to the batter, with the first egg white, ½ cup finely chopped nuts and ½ cup chopped maraschino cherries, well drained. Frost with White Mountain Icing (p. 167). Decorate with bright red cherries.

Lady Baltimore Cake: Bake in layers. Finish with Lady Baltimore Filling and Icing (below).

Lady Baltimore Filling and Icing: Make 1½ times recipe for White Mountain Icing (p. 167). Into ⅓ of icing, blend ⅓ cup raisins, cut fine; ⅓ cup figs, cut in strips; ½ cup chopped walnuts. Spread both cooled layers with this filling. Put layers together. Cover top and sides with remaining icing.

WHOLE-EGG OR YELLOW CAKE

Fluffy, fine-textured and full-flavored. Follow easy directions on pkg. of Betty Crocker Yellow Cake Mix. Finish with your favorite topping or icing (pp. 166-169). Or serve un-iced, warm from the oven.

VARIATIONS

Banana Cake: Stir ⅛ tsp. soda into the Mix before adding liquid. Use only ⅓ cup water and add ⅓ cup mashed very ripe bananas in first mixing period. In place of second ½ cup water, add, in 4 parts, ⅔ cup mashed bananas. Finish with whipped cream and sliced bananas.

Orange Cake: Fold 1 tbsp. grated orange rind into the batter. Frost with Orange Butter Icing (p. 166). Decorate with fresh orange sections (membrane removed).

Peanut Butter Cake: Add 1 tbsp. peanut butter with the first ½ cup water. Fold in ½ cup finely chopped peanuts. Finish with Broiled Peanut Butter Icing (p. 166).

Coconut Cream Cake: Prepare 1 pkg. quick vanilla pudding as directed on pkg. Chill. Meanwhile, bake cake in layers. Add about ½ cup shredded coconut to ⅓ of the cooled vanilla filling; spread between layers. Cover top and sides with rest of filling. Sprinkle with coconut (1½ cups).

Maple Nut Cake: Add 1½ tsp. maple flavoring with the water, and add ½ cup finely chopped nuts with the first egg. Frost with Maple Butter Icing (p. 166) or Satiny Beige Icing (p. 167).

MARBLE CAKE
See color picture on p. 239.
Fluffy, tender yellow cake marbled with chocolate. Make it deliciously and quickly from simple directions on pkg. of Betty Crocker Marble Cake Mix. Frost with Glossy Chocolate Icing (p. 167).

CHOCOLATE DEVILS FOOD CAKE

Rich, dark, chocolatey, smooth as velvet. Easy to make as directed on pkg. of Betty Crocker Chocolate Devils Food Cake Mix. Serve uniced, warm from the oven, or finish with your favorite icing or topping (pp. 166-169).

VARIATIONS

Mocha Devils Food Cake: Stir 3 tbsp. powdered coffee into the Mix before adding liquid. Or add 1 cup cold strong coffee in place of water. Frost with Mocha Butter Icing (p. 166).

Cherry-Chocolate Cake: Bake in layers or oblong. Frost with Cherry Butter Icing (p. 166) to which ½ cup finely chopped well drained maraschino cherries has been added.

Fudge Nut Cake: Fold into the batter ⅔ cup finely chopped nuts. Frost with Browned Butter or Glossy Chocolate Icing (pp. 166, 167).

Pep-o-mint Devils Food Cake: Fold into the batter ¼ tsp. peppermint extract or 2 drops oil of peppermint. Frost with White Mountain Icing (p. 167). Sprinkle with bits of peppermint stick candy.

Candle Cupcakes: Bake in cupcakes as directed on pkg. Frost with White Mountain Icing (p. 167). Place a candle in center of each. For Christmas, use red candles and decorate around them with holly clusters made of small petal-like pieces of maraschino cherries and thin pieces of cut-up citron or green gumdrops. Light candles just before serving.

CUPCAKES

Directions for White, Yellow, Chocolate and Honey Spice Cupcakes appear on boxes of Betty Crocker Cake Mixes. Bake the variety you want, the good and easy way.

HONEY SPICE CAKE

Rich and tender, with honey and spice and everything nice. Follow simple directions on pkg. of Betty Crocker Honey Spice Cake Mix. Finish with your favorite icing or topping (pp. 166-169). Delicious, too, served uniced, warm from the oven.

VARIATIONS

Mocha Spice Cake: In place of water, use 1 cup cold coffee. Frost with Mocha Butter Icing (p. 166). If you use powdered instant coffee, dissolve 2 tbsp. of it in ½ cup boiling water, then fill cup with cold water. Coffee must be cold when added to Mix.

Quick Prune Cake: Stir into the batter 1½ cups cut-up pitted well drained cooked prunes (easily cut with coarse blade of food chopper) and ⅓ cup finely chopped nuts. Frost with White Butter Icing (p. 166) or Easy Penuche Icing (p. 167).

Pumpkin-Walnut Cake: Stir ½ tsp. soda into the Mix before adding water. In place of second ½ cup water, add 1 cup mashed cooked pumpkin (canned). Fold in ½ cup finely chopped nuts. Finish with White Butter or Browned Butter Icing (p. 166). Or serve warm from oven as a dessert with Hard Sauce (p. 170).

Honey-Coconut Spice Cake: Bake in oblong pan. Spread warm cake in pan with Honey-Coconut Topping (below).

Applesauce Cake: Stir ¼ tsp. soda into the Mix before adding water. In place of second ½ cup water, add 1 cup thick applesauce (sweetened or unsweetened). Fold in ⅓ cup chopped nuts. Finish with Lacy Sugar Topping (p. 81) or Easy Penuche Icing (p. 167).

Black Walnut Spice Cake: Fold into the batter ⅔ cup finely chopped black walnuts. Frost with White or Browned Butter Icing (p. 166).

Honey-Coconut Topping: Mix 4 tbsp. soft butter, ⅓ cup honey, 2 tbsp. cream, 1 cup shredded coconut, dash of salt. After spreading on cake, place 3″ under broiler (low heat) until mixture bubbles and browns (3 to 5 min.). Do not burn.

ANGEL FOOD CAKE

Fluffy, high and deliciously tender. Just follow the easy directions on pkg. of Betty Crocker Angel Food Cake Mix. Preferred by many uniced. Whipped cream toppings (p. 168) and butter icings (p. 166) make a beautiful finish. See picture, p. 240.

VARIATIONS

Cherry-Nut Angel Food Cake: At the last, fold in gently ½ cup chopped maraschino cherries, drained on paper towel, and ½ cup chopped nuts. Frost with Cherry Butter Icing (p. 166).

Coconut Angel Food Cake: At the last, gently fold in 1 cup finely shredded coconut. Frost with White Mountain Icing (p. 167) and sprinkle generously with shredded coconut.

LEMON CUSTARD ANGEL FOOD
Sunshine gold...with the delicate tang of fresh lemon...the rich moistness of custard...the high lightness of 13-egg angel food. So easy to make with Betty Crocker Lemon Custard Angel Food Mix. Arrange slices of it around a bowl of rich vanilla ice cream for an extra-special treat.

Mocha Angel Food Cake: Mix 1 tbsp. powdered instant coffee with the flour mixture. Frost with Mocha Butter Icing (p. 166).

Maple Nut Angel Food Cake: Omit almond extract and vanilla and use 1 tsp. maple flavoring. Gently fold in at the last ⅓ cup finely chopped pecans. Frost with Maple Butter Icing (p. 166).

Marble Angel Food Cake: Omit almond extract and use 2 tsp. vanilla. Divide batter into 2 parts. Into one half of batter, fold gently 2 tbsp. sifted cocoa. Drop spoonfuls into pan alternating white and chocolate batter. Cut through batter several times with spoon. Frost with Chocolate, White or Lemon Butter Icing (p. 166).

LOVELIGHT YELLOW CHIFFON CAKE

2 eggs, separated
1½ cups sugar
2¼ cups sifted
   Softasilk Cake Flour
3 tsp. baking powder
1 tsp. salt
⅓ cup cooking (salad) oil
1 cup milk
1½ tsp. flavoring

Heat oven to 350° (mod.). Grease generously and dust with flour 2 round layer pans, 8" by at least 1½" deep, or 9x1½" or one oblong pan, 13x9½x2".

Beat egg whites until frothy. Gradually beat in ½ cup of the sugar. Continue beating until very stiff and glossy.

Sift rest of sugar, flour, baking powder, salt into another bowl. Add oil, half of milk, flavoring. Beat 1 min. medium speed on mixer or 150 strokes by hand. Scrape sides and bottom of bowl constantly. Add rest of milk, egg yolks. Beat 1 more min., scraping bowl constantly. Fold in meringue. Pour into prepared pans. Bake layers 30 to 35 min., oblong 40 to 45 min., until top springs back when lightly touched. Remove from pans. Cool. Spread Clear Orange Filling (p. 169) between layers and White Mountain Icing (p. 167) over top and sides.

With Whipped Cream and Fruit: Fill and top with sweetened whipped cream and berries or other cut-up fruit.

LOVELIGHT CHOCOLATE CHIFFON CAKE

2 eggs, separated
1½ cups sugar
1¾ cups sifted
   Softasilk Cake Flour
¾ tsp. soda
¾ tsp. salt
⅓ cup cooking (salad) oil
1 cup buttermilk (or
   sweet milk)
2 sq. unsweetened
   chocolate (2 oz.), melted

Heat oven to 350° (mod.). Grease generously and dust with flour 2 round layer pans, 8" by at least 1½" deep or 9x1½", or one oblong pan, 13x9½x2".

Beat egg whites until frothy. Gradually beat in ½ cup of the sugar. Continue beating until very stiff and glossy. Sift rest of sugar, flour, soda, salt into another bowl. Add oil, half of buttermilk. Beat 1 min. medium speed on mixer or 150 strokes by hand. Scrape sides and bottom of bowl constantly. Add remaining buttermilk, egg yolks, chocolate. Beat 1 more min., scraping bowl constantly. Fold in meringue. Pour into prepared pans. Bake layers 30 to 35 min., oblong 40 to 45 min. Remove from pans. Cool. Frost.

Orange Chiffon Cake . . . with the fresh fruit flavor of oranges. **Cocoa Chiffon Cake** . . . chocolatey-rich with the best cocoa. Both so easy . . . high . . . and light, made with Betty Crocker Chiffon Cake Mixes.

163

ONE-EGG CAKE

A good-and-easy butter cake.

2 cups sifted Softasilk
    Cake Flour
1 ¼ cups sugar
2 ½ tsp. baking powder
1 tsp. salt
⅓ cup soft shortening
    (such as Snowdrift or
    Crisco)
1 tsp. vanilla
1 cup milk
¼ cup unbeaten egg
    (1 large)

Heat oven to 350° (mod.).
Grease well and dust with flour
2 round layer pans, 8x1½" or 1
square pan, 9x9x1¾".
Sift dry ingredients into bowl.
Add shortening, vanilla, ⅔ of
milk. Beat 2 min. medium speed
on mixer or 300 strokes by hand.
Scrape sides and bottom of bowl
constantly. Add remaining milk,
egg. Beat 2 more min. Pour into
prepared pans. Bake layers 25 to
30 min., square 30 to 35 min.,
until top springs back when
lightly touched. Frost with your
favorite icing.

Marble One-egg Cake: Follow
recipe for One-egg Cake (above)
except—to ½ of batter add mixture of 1 sq. unsweetened chocolate (1 oz.), melted, ¼ tsp. soda,
2 tbsp. water. Beat ½ min. Spoon
chocolate and white batter alternately into prepared pans. Draw
knife through several times for
marbled effect. Frost cooled cake
with Glossy Chocolate Icing
(p. 167).

ONE-EGG CHOCOLATE CAKE

2 sq. unsweetened chocolate
    (2 oz.), cut up
½ cup boiling water
1 cup sifted Softasilk
    Cake Flour
1 cup sugar
½ tsp. soda
¼ tsp. baking powder
½ tsp. salt
¼ cup soft shortening
    (such as Crisco or Spry)
¼ cup buttermilk or
    sour milk
½ tsp. vanilla
1 egg, unbeaten

Heat oven to 350° (mod.).
Grease well and dust with flour
one square pan 8x8x2". Stir chocolate and water in mixing bowl
until chocolate is melted. Sift
dry ingredients together and stir
in. Add shortening. Beat 1 min.
medium speed on mixer or 150
strokes by hand. Scrape sides
and bottom of bowl constantly.
Add buttermilk, vanilla, egg.
Beat 1 more min. Pour into prepared pan. Bake 35 to 40 min.,
until top springs back when
lightly touched. When cool, frost
with your favorite icing.

Orange One-egg Cake: Follow
recipe for One-egg Cake (left)
except—add ¼ tsp. soda with dry
ingredients, and in place of 1 cup
milk, use ¼ cup fresh or diluted
frozen orange juice and ¾ cup
milk. Omit vanilla. Beat in 1 tsp.
grated orange rind with egg.
When cool, ice with Orange Butter Icing (p. 166).

GOLDEN DATE CAKE

Dates in the cake, orange in the icing—delectable combination.

- 2 cups plus 2 tbsp. sifted Gold Medal Flour
- 1½ cups sugar
- 3 tsp. baking powder
- 1 tsp. salt
- ½ cup soft shortening (such as Snowdrift or Crisco)
- 1 cup milk
- 1½ tsp. vanilla
- ⅓ to ½ cup unbeaten eggs (2 medium)
- 1 cup pitted dates, cut up
- ½ cup coarsely chopped nuts

Heat oven to 350° (mod.). Grease well and dust with flour 2 round layer pans, 8 or 9x1½", or 1 oblong pan, 13x9½x2".

Sift flour, sugar, baking powder, salt together into bowl. Add shortening, milk, vanilla. Beat 2 min. medium speed on mixer or 300 vigorous strokes by hand. Scrape sides and bottom of bowl constantly. Add eggs, dates. Beat 2 more min., scraping bowl constantly. Fold in nuts. Pour into prepared pans. Bake layers 35 to 45 min., oblong 40 to 45 min., until top springs back when lightly touched. Cool. Frost with Orange Butter Icing (p. 166).

HOT WATER SPONGE CAKE

Sometimes called Mock Sponge Cake.

- 1¼ cups sifted Softasilk Cake Flour
- 1½ tsp. baking powder
- ½ tsp. salt
- 3 eggs
- ¾ cup sugar
- ⅓ cup hot water
- 1 tsp. vanilla
- ½ tsp. lemon flavoring

Heat oven to 350° (mod.). Grease generously and dust with flour a square pan, 9x9x1¾". Sift together flour, baking powder and salt; set aside. Beat eggs in small mixer bowl until very thick and lemon-colored (about 5 min.). Pour into large mixer bowl and beat in sugar gradually. Beat in on low speed hot water and flavorings. Quickly and thoroughly beat in dry ingredients. Immediately pour into prepared pan. Bake 25 to 30 min., until top springs back when lightly touched. Cool. Serve fresh with fruit, or top pieces of cake with sweetened whipped cream and berries, sliced peaches or bananas.

Cut dates up fine with wet scissors, after measuring.

WHITE BUTTER ICING

Easy uncooked icing.

⅓ cup soft butter or
    other shortening
3 cups sifted
    confectioners' sugar
1½ tsp. vanilla
about 3 tbsp. cream
    or rich milk

Blend shortening and sugar. Stir in vanilla and cream until smooth.

VARIATIONS

Chocolate Butter Icing: Add 3 sq. unsweetened chocolate (3 oz.), melted.

Orange or Lemon Butter Icing: Use 1½ tbsp. grated rind and 3 tbsp. orange or lemon juice in place of vanilla and cream.

Maple Butter Icing: Use ½ cup maple syrup in place of vanilla and cream.

Mocha Butter Icing: Use 3 tbsp. strong black coffee in place of vanilla and cream.

Cherry or Strawberry Butter Icing: Use about 4 tbsp. maraschino cherry juice or 3 tbsp. crushed fresh or frozen strawberries (including juice) in place of cream.

Browned Butter Icing: Use all butter for shortening, and brown butter before blending with sugar.

PEPPERMINT PATTY ICING

Place chocolate peppermint patties on cake immediately after removing cake from oven. As patties melt, spread the chocolate and fondant to cover cake.

BROILED COCONUT ICING

3 tbsp. soft butter or
    other shortening
⅓ cup brown sugar
    (packed)
2 tbsp. rich milk or cream
½ cup Wheaties or
    shredded coconut
¼ cup chopped nuts

Mix together. Spread over warm 8″ sq. cake in pan. Place 3″ under broiler (low heat) until mixture bubbles and browns (3 to 5 min.). Do not burn.

BROILED PEANUT BUTTER ICING

¼ cup soft butter or
    other shortening
⅔ cup brown sugar
    (packed)
4 tbsp. rich milk or cream
1 cup finely chopped peanuts
4 tbsp. peanut butter

Mix together. Spread over cooled 13 x 9″ oblong cake in pan. Place 3″ under broiler (low heat) until mixture bubbles and browns (3 to 5 min.). Do not burn.

To SAVE TIME AND WORK Choose from the Betty Crocker Instant Frosting Mixes at your grocer's. Open the box. Add boiling water. Stir ... and spread.

GLOSSY CHOCOLATE ICING

2 or 3 sq. unsweetened
  chocolate (2 or 3 oz.)
3 tbsp. shortening
⅓ cup milk
2 cups sifted confectioners'
  sugar
¼ tsp. salt
1 tsp. vanilla

Melt over hot water chocolate
and shortening. Blend in milk,
confectioners' sugar, salt, vanilla.
Stir until smooth and thick
enough to spread.

To thicken, stir over ice water.

To thin, stir over hot water.

EASY PENUCHE ICING

½ cup butter
1 cup brown sugar (packed)
¼ cup milk
1¾ cups sifted
  confectioners' sugar

Melt butter in saucepan. Stir in
brown sugar. Boil and stir over
low heat 2 min. Stir in milk.
Bring to boil, stirring constantly. Cool to lukewarm. Gradually
add confectioners' sugar. Beat
until thick enough to spread. If
icing becomes too stiff, add a
little hot water.

QUICKEST-EVER FROSTINGS

Easy. And so delicious. With Betty
Crocker Instant Frosting Mixes.
Your grocer has them in your
choice of favorite flavors ... each
one creamy smooth. Just add
boiling water as directed on pkg.
Stir. Spread on cooled cake.

WHITE MOUNTAIN ICING

½ cup sugar
¼ cup white corn syrup
2 tbsp. water
¼ cup egg whites
1 tsp. vanilla

Blend sugar, syrup, water
in saucepan. Boil rapidly
until mixture spins a 6 to
8″ thread (or 242°). When
mixture begins to boil, beat
egg whites until stiff enough
to stand in peaks. Pour hot
syrup in thin steady stream
into beaten whites, beating
constantly with rotary or
electric beater until it
stands in very stiff peaks.
Blend in vanilla.

DELICIOUS VARIATIONS

Pink Mountain: Use 2 tbsp.
maraschino cherry juice in
place of water.

Peppermint: Fold in, after
beating, ½ tsp. peppermint
extract or 1 stick crushed
peppermint candy.

Satiny Beige: Use brown
sugar (packed) in place of
granulated.

Allegretti: Ice cake with
White Mountain Icing. Melt
1 sq. unsweetened chocolate
(1 oz.) with ¼ tsp. shortening. Using teaspoon, drip
chocolate around top edge
of iced cake and let run
down sides.

SWEETENED WHIPPED CREAM TOPPING

1 cup chilled heavy cream
¼ cup sifted confectioners' sugar

Beat together until stiff in chilled deep bowl with cold rotary or electric beater.

VARIATIONS

Chocolate Fluff Topping: Fold in 2 milk chocolate nut bars (chopped into slivers).

Peanut Crunch Topping: Fold in ½ cup finely crushed peanut brittle.

Banana Cream Topping: Place banana slices on whipped cream on cake.

Mocha Cream Topping: Fold in 1 tbsp. powdered coffee.

Pineapple-Cherry Cream Topping: Fold in ¾ cup well drained crushed pineapple and ⅓ cup well drained maraschino cherries, cut in quarters.

STRAWBERRY FLUFF TOPPING

1 egg white
¾ cup sugar
¾ cup crushed strawberries with juice

Beat egg white until stiff. Beat in alternately sugar and strawberries (about 2 tbsp. at a time), beating well between additions and until mixture is very stiff. Serve at once.

COCOA FLUFF TOPPING

1 cup chilled heavy cream
½ cup sifted confectioners' sugar
¼ cup cocoa
dash of salt

Mix in chilled bowl. Beat until stiff.

Delicious Addition: Sprinkling of toasted or salted almonds.

Choco-Mint Cream Topping: Fold in ⅓ cup cut-up solid chocolate peppermint wafers. Garnish with a few curls shaved from a wafer.

BANANA WHIP

Make not more than an hour before serving.

1 ripe banana, sliced
1 egg white, unbeaten
⅓ cup sugar
dash of salt
½ tsp. vanilla
½ tsp. lemon juice

Beat together until light and fluffy.

WHIPPED ICE CREAM

Whip ice cream with electric beater at medium speed or with wooden spoon until softened and smooth. Do not melt.

With Fruit: Spoon Whipped Ice Cream over cake and top with crushed raspberries or strawberries, or sliced bananas or sweetened sliced peaches.

CLEAR LEMON FILLING

1 cup sugar
4 tbsp. cornstarch
½ tsp. salt
1 cup water
2 tbsp. grated lemon rind
½ cup lemon juice
2 tbsp. butter

Mix in saucepan. Bring to boil; boil 1 min., stirring constantly. Chill before using.

CLEAR ORANGE FILLING

Make same as Lemon Filling above except—use 1 cup orange juice in place of water and 2 tbsp. orange rind in place of lemon. Use 1½ tbsp. lemon juice.

STRAWBERRY CREAM FILLING

1 pt. ripe strawberries
2 tbsp. sugar
1 tsp. gelatin soaked in
 1 tbsp. cold water and
 dissolved over hot water
1 cup whipped cream
 (sweetened)

Mash most of berries. Stir in sugar. Blend in gelatin. Chill. When partially set, fold in cream. Garnish with unmashed berries.

DARK CHOCOLATE FILLING

1 large egg yolk
½ cup sugar
3 tbsp. cream
1 sq. unsweetened
 chocolate (1 oz.), cut up
1 tbsp. butter

Mix in saucepan. Cook and stir over med. heat only until bubbles appear around edge. Remove from heat. Beat until thick. Cool.

CUSTARD CREAM FILLING

⅓ cup sugar
¼ cup Gold Medal Flour
¼ tsp. salt
1¼ cups rich milk
1 egg or 2 egg yolks,
 slightly beaten
1½ tbsp. butter
1 tsp. vanilla or rum flavoring

Mix sugar, flour, salt in saucepan. Stir in milk. Cook over low heat, stirring until it boils. Boil 1 min. Remove from heat. Slowly stir half the hot mixture into beaten egg; blend into hot mixture in saucepan, bring to boil. Stir in butter and flavoring. Cool.

Almond Cream Filling: Use part almond flavoring. Add about ½ cup toasted chopped blanched almonds when cool.

Date or Fig Cream Filling: Fold in about ½ cup each cut-up dates or figs and toasted nuts.

TIME-SAVING FILLINGS

Some of the quick pudding mixes at your grocer's make delicious fillings for cakes.

DESSERT SAUCES

Easy sauces to top fresh-from-the-oven cakes, ice cream or other desserts.

VANILLA, LEMON OR NUTMEG SAUCE

1 cup sugar
2 tbsp. cornstarch
2 cups boiling water
4 tbsp. butter
2 tsp. vanilla or 2 tsp. lemon juice with 1 tbsp. grated lemon rind or 2 tsp. nutmeg

Mix sugar and cornstarch in saucepan. Gradually stir in water. Boil 1 min., stirring constantly. Stir in butter and flavoring. Serve hot. *2 cups sauce.*

CLEAR ORANGE SAUCE

1 cup sugar
¼ tsp. salt
2 tbsp. cornstarch
1 cup orange juice
¼ cup lemon juice
¾ cup boiling water
1 tbsp. butter
1 tsp. each grated orange and lemon rind

Mix sugar, salt, cornstarch in saucepan. Stir in juices, water. Boil 1 min., stirring constantly. Remove from heat. Stir in butter and grated rind. Keep hot until time to serve. *2 cups sauce.*

HARD SAUCE

Cream ½ cup soft butter, add 1½ cups sifted confectioners' sugar gradually and cream until fluffy. Blend in 2 tsp. vanilla. Thin with cream as desired.

CARAMEL SAUCE

½ lb. vanilla caramels (about 36)
4 tbsp. water

Melt caramels in water over hot (not boiling) water. Stir to blend well. *1 cup sauce.*

GLOSSY CHOCOLATE SAUCE

2 sq. unsweetened chocolate (2 oz.)
1 cup light corn syrup
½ tsp. vanilla
1 tbsp. butter

Melt chocolate in corn syrup over low heat. Remove from heat. Stir in vanilla and butter. *1 cup sauce.*

BUTTERSCOTCH SAUCE

1½ cups brown sugar (packed)
½ cup white corn syrup
4 tbsp. butter
½ cup cream
1 tsp. vanilla

Mix brown sugar, syrup and butter in saucepan. Bring to boil over low heat. Remove from heat. Stir in cream and vanilla. *1 cup sauce.*

TO SAVE TIME AND WORK

Use packaged quick pudding and pie filling mixes for dessert sauces. Many flavors are available at your grocer's.

SNOWBALLS

Make batter as directed on pkg. of Betty Crocker White Cake Mix. Pour into 12 well greased custard cups (⅔ full). Tie waxed paper or aluminum foil loosely over tops. Steam 30 min. Serve warm, inverted in sauce dishes with hot Clear Red Sauce. *12 servings.*

CLEAR RED SAUCE

½ cup sugar
2 tbsp. cornstarch
1 cup boiling water
¾ cup juice from cherries
    or raspberries
¼ tsp. almond extract
few drops red food coloring

Mix sugar and cornstarch in saucepan. Gradually stir in water and juice. Boil 1 min., stirring constantly. Stir in flavoring, coloring.

CRANBERRY HOLIDAY PUDDING

1¼ cups washed raw
    cranberries
1½ cups Bisquick
½ cup sorghum or molasses
½ cup warm water
2 tsp. soda

Mix cranberries and Bisquick. Mix sorghum, water, soda. Combine the two mixtures; mix well. Pour into greased and floured 1-qt. mold, or 3-lb. shortening can, or 2-lb. coffee can (⅔ full). Tie waxed paper loosely over top. Steam 2½ to 3 hr. Unmold onto serving platter. Serve hot with hot Easy Vanilla or Rum Sauce. *8 servings.*

CHOCOLATE PUDDING

Make batter as directed on pkg. of Betty Crocker Chocolate Devils Food Cake Mix. Pour into 3 well greased no. 2 cans (⅔ full). Tie waxed paper or aluminum foil loosely over tops. Steam 1½ hr. Remove from cans. Slice and serve warm with Easy Vanilla or Rum Sauce (below) or Hard Sauce (p. 170). Leftover pudding may be frozen for later use.

EASY VANILLA OR RUM SAUCE

1 cup sugar
½ cup cream or rich milk
½ cup butter, melted
1 tsp. vanilla or
    rum flavoring

Mix sugar and cream. Heat, but do not boil. When ready to serve, beat in butter with rotary beater. Stir in flavoring.

CREAMY SAUCE

1 egg, beaten until foamy
⅓ cup melted butter
1½ cups sifted confectioners'
    sugar
1 tsp. vanilla
1 cup cream, whipped stiff

Into beaten egg blend butter, sugar and vanilla. Fold in the whipped cream.

To SAVE TIME AND WORK
Choose your favorite steamed puddings, convenient in cans or packages on your grocer's shelves. Delicious fig, date, English plum and other varieties are ready to serve.

SOFT CUSTARD DESSERT OR SAUCE

4 egg yolks or 2 whole eggs
¼ cup sugar
¼ tsp. salt
1½ cups milk, scalded
1 tsp. vanilla

Beat egg yolks or eggs in top of double boiler. Blend in sugar, salt, scalded milk. Cook over simmering water, stirring constantly, until mixture coats spoon. Cool quickly. Blend in vanilla. Serve in sherbet glasses topped with whipped cream. Or use as a sauce over cake or other desserts.

To Save Time: Use vanilla pudding mix for Soft Custard. And by using 1½ times as much milk as recipe on pkg. calls for, you can make a creamy Custard Sauce in no time.

Hidden Fruit: Pour chilled Soft Custard over chilled berries or fruit (cut-up grapes, oranges, bananas, peaches).

Baked Islands: Heat oven to 275° (slow). Drop meringue by small spoonfuls on brown paper on baking sheet. Bake 20 min., cover with brown paper and bake 20 min. more. Turn off heat. Leave in oven until cool.

Floating Island: Make Soft Custard, using 2 egg yolks and 1 whole egg. Beat the 2 leftover egg whites with ⅛ tsp. cream of tartar until frothy, then beat in gradually ¼ cup sugar. Beat until stiff and glossy. Bake (below, left) and float on custard. Or drop unbaked as "islands" on hot custard in serving dish. Chill.

BAKED CUSTARD

2 large eggs (or 4 egg yolks)
⅓ cup sugar
¼ tsp. salt
2 cups milk, scalded
nutmeg, for flavoring

Heat oven to 350° (mod.). Beat eggs, sugar and salt together slightly to mix. Pour in the hot scalded milk. Strain into 6 custard cups or a 1½-qt. casserole and set in pan of hot water (1" up on cups or casserole). Sprinkle nutmeg over tops. Bake in oven or, tightly covered, on top of range 30 to 35 min., until silver knife thrust into custard comes out clean. Cool and serve.

Molded Custard: Add 1 more egg or 2 egg yolks and pour into buttered molds. Bake. Chill. Unmold. Serve with cream or fruits or fruit juice.

Molded Maple Custard: Before straining Molded Custard into cups, pour 1 to 1½ tbsp. maple syrup into each cup. Pour custard mixture in carefully in order not to disturb the syrup. Cool thoroughly before unmolding.

COOKED PUDDING AND PIE FILLING MIXES

These contain no eggs but make puddings that taste much like old-time creamy custards. Available in a number of flavors including vanilla, chocolate, lemon, butterscotch and caramel, they cook in only a few minutes. Directions on each pkg.

FOR EXTRA RICHNESS

Proceed as directed on pkg. After removing from heat, stir in 2 tsp. butter and, if desired, extra flavoring to taste. Then beat with rotary beater and cool slightly.

FLAVOR·ADDITIONS

To Vanilla Pudding: Add 5 or 6 chocolate-covered cream-center mints, cut in small pieces. Stir just enough to swirl streaks of chocolate through the pudding.

To Lemon Pudding: Add 2 or 3 drops of lemon extract.

To Chocolate Pudding: Add ½ tsp. vanilla and dash of nutmeg. 1 sq. unsweetened chocolate (1 oz.) may be added before cooking.

To Butterscotch Pudding: Add ¼ tsp. maple flavoring and 2 drops of brandy flavoring.

INSTANT PUDDING AND PIE FILLING MIXES

You can make these in only 30 seconds. No cooking. Just follow directions on each pkg. Banana cream, pineapple cream and coconut cream puddings may be made from the vanilla mix by adding sliced bananas, drained crushed pineapple or shredded coconut. There are other flavors, such as chocolate and lemon.

Chocolate Malted Milk Pudding: Mix 1 to 2 tbsp. chocolate malted milk powder with 1 pkg. chocolate instant pudding mix. Use milk for liquid. Proceed as directed on pkg.

FLAVORED GELATIN DESSERT MIXES

Only liquid need be added to pkg. contents in a variety of flavors. Follow directions on pkg. Then as you choose, add drained cut-up fruit, marshmallows or nuts when slightly thickened. Use your ingenuity in making delectable variations, such as:

Lime Ginger Jelly: Dissolve 1 pkg. lime-flavored gelatin in 1 cup hot water. Chill. As mixture thickens, beat with egg beater until frothy and stir in 1 cup ginger ale. Turn into mold. When set, unmold. Surround with apricot halves on pineapple slices. Serve with Custard Sauce (p. 172) as a change from whipped cream.

LEMON SURPRISE CAKE

White cake baked with lemon filling beneath.

Prepare 1 pkg. quick lemon pie filling as directed on pkg. Spread in oblong pan, 13x9½x2″. Let stand while making cake batter. Heat oven to 350° (mod.). Make batter as directed on pkg. of Betty Crocker White Cake Mix. Pour batter over lemon filling. Bake 35 to 40 min., until top springs back when lightly touched. Sift confectioners' sugar over top. Serve warm.

FRESH PEACH OR BANANA SHORTCAKE

Bake cake in oblong pan as directed on pkg. of Betty Crocker Honey Spice, Yellow, Chocolate or White Cake Mix. Cut in squares and top with whipped cream and sliced peaches or bananas.

BOSTON CREAM PIE

Now you can make the old-time favorite easily with Betty Crocker Boston Cream Pie Mix. All in one package, you get mixes for (1) light, tender, homemade Yellow Cake, (2) soft, smooth, creamy, fresh-tasting Boston Cream Pie Filling and (3) perfect Chocolate Icing to top it off. Quick, complete directions are right on the package.

LITTLE UPSIDE-DOWN CAKES

In each of 24 muffin cups put:
½ tsp. butter
1 tsp. brown sugar
about 1 tbsp. fresh or well drained canned fruit (thinly sliced or crushed)

Heat oven to 400° (mod. hot). Make Cupcake batter as directed on pkg. of Betty Crocker Yellow, White or Honey Spice Cake Mix. Pour half of batter over fruit, filling cups not more than ⅔ full. Fill remaining cups a scant ½ full for plain cupcakes. Bake 15 to 18 min., until tops spring back when lightly touched. Loosen and invert at once on platter. Serve warm with whipped cream.

THIN CHOCOLATE ICING

1 tbsp. shortening
1 sq. unsweetened chocolate (1 oz.)
1 cup sifted confectioners' sugar
2 tbsp. boiling water

Melt shortening and chocolate over low heat. Blend in sugar and water. Beat only until smooth, not stiff.

174

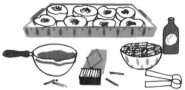

FLAMING PEACHES

Sprinkle brown sugar in hollows of peach halves in baking dish. Dot with butter. Broil slowly until sugar crusts. Center each with sugar lump soaked 15 to 20 min. in lemon extract; light lumps and bring to table flaming. Pass ice cold Soft Custard Sauce (p. 172).

PEAR HÉLÈNE

Place a drained chilled canned or thawed frozen or poached fresh pear half (p. 69) in each individual dessert dish. Top with vanilla ice cream. Cover with ready-made or Glossy Chocolate Sauce (p. 170).

PARTY PEACH MELBA

6 peach halves (poached,
    if fresh—p. 69)
toasted almonds
8-oz. can red raspberries,
    1 pkg. thawed frozen rasp-
    berries or 1 cup sweetened
    fresh raspberries
1 pt. vanilla ice cream
rum flavoring

Stud peach halves with almonds; put one in each individual dessert dish. Spoon raspberries over peaches. Chill. Whip ice cream (p. 168) to pouring consistency; blend in flavoring; pour over peaches. *6 servings.*

POT DE CRÊME AU CHOCOLAT

¼ lb. German sweet
    chocolate
1 tbsp. sugar
½ cup cream
2 egg yolks, slightly beaten
½ tsp. vanilla
whipped cream

Melt chocolate over hot water. Gradually stir in the sugar and the cream until smooth. Remove from heat. Slowly blend in egg yolks and vanilla. Pour into small individual dessert dishes, such as demitasse cups. Chill. Serve with garnish of whipped cream. *4 servings.*

EASY REFRIGERATOR PUDDING

Crumble a layer of crisp cookies in bottom of each individual dessert dish. Cover with layer of whipped cream. Repeat layers. Chill several hr.

EASY SNOW PUDDING

1 pkg. lemon-flavored gelatin
2 to 3 tsp. grated lemon rind
2 egg whites, stiffly beaten
    with 2 tsp. sugar
Custard Sauce (p. 172)

Prepare gelatin as directed on pkg. except — add lemon rind when gelatin is almost set, beat with rotary beater until frothy. Beat in egg whites, continuing until mixture holds its shape. Pile into sherbet glasses. Chill. Serve with cold Custard Sauce. *6 servings.*

STIR-N-ROLL PASTRY

Insures a brown, flaky undercrust in fruit pies. Ideal for refrigerator pies, too.

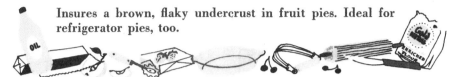

8 OR 9" TWO-CRUST PIE

2 cups sifted Gold Medal Flour
1½ tsp. salt
½ cup cooking (salad) oil
¼ cup cold whole milk
filling (see recipe for special pie being made)

Heat oven to 425° (hot). Mix flour, salt. Pour oil, milk into one measuring cup (but don't stir). Pour into flour. Mix well. Press into ball. Cut into halves; flatten slightly.

Bottom Crust: Roll out one-half between waxed papers 12" square. Damp table top prevents slipping. Peel off top paper. If dough tears, mend without moistening. Place paper side up in pie pan. Peel off paper. Ease pastry into pan. Add filling. Trim crust evenly.

Top Crust: Roll as above. Peel off top paper. Place over filling, paper side up. Peel off paper. Trim evenly. Seal with fork or flute edge. Make 3 or 4 slits near center. Bake until golden brown, about 40 min.

BAKED 8 OR 9" PIE SHELL

Filling is piled into baked shell.

1⅓ cups sifted Gold Medal Flour
1 tsp. salt
⅓ cup cooking (salad) oil
3 tbsp. cold whole milk

Heat oven to 475° (very hot). Make Stir-N-Roll Pastry as for 8" Two-crust Pie at left. Roll out as for bottom crust. After placing rolled dough in pie pan, trim evenly. Flute edge. Prick bottom and sides thoroughly with fork. Bake 8 to 10 min., until golden brown.

8 OR 9" ONE-CRUST PIE

Filling and crust are baked together.

Follow recipe for 8 or 9" Pie Shell, but do not prick and do not bake until filling is added. Then bake as directed for special pie being made.

Roast Beef (p. 96) with satin-smooth Pan Gravy (p. 121) and fluffy mashed potatoes is a universal favorite.

Main Dishes

Tossed Green Salad

Use a selection of interesting greens
and garnishes. Season with salt and
freshly grated pepper. Add salad oil,
then vinegar, and toss. Serve at once (p. 146).

Even Filled Cookies can be easy (p. 195).

Good Cookies the Easy Way

For many delicious cooky recipes, see pp. 82-83, 194-199.

Easy Sugar Cookies...they're Stir-N-Drop (p. 194).

Frosting a Cake

Swirl icing on cake with light, sweeping strokes.

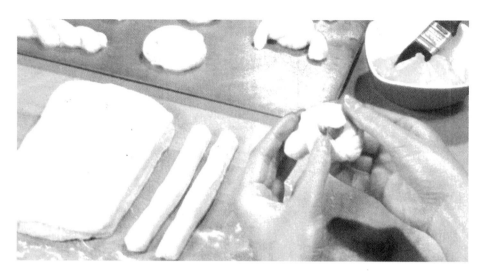

Spread dough with soft butter, fold over, cut in
narrow strips, tie in knots or form in twists.

Easy Refrigerator Rolls

Make hot, tempting rolls in a variety of shapes (p. 154).

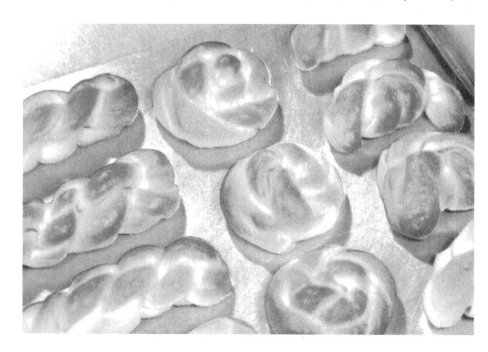

STANDARD PASTRY
8 OR 9" TWO-CRUST PIE

2 cups sifted Gold Medal Flour
1 tsp. salt
⅔ cup shortening (add 2 tbsp.
  if using hydrogenated)
4 tbsp. water
filling (for pie chosen)

Mix flour, salt. Cut in shortening.
Sprinkle with water; mix with
fork. Round into ball. Roll half
of dough 1" larger than inverted
pie pan. Ease into pan, fill and
trim edge. Roll out other half
same way. Cut slits near center.
Fit over filling, seal and flute.
Bake as directed for special pie
being made.

BAKED 8 OR 9" PIE SHELL

Filling is piled into baked shell.
1 cup sifted Gold Medal Flour
½ tsp. salt
⅓ cup shortening (add 1 tbsp.
  if using hydrogenated)
3 tbsp. water

Heat oven to 475° (very hot).
Mix flour, salt. Cut in shortening.
Sprinkle with water; mix with
fork. Round into ball. Roll out
1" larger than inverted pie pan.
Ease into pan, flute and prick
pastry. Bake 8 to 10 min., until
golden brown.

8 OR 9" ONE-CRUST PIE

Filling and crust are baked together. Follow recipe for 8 or 9"
Pie Shell, but do not prick and
do not bake until filling is added.
Then bake as directed for special pie being made.

PASTRY MADE WITH
A MIX

Just follow simple directions on
pkg. of Betty Crocker Homogenized Pie Crust Mix in sticks for
two-crust pie, one-crust pie,
baked pie shell.

LEFTOVER
PASTRY DAINTIES

Roll out trimmings from pie
crust. Sprinkle with grated
cheese, or with sugar and cinnamon mixed. Cut into fancy
shapes. Bake as for tarts. Serve
with salads, tea.

QUICK PIE FILLINGS

Prepared fruit pie fillings,
canned or packaged, include
apple, cherry, mincement, blueberry, other fruit.

Prepared cream pie fillings
(quick pudding mixes) include
vanilla, butterscotch, chocolate,
lemon, lime, orange, other flavors.

Canned pumpkin (cooked and
smoothly mashed).

Canned sliced apples.

Sweetened fresh frozen fruit
(use only half the amount of
sugar called for in a fresh fruit
recipe).

APPLE PIE

Pastry for 8″ Two-crust Pie
  (pp. 176, 185)
6 cups sliced tart, juicy apples
½ to ¾ cup sugar
¾ tsp. cinnamon or nutmeg
1 tbsp. butter

Heat oven to 425° (hot). Mix apples, sugar, spice. Heap in pastry-lined pie pan. Dot with butter. Cover with top crust. Seal and flute. Bake 50 to 60 min., until apples cook through.

VARIATIONS

Brown Sugar Apple Pie: Use brown sugar in place of granulated.

Dutch Apple Pie: 5 min. before pie is done, remove from oven and pour ½ cup heavy cream through slits in top crust. Return to oven and bake 5 min. more.

Compote Apple Pie: Before putting on top crust, thinly slice ¼ cup firm butter over the apples.

Spicy Apple Pie: Use in filling ¾ tsp. each nutmeg, ginger and cinnamon.

French Apple Pie: Use a single unbaked crust. Sprinkle over the filling a "crumb" or "rubbed-together" mixture of ½ cup butter, ½ cup brown sugar and 1 cup sifted Gold Medal Flour.

Cinnamon Candy Apple Pie: Omit spices and sprinkle over apples ¼ cup little red cinnamon candies.

Cheese-topped Apple Pie: Brush top crust of baked pie lightly with melted butter. Arrange thin slices of American cheese attractively over it, or sprinkle with grated cheese. Sprinkle lightly with nutmeg and set in mod. oven (350°) until cheese is lightly browned, about 10 min. Serve at once.

TO SAVE TIME

Use Betty Crocker Homogenized Pie Crust Mix in sticks for your pastry.
Use packaged sliced fresh apples or sliced unpeeled fresh red apples for the filling.

PEACH PIE

Pastry for 8″ Two-crust Pie
  (pp. 176, 185)
⅔ cup sugar
3 tbsp. flour
⅓ tsp. cinnamon
3 cups sliced firm peaches
1 tbsp. butter

Heat oven to 425° (hot). Mix sugar, flour, cinnamon. Mix lightly through peaches. Heap in pastry-lined pie pan. Dot with butter. Cover with top crust. Bake 35 to 45 min.

186

FRESH BERRY PIE

Pastry for 8″ Two-crust Pie
(pp. 176, 185)
⅔ to ¾ cup sugar
4 tbsp. Gold Medal Flour
⅓ tsp. cinnamon
3 cups fresh berries
(blueberries, blackberries,
raspberries, strawberries,
boysenberries)
1 tbsp. butter

Heat oven to 425° (hot). Mix sugar, flour, cinnamon. Mix lightly through berries. Pour into pastry-lined pie pan. Dot with butter. Cover with top crust. Seal and flute. Bake 35 to 45 min.

FRESH CHERRY PIE

Follow directions for Fresh Berry Pie (above) except—use pitted sour pie cherries in place of berries, add 1 cup sugar and 3 drops almond extract.

CHERRY-BERRY PIE

Make same as Fresh Berry Pie (above) except—use 1½ cups each fresh red raspberries and pitted fresh red pie cherries. Use ⅔ to 1 cup sugar.

TOP-CRUST FRUIT AND BERRY PIES

Make and bake same as Two-crust Pies except—place fruit or berries directly in empty pie pan; make Pastry for One-crust Pie (pp. 176, 185) and place over filling. Trim evenly. Seal to rim of pan with fork or flute edge. Cut slits near center.

CANNED BERRY PIE

Pastry for 8″ Two-crust Pie
(pp. 176, 185)
½ to ⅔ cup sugar
2½ tbsp. flour
¼ tsp. cinnamon
⅓ cup juice from berries
2⅓ cups drained canned
berries (any kind you
choose)
1 tbsp. butter

Heat oven to 425° (hot). Mix sugar, flour, cinnamon and juice. Cook over med. heat, stirring constantly until mixture thickens and boils. Boil 1 min. Mix lightly with drained berries. Pour into pastry-lined pie pan. Dot with butter. Cover with top crust. Seal and flute. Bake 35 to 45 min.

CANNED CHERRY PIE

Follow directions for Canned Berry Pie (above) except—use pitted sour red pie cherries and juice; use ¼ tsp. almond extract in place of cinnamon; may add a few drops red food coloring.

CANNED PEACH OR APRICOT PIE

Follow directions for Canned Berry Pie (above) except—use sliced peaches or apricots and juice instead of berries and juice.

> **TO SAVE TIME AND WORK**
> Use prepared fruit or berry pie-filling mix available at your grocer's in many flavors. Just pour the filling into the crust!

DEEP DISH FRESH FRUIT PIES

Pastry for 8″ One-crust Pie (pp. 176, 185)
2 cups peeled peaches, quartered
2 cups quartered plums
¾ to 1 cup sugar
2 tbsp. flour
2 tbsp. butter

Heat oven to 425° (hot). Place fruit in square pan, 8x8x2″, or 1½-qt. casserole. Mix sugar and flour and sprinkle over fruit. Dot with butter. Cover with top crust. Bake 30 to 40 min. *Serves 6 to 8.*

Note: For a thinner pie, omit flour.

VARIATIONS

In place of the plums in recipe above, use pitted sweet or sour cherries, raspberries or blueberries.

Or try pitted sour and sweet cherries instead of both peaches and plums.

Or use 6 cups sliced apples instead of peaches and plums, mixing 1 tsp. cinnamon with the sugar.

HOLIDAY MINCE PIE

Pastry for 8″ Two-crust Pie (pp. 176, 185)
2½ cups mincemeat (chopped apple mixed in makes it extra fruity)

Heat oven to 425° (hot). Fill pastry-lined pie pan with mincemeat. Cover with top crust. Seal and flute. Bake 30 to 40 min., until golden brown.

Apricot-Mince Pie: Arrange layer of drained sweetened cooked apricots on bottom of pastry-lined pan (8″). Spread mincemeat over apricots, cover with top crust, seal and flute. Bake 40 to 45 min.

Blackberry-Mince Pie: Substitute well drained canned blackberries for ½ the mincemeat in filling for Holiday Mince Pie. Serve warm with Hot Blackberry sauce (below).

HOT BLACKBERRY SAUCE

1 tbsp. each sugar and cornstarch
1 cup blackberry juice (drained from canned berries)
1 tbsp. butter
⅛ tsp. salt
2 tbsp. lemon juice

Mix sugar and cornstarch in saucepan. Blend in blackberry juice. Cook until smooth and thickened, stirring constantly. Remove from heat. Stir in butter, salt, lemon juice.

SOUTHERN CHESS PIE
Much like Southern Pecan Pie.

> Pastry for 8" One-crust Pie
> (pp. 176, 185)
> 1 cup brown sugar (packed)
> ½ cup granulated sugar
> 1 tbsp. flour
> 2 eggs
> 2 tbsp. milk
> 1 tsp. vanilla
> ½ cup butter, melted
> 1 cup pecans

Heat oven to 375° (quick mod.). Mix together sugars and flour. Beat in thoroughly eggs, milk, vanilla, butter. Fold in nuts. Pour into pastry-lined pan. Bake 40 to 50 min. Serve slightly warm, plain or with whipped cream.

CREAMY PUMPKIN PIE

> Pastry for 9" One-crust Pie
> (pp. 176, 185)
> 1¾ cups canned pumpkin
> (no. 300 can)
> 1⅓ cups sweetened con-
> densed (not evaporated)
> milk (15-oz. can)
> 1 large egg
> ½ tsp. salt
> ½ tsp. cinnamon
> ¼ tsp. nutmeg
> ¼ tsp. ginger
> 1 cup hot water

Heat oven to 375° (quick mod.). Line pie pan with pastry. Beat remaining ingredients together with rotary beater or electric mixer; pour into pastry-lined pan. Bake 50 to 55 min., until knife inserted in side of filling comes out clean. Just before serving, garnish if desired with thin layer of whipped cream.

QUICK EGGNOG PIE

A heavenly dessert for holiday and special entertaining.

> Baked 9" Pie Shell
> (pp. 176, 185)
> 1 envelope unflavored gelatin
> 3 tbsp. cold water
> 2 cups commercially
> prepared eggnog
> (available from milk
> dealers)
> 1 cup heavy cream, whipped
> ¼ cup sugar
> ¼ tsp. salt
> 2 tsp. vanilla or 1 tsp. rum
> flavoring
> ½ tsp. almond extract

Soften gelatin in cold water. Warm eggnog over direct low heat; stir in the softened gelatin and continue heating until completely dissolved. Chill until partially set. Then beat until smooth. Into stiffly whipped cream, beat sugar, salt and flavorings; fold into eggnog mixture. Pour into baked pie shell. Chill 2 to 4 hr.

Garnish with grated nutmeg, toasted slivered almonds, shredded coconut or holly clusters made from cut-up maraschino cherries and angelica.

VANILLA CREAM PIE

Baked 8" Pie Shell
  (pp. 176, 185)
½ cup sugar
½ tsp. salt
2 tbsp. cornstarch
2 cups rich milk
2 egg yolks, slightly beaten
2 tsp. butter
1 tsp. vanilla

Mix sugar, salt and cornstarch in saucepan. Slowly stir in milk. Boil 1 min. over med. heat, stirring constantly. Remove from heat. Stir half of mixture into egg yolks, then blend into hot mixture in saucepan. Boil 1 more min., stirring constantly. Remove from heat. Blend in butter, vanilla. Pour into baked pie shell, and chill for about 2 hr. Just before serving, top with whipped cream.

VARIATIONS

Apricot Cream: Garnish cooled filling or whipped cream topping with ring of apricot halves.

Banana, Orange: Slice bananas or orange in bottom of pie shell before pouring in cooled filling.

Berry Cream: Cover cooled filling with raspberries, blueberries, sliced strawberries or sweetened blackberries. Top with whipped cream.

Bittersweet: Sprinkle whipped cream topping with finely grated or shaved unsweetened or semisweet chocolate.

Butterscotch: Substitute dark brown sugar (packed) for granulated sugar; increase butter to 1 or 2 tbsp.

Chocolate Cream: Use 1⅛ cups sugar and add 2¼ sq. cut-up unsweetened chocolate (2¼ oz.) with the milk. Delicious with layer of freshly sliced bananas under cooled chocolate filling.

Coconut: Fold ¾ cup moist shredded coconut into cooled filling just before pouring into pie shell. Sprinkle ¼ cup coconut over whipped cream topping.

Date: Add ¾ cup chopped pitted dates to cooled filling.

Serving Note: Remove cream pies from refrigerator 20 min. before serving to take chill from crusts.

TIME-SAVER

Use packaged quick pudding mixes for your cream pie fillings. Vary them by using some of the suggestions on page 173.

MR.-AND-MRS. PIE

Choice of fillings in a single shell. Make up 2 prepared pudding mix fillings, such as vanilla-banana and butterscotch. Cool. Place cardboard divider upright in baked pie shell. Place one filling on one side, other filling on other side of divider. Chill. Remove divider.

LEMON MERINGUE PIE

Baked 8 or 9" Pie Shell
  (pp. 176, 185)
1½ cups sugar
⅓ cup cornstarch
1½ cups water
3 egg yolks, slightly beaten
3 tbsp. butter
¼ cup lemon juice
1 tbsp. grated lemon rind
Meringue (below) made with
  3 egg whites

Heat oven to 400° (mod. hot). Mix sugar and cornstarch in saucepan. Gradually stir in water. Stir over med. heat until mixture thickens and boils. Boil 1 min. Slowly stir half of hot mixture into slightly beaten egg yolks. Beat into remaining hot mixture. Boil 1 min., stirring constantly. Remove from heat. Continue stirring until smooth. Blend in butter, lemon juice and lemon rind. Pour hot filling into baked pie shell. Cover with Meringue (below). Bake 8 to 10 min., until a delicate brown.

MERINGUE

For 2 eggs:	For 3 eggs:
¼ tsp. cream of tartar	¼ tsp. cream of tartar
4 tbsp. sugar	6 tbsp. sugar

Beat egg whites with cream of tartar until frothy. Gradually beat in sugar. Beat until stiff and glossy.

FRUIT SUNDAE PIE

Baked 9" Pie Shell
  (pp. 176, 185)
1 qt. firm vanilla ice cream
1 pkg. frozen fruits,
  thawed and drained
  or 1 qt. sweetened fresh
  berries or fruit

Quickly fill cooled baked pie shell with ice cream. Top with berries or fruit. Serve at once.

QUICK ORANGE MERINGUE PIE

Baked 8" Pie Shell
  (pp. 176, 185)
1 cup sugar
4 tbsp. cornstarch
1⅓ cups diluted frozen
  orange juice
2 egg yolks
2 tbsp. butter
Meringue made with 2 egg
  whites

Heat oven to 400° (mod. hot). Mix sugar, cornstarch in saucepan. Add orange juice gradually. Stir over med. heat until thick. Boil 1 min. Beat half of hot mixture into egg yolks. Beat into remaining hot mixture. Boil 1 min., stirring constantly. Blend in butter. Pour into baked pie shell. Cover with Meringue. Bake 8 to 10 min., until a delicate brown.

FROSTY FRUIT PIE

Use crushed pineapple, apple-sauce, apple juice, orange juice, grape juice, prune juice, apricot nectar or pineapple juice.

Baked 9" Pie Shell
  (pp. 176, 185)
1¼ cups fruit or juice
1 pkg. lemon-flavored
  gelatin
¾ to 1 cup sugar
  (to sweeten fruit)
1 cup chilled evaporated milk
1 tbsp. lemon juice

Bring fruit to a boil. Stir in gelatin until dissolved. Mix in sugar. Cool until almost stiff. Whip evaporated milk with lemon juice until stiff. Beat slowly into gelatin mixture. Pour into baked pie shell. Chill at least 1 hr. Garnish with shaved chocolate.

STRAWBERRY MINUTE PIE

Baked 8" Pie Shell
  (pp. 176, 185)
1 pkg. strawberry-flavored
  gelatin
1 cup hot water
1 pkg. unthawed frozen
  sweetened sliced
  strawberries

Dissolve flavored gelatin in hot water. Add unthawed frozen berries. Break up berries with a fork. As berries thaw, gelatin thickens. When partially set, pour into cooled pie shell. Chill until completely set. Just before serving, garnish with sweetened whipped cream.

GLAZED STRAWBERRY PIE

Baked 9" Pie Shell
  (pp. 176, 185), cooled
1 qt. drained hulled
  strawberries
3-oz. pkg. white cream cheese,
  softened
1½ cups juice
1 cup sugar
3 tbsp. cornstarch

Spread softened cream cheese over bottom of pastry shell. Cover with half the berries (choicest). Mash and strain rest of berries until juice is extracted; add water, if needed, to make 1½ cups juice. Bring juice to boil; stir in sugar and cornstarch. Cook over low heat, stirring constantly, until boiling. Boil 1 min. Pour over berries in pie shell. Chill 2 hr. Just before serving, decorate with whipped cream.

RASPBERRY MINUTE PIE

Make same as Strawberry Minute Pie (left) except—use raspberry-flavored gelatin in place of strawberry-flavored and frozen raspberries instead of strawberries.

SERVING NOTE: Remove refrigerator pies from refrigerator 20 min. before serving to take chill from crust.

EASY-PERFECT PATTY SHELLS

For creamed chicken or sea foods, or for ice cream and fruit or cream pie fillings.

In Advance: Roll pastry for Two-crust Pie (pp. 176, 185) to thickness of pie crust. Cut into 5" rounds. Prick with fork. Stack, with waxed paper between rounds. Place in plastic bag or in aluminum foil and freeze.

When Ready to Use: Heat oven to 475° (very hot). Place frozen circles on inverted custard cups on baking sheet or on backs of muffin cups. Bake 8 to 10 min. During baking, pastry takes shape of cups. *8 patty shells.*

SIMPLIFIED TARTS

Crispy pastry rounds or squares make a delicious dessert when topped with a favorite filling.

Heat oven to 475° (very hot). Roll Pastry (pp. 176, 185) thin. Cut into 3" rounds or squares. Place on ungreased baking sheet. Prick with fork. Bake until delicately browned, 8 to 10 min.

Top Tarts with softened cream cheese, then with sweetened or glazed fruit. Or top with chocolate or other cream pie filling, and then with whipped cream.

Put together, shortcake fashion, with sweetened fresh or frozen fruit and Soft Custard (p. 172); top with more fruit and Soft Custard or whipped cream.

RING-TOPPED TARTS

Remove centers from half the ⅛" thick Pastry rounds (see Simplified Tarts) when cutting. When baked, place pastry rings on sweetened fruit or cream pie filling on uncut rounds. Garnish with more filling, whipped cream, berries and a sprig of mint.

ALASKA SURPRISE

Heat oven to 400° (mod. hot). On each Simplified Tart (left), spread cooled Lemon or Orange Filling (p. 169) or use packaged pudding mix, leaving ½" edge of pastry all around.

Completely cover with Meringue (p. 191) down to the pastry. Bake 6 to 8 min., until delicately browned.

FRUIT TARTS À LA MODE

Fill baked tart shells with fruit (sweetened whole or sliced strawberries, blueberries, green or Tokay grapes or raspberries; peaches; crushed pineapple or applesauce). Top with ice cream or with whipped cream or Soft Custard (p. 172).

GLAZED FRUIT TARTS

Heat currant jelly just until it melts. Spoon about 1 tbsp. over fruit in each fruit-filled baked tart shell. Or drop the fruit into the melted jelly and pile back into baked shells.

STIR-N-DROP SUGAR COOKIES

See picture, p. 182.

2 eggs
2/3 cup cooking (salad) oil
2 tsp. vanilla
1 tsp. grated lemon rind
3/4 cup sugar
2 cups sifted
    Gold Medal Flour
2 tsp. baking powder
1/2 tsp. salt

Heat oven to 400° (mod. hot). Beat eggs with fork until well blended. Stir in oil, vanilla, lemon rind. Blend in sugar until mixture thickens. Sift together flour, baking powder, salt and stir into oil mixture. Drop with teaspoon 2" apart on ungreased baking sheet. Flatten with greased glass dipped in sugar. Bake 8 to 10 min., just until a delicate brown. Remove immediately from baking sheet. *About 3 doz. cookies.*

STIR-N-DROP OATMEAL COOKIES

1 cup sifted
    Gold Medal Flour
1 tsp. baking powder
1/2 tsp. salt
1/2 tsp. cinnamon
1/2 tsp. ginger
1 cup brown sugar (packed)
1 cup quick rolled oats
1/4 cup cooking (salad) oil
2 tbsp. milk
1 egg
3/4 cup Spanish peanuts

Heat oven to 375° (quick mod.). Sift flour, baking powder, salt, spices into bowl. Add brown sugar, rolled oats. Mix in thoroughly oil, milk, egg. Add peanuts. Drop with teaspoon 2" apart on lightly greased baking sheet. Bake 10 to 12 min., just until a light touch with finger leaves no imprint. *About 3 doz. cookies.*

COCOA DROP COOKIES

1/2 cup soft shortening
1 cup sugar
1 egg
3/4 cup buttermilk or
    sour milk
1 tsp. vanilla
1 3/4 cups sifted
    Gold Medal Flour
1/2 tsp. soda
1/2 tsp. salt
1/2 cup cocoa
1 cup chopped nuts
    or raisins

Mix thoroughly shortening, sugar and egg. Stir in buttermilk and vanilla. Sift together and stir in flour, soda, salt and cocoa. Stir in nuts or raisins. Chill at least 1 hr. Heat oven to 400° (mod. hot). Drop with teaspoon 2" apart on lightly greased baking sheet. Bake 8 to 10 min., just until a light touch with finger leaves no imprint. Frost cooled cookies with Browned Butter Icing. *About 3 1/2 doz. cookies.*

Browned Butter Icing: Melt 1/4 cup butter, then keep over low heat until golden brown. Blend in 2 cups sifted confectioners' sugar. Stir in cream or undiluted evaporated milk until easy to spread (about 2 tbsp.) and 1 tsp. vanilla.

JUBILEE JUMBLES

½ cup soft shortening
1 cup brown sugar (packed)
½ cup sugar
2 eggs
1 cup undiluted evaporated
    milk or cultured sour
    cream
1 tsp. vanilla
2¾ cups sifted
    Gold Medal Flour
½ tsp. soda
1 tsp. salt
1 cup moist shredded coconut
    or finely cut dates or seed-
    less raisins or a 6-oz. pkg.
    semisweet chocolate pieces
1 cup cut-up nuts, if desired

Heat oven to 375° (quick mod.).
Mix thoroughly shortening, sugars and eggs. Stir in milk and vanilla. Sift together; stir in flour,
soda and salt. Blend in remaining ingredients. Chill. Drop with
tablespoon 2″ apart on greased
baking sheet. Bake until a light
touch with finger leaves no imprint, about 10 min. While cookies are still warm, frost, if desired, with Browned Butter Icing.
(p. 194). *About 4 doz. cookies.*

EASY FILLED COOKIES
See picture, p. 182.

Date Filling (recipe below)
1 cup soft shortening
2 cups brown sugar (packed)
2 eggs
½ cup water or buttermilk
1 tsp. vanilla
3½ cups sifted
    Gold Medal Flour
1 tsp. salt
1 tsp. soda
⅛ tsp. cinnamon

Heat oven to 400° (mod. hot).
Mix thoroughly shortening,
brown sugar and eggs. Stir in
water and vanilla. Sift together
and stir in flour, salt, soda and
cinnamon. Drop with teaspoon
on ungreased baking sheet. Place
½ tsp. Date Filling on dough;
cover with another ½ tsp. dough.
Bake until lightly browned, 10
to 12 min. *5 to 6 doz. cookies.*

DATE FILLING

2 cups dates, finely cut up
¾ cup sugar
¾ cup water
½ cup chopped nuts,
    if desired

Cook together slowly, stirring
constantly until thickened, dates,
sugar, water. Add nuts. Cool.

Quick, Luscious Date Bars:
An old favorite, made the new way
with Betty Crocker Date Bar Mix.
Just add water. Then follow simple directions on the pkg.

HONEY DROPS

1 cup soft shortening
(part butter)
1 cup brown sugar (packed)
2 eggs
¼ cup plus 2 tbsp. honey
1 tsp. vanilla
3½ cups sifted
Gold Medal Flour
2 tsp. soda
apricot or other jam

Mix thoroughly shortening, brown sugar, eggs. Stir in honey and vanilla. Sift together and stir in flour and soda. Chill until firm, several hr. or overnight. Heat oven to 350° (mod.). Form dough into balls; place on ungreased baking sheet. Bake 10 to 12 min., until golden brown and top springs back when lightly touched. Cool slightly. Put together in pairs with apricot jam between. *3 doz. double cookies.*

CHOCOLATE LOGS

½ cup soft shortening
(part butter)
1 cup sugar
1 egg
2 sq. unsweetened chocolate
(2 oz.), melted
2 tsp. vanilla
2 cups sifted
Gold Medal Flour
½ tsp. salt
¾ cup nuts, finely chopped

Mix thoroughly shortening, sugar, egg, melted chocolate and vanilla. Stir in flour and salt. Mix in nuts. Shape into 8x12″ rectangle on well greased baking sheet. Cover with waxed paper; chill until firm. Heat oven to 375°

(quick mod.). Cut dough into 48 logs, 4x½″. Place a little apart on ungreased baking sheet. Bake 10 to 12 min., just until set but not hard. *48 logs.*

HIDDEN CHOCOLATE COOKIES

It's a delicious surprise to find a chocolate mint in the center.

½ cup soft shortening
(part butter)
½ cup sugar
¼ cup brown sugar (packed)
1 egg
1 tbsp. water
½ tsp. vanilla
1½ cups plus 2 tbsp.
sifted Gold Medal Flour
½ tsp. soda
¼ tsp. salt
½ pkg. chocolate mint
wafers (9½ oz.)

Heat oven to 400° (mod. hot). Mix thoroughly shortening, sugars, egg. Stir in water and vanilla. Sift together and stir in flour, soda and salt. Shape cookies by enclosing each chocolate mint wafer in about 1 tbsp. dough. Place about 2″ apart on greased baking sheet. Bake until a light touch with finger leaves almost no imprint, 8 to 10 min. *About 3 doz. cookies.*

BROWNIES

2 sq. unsweetened chocolate (2 oz.)
⅓ cup shortening
1 cup sugar
2 eggs
¾ cup sifted
  Gold Medal Flour
½ tsp. baking powder
½ tsp. salt
½ cup broken nuts

Heat oven to 350° (mod.). Melt chocolate and shortening together over hot water. Remove from heat and beat in sugar and eggs. Sift together and beat in flour, baking powder and salt. Mix in nuts. Spread in well greased square pan, 8x8x2". Bake until a light touch with finger leaves slight imprint, 30 to 35 min. Cool slightly, then cut into squares. *16 2" squares.*

Chocolate-frosted Brownies: Before cutting, spread cooled sheet of Brownies with Marie's Chocolate Icing (opposite).

Chocolate Peppermint Brownies: As soon as you remove baked Brownies from oven, place about 16 chocolate peppermint patties on top. Return to oven a couple of minutes to soften patties; then, as they melt, spread over top with a spatula.

BUTTERSCOTCH BROWNIES

¼ cup shortening
1 cup light brown sugar (packed)
1 egg
¾ cup sifted
  Gold Medal Flour
1 tsp. baking powder
½ tsp. salt
½ tsp. vanilla
½ cup broken nuts

Heat oven to 350° (mod.). Melt shortening over low heat. Remove from heat and blend in brown sugar. Cool. Stir in egg. Sift together and stir in flour, baking powder and salt. Stir in vanilla and nuts. Spread in well greased and floured square pan, 8x8x2". Bake 20 to 25 min., until a light touch with finger leaves slight imprint. Cut into bars while warm. *18 bars (1x2½").*

Marie's Chocolate Icing: Melt over hot water 1 tbsp. butter and 1 sq. unsweetened chocolate (1 oz.). Blend in 1½ tbsp. warm water. Stir and beat in about 1 cup sifted confectioners' sugar until icing will spread easily.

QUICKER BROWNIES

Easier than ever to make with Betty Crocker Brownie Mix. Just follow simple directions on pkg.

CHINESE ALMOND CAKES

Shortbread type. Perfect with fresh fruit or with orange ice to finish a chow mein supper.

1 cup sifted Gold Medal Flour
½ cup shortening
(half butter)
½ tsp. salt
¼ cup plus 2 tbsp. sugar
½ tsp. almond extract or
vanilla
1 egg yolk
1 tbsp. water
¼ cup blanched almonds

Place flour in bowl. Cut in shortening finely. Use hands to work in salt, sugar and flavoring. Shape into long roll, 1" in diameter, and wrap in waxed paper. Chill about 1 hr. Heat oven to 400° (mod. hot). Cut roll into ¼" slices. Place 1" apart on lightly greased baking sheet. Brush each slice with mixture of egg yolk and water. Press ½ blanched almond into top of each. Bake until light golden brown, 8 to 10 min. *About 2 doz. cakes.*

CARAMEL NUT SLICES

½ cup soft shortening
(part butter)
1 cup brown sugar (packed)
1 egg
1¾ cups sifted
Gold Medal Flour
¼ tsp. salt
½ tsp. soda
½ cup finely chopped nuts

Mix thoroughly shortening, sugar and egg. Sift together and stir in flour, salt, soda. Blend in nuts. Form into two rolls, 2" in diameter. Wrap in waxed paper and chill overnight. Heat oven to 400° (mod. hot). Cut slices ⅛" thick; place a little apart on ungreased baking sheet. Bake 8 to 10 min., until set but not hard. *About 6 doz. cookies.*

ISLAND COOKIES

½ cup soft shortening
¼ cup granulated sugar
¼ cup brown sugar (packed)
1 egg
¾ tsp. vanilla
1¼ cups plus 2 tbsp.
sifted Gold Medal Flour
¼ tsp. soda
½ tsp. salt

Mix thoroughly shortening, sugars, egg and vanilla. Sift together and stir in flour, soda and salt. Mold into long smooth roll, 2½" in diameter. Wrap in waxed paper and chill overnight. Heat oven to 400° (mod. hot). Cut roll into ⅛" slices and place a little apart on ungreased baking sheet. Put a spoonful of Topping (below) on each. Bake until lightly browned, 6 to 8 min. *About 3 doz. cookies.*

Topping: Cook together until thick, about 5 min., 1 cup chopped dates, apricots, raisins or figs; 1 cup chopped walnuts; ½ cup sugar; ½ cup water.

QUICK PARTY COOKIES
Use drop or rolled cookies of appropriate color and shape, made from foregoing recipes (pp. 194-198) or bought ready-made from your neighborhood baker or grocer. Use Simple White Icing (tinted with a drop or two of food coloring as desired).

SIMPLE WHITE ICING
1 cup sifted confectioners'
  sugar
¼ tsp. salt
½ tsp. vanilla
about 1½ tbsp. milk, water
  or cream

Into sugar, salt and vanilla, blend enough liquid to spread easily.

New Year's Clocks: Cover round cookies with white frosting for faces. Mark hands and hours with melted chocolate (using toothpick for outlining).

Valentine Hearts: Spread pink icing on heart-shaped cookies. Or center pink-frosted rounds with candy hearts.

Flags: Spread bar cookies with white icing; tint icing blue for field of blue; use silver dragees for stars and red cinnamon candies for stripes.

Shamrocks: Frost shamrocks (cut with club cutter) with pale green icing. Or put candy shamrocks on green-frosted squares or rounds.

Jack-o'-Lanterns: Spread orange-tinted icing on rounds. Make faces with melted chocolate.

Easter Eggs: Cover oval or egg-shaped cookies with pastel-tinted icings (yellow, lavender, green or pink). Or in center of each pastel-frosted round or square, put little candy egg (jelly bean).

Goldilocks: On white-frosted round cooky, use small lavender gumdrops for eyes, silver dragees for eyebrows and nose, yellow gumdrops for hair, cinnamon candies for mouth.

Place Cards: Write names on frosted or unfrosted cookies with melted chocolate or colored icing.

GOOD AND EASY USES FOR LEFTOVERS

BACON	Use as soup garnish (p. 37). Use in Peanut Butter-Bacon Sandwich (p. 42).
BAKED HAM	Use in Macaroni Cups (p. 48). Use in Creamed Ham and Eggs (p. 52). Use in Ham-Cheese Fondue (p. 53). In omelets, salads (bits and slivers).
BEEF	Use in sandwich fillings (p. 42). Use in Sure-fire Special (p. 46). Use in Ruth's Hash (p. 54). Use in Chef's Salad (p. 59). Heat sliced meat in gravy; serve as hot sandwich on bread. Combine cut-up pot roast, leftover vegetables, leftover gravy. Top with moist mashed potato and bake. Spread chopped meat, onion, green pepper on biscuit dough; roll up, slice, bake and serve with gravy.
BREAD (Crumbs or Cubes)	Use in Croquettes (p. 203). Use in City Chicken (p. 103). Use in Croutons (p. 38). Use in Stuffings (p. 120).
CHEESE	Grate and add to salad, cream sauce, scalloped potatoes or onions.
CHICKEN	Use in Chicken Salads (p. 60). Use in Chicken-Wild Rice Casserole (p. 134). Use in Chicken à la King (p. 111). Use in Yankee Chicken Hash (p. 131). Use in Macaroni Salad (p. 59). For croquettes with rice.
EGG WHITES	Use in Meringues (p. 191). Use in Icings (p. 167). Use in Omelets (p. 10). Beat and fold into applesauce. Beat stiff with small glass of tart jelly for cake icing.

EGG YOLKS	Use in Almond Sauce (p. 123). Use in Mushroom Sauce (p. 123). Use in Easy Hollandaise (p. 122). Use in Fluffy Hollandaise (p. 203). Use in Fillings (p. 169). Use in Custard (p. 172).
FRUITS	Use as topping for puddings, ice cream, tapioca and cake. Use fruit juice in gelatin salads and in sauce for dessert. Use in mixed fruit juice cocktail. Add to custards.
LAMB	Serve as curried lamb with rice (p. 135).
PIE FILLING	Serve as pudding with a whipped cream topping. Thin with fruit juice, milk or cream and serve in sherbet glasses.
PORK	Use in Chinese Pork and Rice (p. 51). Heat slices in Barbecue Sauce (p. 117), serve on a bun.
SHRIMP	Use in Shrimp-Cheese Fondue (p. 53). Use in Canapés (p. 93).
TUNA OR SALMON	Use in Creamed Tuna or Salmon (p. 52). Use in Canapés (p. 93).
VEAL	Use in Macaroni Salad (p. 59). Serve as curried veal with rice. Heat slices in Barbecue Sauce (p. 117), serve on a bun.
VEGETABLES	Use in Vegetable Soups (pp. 34-35). Use in Vegetable Salads (pp. 58, 149). Use in Meat Supper Pie (p. 202). Use in Garden Supper Casserole (p. 203). Use in Quick Pickled Beets (p. 126). Use in sauce over meat loaves and casseroles. Save vegetable juices and cooking water for soup.

The smart cook plans on using leftovers for good, time-saving, economical extra meals. Using leftovers temptingly takes a bit of imagination. Here are a few sample recipes:

MEAT SUPPER PIE

2 cups leftover mashed potato
1 egg, beaten
½ tsp. salt
milk
1 cup cubed cooked meat
1 cup gravy
½ cup diced cooked carrots
    or other vegetable
½ cup cooked peas
½ cup diced onion
salt and pepper to taste
¼ tsp. sage

Heat oven to 375° (quick mod.). Blend potato, egg, ½ tsp. salt, moistening with enough milk to spread easily. Spread half on bottom and up the sides of 9″ pie plate. Mix together rest of ingredients; spread over mashed potato in pie plate; top with rest of potato. Bake 30 min. *4 servings.*

POTATO SCONES

1½ cups cold mashed potato
1 egg, beaten
1 tbsp. grated onion
2 tbsp. minced parsley
1 tsp. Worcestershire sauce
1 cup Bisquick

Mix ingredients, adding milk if too stiff. Roll out ⅜″ thick on Bisquick-covered cloth. Cut rounds with floured 3″ cutter. Sauté in butter until brown; turn. Delicious with pot roast. *1 doz. scones.*

MEXICAN RICE AND MEAT

3 cups cooked rice
    (or 1 cup uncooked)
½ cup chopped onion
4 tbsp. fat
no. 2 can tomatoes (2½ cups)
¾ to 1 cup cut-up
    cooked meat
¼ cup meat stock or
    gravy mixed with ¼ cup
    water or 1 bouillon cube
    in ½ cup hot water
salt and pepper to taste
⅛ tsp. dry mustard

Heat oven to 350° (mod.). Mix ingredients. Place in greased 1½-qt. baking dish. Bake 30 min. *6 servings.*

CURRIED PORK SLICES

Heat oven to 350° (mod.). Arrange slices of leftover pork in baking dish; top each slice with canned apricot halves. Pour Curry Sauce (p. 122) over them; top with a few sautéed fresh or canned mushrooms. Heat in oven, about 15 to 20 min., until sauce bubbles.

CROQUETTES

2 cups ground or chopped
  cooked meat or chicken
1 cup Thick Cream Sauce
  (p. 122)
1 tsp. minced onion
1 tsp. minced parsley
½ tsp. flavor extender
  (p. 124)
1 egg, slightly beaten
2 tbsp. water
fine dry bread crumbs

Mix meat, Cream Sauce, onion, parsley and flavor extender; spread in 8″ sq. pan. Chill until stiff. Cut in squares or oblongs. Coat with flour; roll in egg mixed with water, then in crumbs. Allow to dry. Fry in deep fat (375°) until brown, about 3 min. Or pan-fry in about ½ cup hot fat over med. heat. Drain on absorbent paper. Serve with Mushroom or Tomato Sauce (p. 123). *12 croquettes.*

CHOPPED BEEF ON TOAST

Heat chopped or ground cooked leftover beef in drippings; add a little water, salt and pepper to taste, chopped onion; cook mixture down to desired consistency. Serve on toast with Tomato, Curry or Mushroom Sauce (pp. 122, 123).

GARDEN SUPPER CASSEROLE

2 cups cubed soft bread
  (about 2 slices)
½ cup grated sharp cheese
2 tbsp. butter, melted
1 cup peas or other cooked
  vegetable
1½ cups Medium Cream
  Sauce (p. 122)
2 tbsp. chopped onion
1 cup chopped cooked meat,
  flaked tuna or
  3 sliced hard-cooked eggs
1 large tomato, sliced

Heat oven to 350° (mod.). Mix bread cubes, cheese and butter; spread half this mixture in greased 1-qt. baking dish. Add peas. Make Cream Sauce, browning onion in the butter. Add meat; pour over peas. Arrange tomato over top and cover with remaining bread mixture. Bake 25 min. *4 to 6 servings.*

FLUFFY HOLLANDAISE

May be kept in refrigerator and served like butter over hot vegetables as needed.

Put 2 hard-cooked egg yolks through sieve. Add ¼ cup soft butter, 1½ tbsp. lemon juice, salt to taste; dash of paprika; beat with electric mixer or rotary beater until fluffy.

ORANGE REFRIGERATOR DESSERT

½ angel food cake
1 envelope unflavored gelatin
  (1 tbsp.)
¼ cup cold water
¼ cup boiling water
1 cup orange juice, fresh or
  diluted concentrated
1 cup sugar
2 cups heavy cream, whipped
grated orange rind, if desired

Break cake in small pieces. Place in oblong pan, 13x9½x2". Soften gelatin in cold water; dissolve in boiling water. Mix orange juice, sugar; blend in gelatin. Chill until slightly thickened. Beat. Mix gelatin mixture and whipped cream. Pour over cake. Chill. Sprinkle orange rind over top. *12 large servings.*

SUBGUM

4-oz. can or ½ cup sliced
  fresh mushrooms
1 tbsp. butter or other fat
1 tbsp. chopped green onion
2 cups diced cooked pork
  from pork roast
2 cups sliced celery
1½ cups leftover gravy
1 tsp. soy sauce
no. 2 can bean sprouts

Save mushroom liquid to add to gravy; sauté mushrooms and onion in butter. Add meat, celery, gravy and soy sauce; cook over low heat until celery is just tender. Add water if it becomes too thick. Add drained bean sprouts; heat through. Serve on hot fluffy rice or crisp Chinese noodles. *6 servings.*

HAM AND EGGPLANT AU GRATIN

½ tsp. dry mustard
¼ tsp. paprika
1 cup Cheese Sauce (p. 122)
4 cups ½" cubes of eggplant
1 cup diced cooked ham
2 tomatoes, sliced
½ cup Wheaties
3 tbsp. butter, melted

Heat oven to 350° (mod.). Add mustard and paprika to hot Cheese Sauce. Alternate layers of eggplant, ham and Cheese Sauce in greased 1½-qt. baking dish. Top with tomato slices; sprinkle with Wheaties mixed with butter. Bake 25 to 30 min *4 to 6 servings.*

CREAMED HAM ON CORN MEAL BISCUITS

2 cups Medium Cream Sauce
  (p. 122)
1 cup cut-up cooked ham
2 tbsp. chopped green onion
salt and pepper to taste
Corn Meal Biscuits (p. 28)

Make Cream Sauce; add ham, onion and seasonings and heat through. Split hot biscuits; spoon hot mixture between and over tops. *8 servings.*

BAKED HAM AND CHICKEN SANDWICH

1½ cups cut-up cooked
   chicken
¾ cup cut-up cooked ham
¾ cup finely diced celery
1 egg, slightly beaten
2 tbsp. rich milk
1 tsp. onion juice
½ tsp. salt
⅛ tsp. pepper
Stir-N-Roll Biscuit dough
   (p. 28)

Heat oven to 450° (hot). Mix together all ingredients except dough. Divide dough in half; roll out between waxed papers to fit 8″ sq. baking pan. Remove top paper; with bottom paper lift and flip dough into pan. Remove paper. Cover evenly with filling. Top with second square of dough; mark surface into squares with fork. Bake 20 to 25 min. Cut in squares and serve with chicken gravy or Mushroom Sauce (p. 123). *9 servings.*

SINGED ANGEL WINGS

Brush cut sides of wedges of Angel Food or Chiffon Cake with melted butter. Lightly brown both sides under broiler, about 1 min. on each side. Serve with Orange Butter Sauce (below).

Orange Butter Sauce: Cream ¼ cup soft butter with ¾ cup sugar; stir in 2 egg yolks, beaten, 1½ tsp. grated orange rind, ⅓ cup orange juice and ⅓ cup milk. Cook over hot water 10 to 15 min. *1½ cups sauce.*

TURKEY BAKE

If you have turkey, stuffing and gravy left, a second-day dish can be as good as the first. Heat oven to 350° (mod.). Place stuffing in baking dish; top with slices and pieces of turkey; pour thinned gravy over (extend with bouillon cubes dissolved in boiling water if you do not have enough). Cover tightly and bake 20 to 30 min.

CHICKEN TURNOVERS

1 tbsp. flour
½ cup chicken stock
1 cup cut-up cooked chicken
2 tsp. minced onion
salt and pepper to taste
¼ tsp. celery salt
⅛ tsp. ginger
Stir-N-Roll Pastry (p. 176)

Heat oven to 425° (hot). Mix together flour and stock; cook over low heat until thickened, stirring constantly. Add remaining ingredients except pastry. Roll pastry ⅛″ thick; cut out 5″ rounds (top of 1- or 2-lb. coffee can). Place filling on half of each round; moisten outside edge with water, and fold pastry over filled side. Seal edge with tines of fork. Make 3 slits in top of each turnover. Bake about 25 min. *6 turnovers.*

Your food freezer can be a great convenience and time-saver. To make sure your food is as good when removed from the freezer as it was when put in, use quality foods, proper packaging materials and care in packaging. The following suggestions may help you.

CHOOSE PROPER MATERIALS

For most solid foods such as meat, cake, pie, bread use freezer-weight paper such as aluminum foil, cellophane, pliofilm for wrapping.

Liquid-packed foods may be packaged in heavily waxed cartons, glass freezer jars, plastic or aluminum containers.

Watch for new and improved packaging materials constantly appearing on the market.

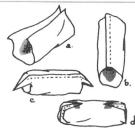

WRAP WITH CARE

The "drugstore wrap" is best for general packaging. Place food in center of wrapping. Bring edges together evenly above the food, then fold them over and over until fold is flat against the food. Press out air. Fold inside edges; seal with freezer locker tape.

LABEL PLAINLY

Label all packages with contents and date. China marking pencils for labeling jars, cartons and packages are available at stationery stores.

LOCKER TAPE

Be sure to buy freezer locker tape for all freezer sealing purposes—not general utility tape. This tape may also be used as a label on hard-to-mark wrapping materials.

GOOD AND EASY FREEZING

Potatoes in the Half Shell (p. 143): Wrap and freeze. When ready to use, unwrap and while still frozen put in mod. hot oven (400°) to thaw and heat.

Hamburger Patties (p. 44): Wrap and freeze. If wrapped separately, just the number needed may be removed. Cook without thawing. Even hamburger buns may be frozen. Split and butter before wrapping for freezing. For serving, toast the buns under the broiler.

Sliced Roast Meat or Turkey: Package in small amounts. Place a double thickness of freezer paper between the layers for easy separation. Thaw in original wrappings.

Fruit Juice Cubes: Freeze concentrated fruit juice in refrigerator tray. When frozen, remove cubes from tray, package in pliofilm or polyethylene bag and keep in food freezer.

Uniced Cake: Wrap and freeze. Thaw in original wrappings in a slow oven (250°) for a short time or at room temperature. Excellent to use as a shortcake or with your favorite fruit or sauce.

LEFTOVERS

Cooked Meat and Chicken: Can be cut up and frozen for use in salads, meat pies and casserole dishes. The gravy can be frozen, too.

Fruit Pies, Chiffon Pies or Cake: Wrap, place in a box in the food freezer. A surprise assortment of pies or cakes may be served.

Whipped Cream: Drop by heaping teaspoons several inches apart on a baking sheet; freeze. When frozen, remove from baking sheet and package in a container or pliofilm or polyethylene bag. For serving, place on dessert while still frozen. Allow 20 min. to thaw.

SPECIAL SUGGESTIONS

Frozen sliced bread may be toasted in the toaster without thawing.

Waffle sections can be frozen and while still frozen, placed in the toaster to reheat.

Pancakes may also be frozen. For serving, place frozen pancakes on broiler pan and heat under broiler.

A roll of cooky dough can be kept in the food freezer, sliced while frozen and baked.

A chiffon pie, dessert or salad with a gelatin base may be chilled in the food freezer for 30 min. or until set.

Pastry circles for pies and tarts may be frozen. See pp. 185, 193.

Sauces for spaghetti and other dishes can be frozen ready to heat for quick use.

Ice Cream for a Crowd: Place scoops or balls of ice cream on baking sheet, put uncovered in food freezer. To keep a day or so, remove from baking sheet, wrap and store in food freezer. When company comes, ice cream is ready to serve.

Quick Punch: Place several fruit ice cubes (frozen fruit juice) in a glass and add ginger ale.

MEALS ON TIME

Ever have the problem of getting all the food for a meal ready at the same time? A little paper-planning will help.

After a few times, this much detail won't be necessary. However, it will still be helpful to list the food for dinner in order of preparation with main starting times jotted down.

And when you are preparing dinner for guests, a detailed list helps you organize your work, keeps you from becoming confused and makes you feel you are accomplishing a lot as you cross off those jobs that are finished.

Rolled Roast of Beef (p. 96)
Mashed Potatoes   Gravy (p. 121)
Buttered Green Beans
Cole Slaw (p. 149)   Hard Rolls
Baked Apple (p. 69)

TIME CHART FOR DINNER AT 6:00 P. M.

APPROXIMATE TIMES FOR PREPARATION	LIST STEPS IN PREPARATION ACCORDING TO TIME REQUIRED
ROAST BEEF 2 hr. 4-lb. rolled roast medium—25 min. per lb. (allow 15 to 20 min. at end for making gravy).	**3:40** Start roast (out at 5:40). **3:40-4:30** Free time.
MASHED POTATOES 35 min. Cook potatoes 30 min. Mash potatoes 5 min.	**4:30** Core apples, add syrup; put in oven at 4:45.
GRAVY 5 min. Prepare from roast drippings.	**4:45** Make cole slaw, let crisp in refrigerator.
GREEN BEANS 20 min. Fresh, cleaned ahead of time.	**5:00** Set table **5:20** Start potatoes. **5:30** Start green beans.
COLE SLAW 10 min. Prepared ahead of time.	**5:40** Take roast and apples from oven. Keep meat warm on platter; place rolls in oven.
BAKED APPLE 1 hr. Start with roast if to be served cold; start 1¼ hr. to 1½ hr. ahead of dinner time if to be served warm.	**5:45** Make gravy. **5:50** Mash potatoes. **5:55** Drain and season beans.
ROLLS 10 min. Put in paper sack, to warm in oven.	**6:00** Dinner's ready!

208

HOLIDAY DINNER

Have a memorable and festive, good-and-easy holiday dinner this year. By planning ahead, you can save time on the holiday itself, and sit down to dinner as relaxed and ready to enjoy it as your family and guests.

AMERICAN TRADITIONAL
Roast Turkey or Chicken with Stuffing
(pp. 112, 109)
Mashed Potatoes   Giblet Gravy
Creamed Onions
Mashed Squash or Rutabagas
Cranberry Sauce   Hot Rolls
Celery Hearts (p. 92)
Mince Pie (p. 188) or
Pumpkin Pie (p. 189)

DO THESE THINGS TWO DAYS AHEAD:

1. Do all possible marketing.

2. Make mince pie and freeze. (Thaw and heat later for holiday dinner.)

3. Take out table linens, silverware, glassware and china needed. See that linens are fresh, and that silverware, glassware and china are shining and bright.

4. Plan centerpiece for table.

DO THESE THINGS ONE DAY AHEAD:

1. Wash and dry the chicken or turkey. Store it on bottom shelf of refrigerator, ready for stuffing.

2. Make stuffing, cool it and store it in plastic bag or covered bowl in refrigerator. (Don't stuff bird until just before roasting.)

3. Prepare celery hearts and store in refrigerator bag or vegetable crisper.

4. Cream onions (use little canned onions, ready-cooked), place them in a casserole, top with buttered crumbs or Wheaties, cover and refrigerate until time to put into oven.

5. Make cranberry sauce (unless you are using canned). If sauce is not jellied, place in serving dish and cover.

6. Make rolls or buy them.

7. Simmer giblets, chop and refrigerate ready for chicken or turkey gravy.

8. Make filling for pumpkin pie (use canned pumpkin) and refrigerate. (Don't freeze pumpkin pie. Bake it the first thing the morning of the holiday dinner.)

9. Arrange centerpiece as completely as possible. (Fresh flowers should be arranged the day of the dinner and kept in cool place until serving time.)

CARVING HELPS

Correct carving lends grace to your dinner table, makes your meat servings more attractive, and gives you a more economical use of the meat. For the carver's sake, keep your carving knife well sharpened!

PORK LOIN ROAST

Your meat retailer will separate backbone from ribs. Backbone can then be removed after roasting.

1. Place roast on platter so rib bones face you. They are your guide for slicing. 2. Insert fork firmly in top of roast. Cut close against both sides of each rib, so that you will have alternately one slice with bone and one without.

ROAST LEG OF LAMB

1. Place leg of lamb with shank bone to the right and meaty section on far side. 2. Insert fork firmly in larger end of leg and cut 2 or 3 slices on near side or where bone is nearest surface. 3. Turn roast so it rests on surface just cut. Insert fork in left of roast; starting at shank end, slice down to leg bone until aitchbone is reached. 4. With fork still in place, run knife along leg bone releasing all the slices.

BLADE POT ROAST

The long, slow cooking process of moist heat softens tissues attached to bone so bone can be slipped out easily when roast is done.

1. Hold pot roast firmly with fork inserted at left. Separate a section by running knife between 2 muscles, and close to bone if bone has not been removed. 2. If desired, turn section on side and cut in slices across grain.

PORTERHOUSE STEAK

A steak is carved *with* the grain because the meat fibers are tender and relatively short.

1. Insert fork at left and cut close around bone. Lift bone to side of platter out of way. 2. Cut across full width of steak, making wedge-shaped portions widest at far side. Each serving will thus have a piece of tenderloin and large muscle. 3. Serve flank end last if additional servings are needed.

STANDING RIB ROAST

Your meat retailer will separate backbone from ribs. Then backbone can be removed in the kitchen after roasting.

1. Insert fork firmly between 2 top ribs. From the far outside edge slice across the grain toward the ribs. **2.** Release each slice by cutting close along the rib with the knife tip. **3.** After each cut, lift slice to side of platter.

ROLLED RIB ROAST

Roast is placed on platter with larger cut surface down.

1. Slice across grain toward the fork from the far right side. **2.** As each slice is carved, lift it to side of platter. Remove each cord only as it is approached in making slices.

BAKED WHOLE HAM

Shank end should always be to carver's right.

1. Find the side nearest the bone and cut 3 or 4 slices. **2.** Turn ham so it rests on surface just cut. Hold ham firmly with fork and cut small wedge from shank end. Keep fork in place to steady ham and cut thin slices down to leg bone. **3.** Release slices by cutting along bone at right angles to slices. For more servings, turn on side and slice at right angle to bone.

BAKED HALF HAM

1. Remove cushion section, turn ham on cut side and make slices beginning at large end. **2.** For more servings, separate from shank by cutting through joint. Remove bone, turn and slice.

CHICKEN OR TURKEY

Place chicken or turkey with leg at right of carver.

1. Cut leg from body, first bending it back with left hand. Sever and lift to plate. **2.** Sever thigh from drumstick. Slice meat from leg. **3.** Then with fork astride breast, cut down sharply on joint joining wing to body. **4.** Cut thin slices of breast where wing was, working up to breast bone.

COMMON FOOD EQUIVALENTS

	Unit	Approximate Measure
Butter, Other Fats	1 lb.	2 cups
Cheese, American or Cheddar	1 lb.	4 cups grated
Chocolate, Unsweetened	½ lb. pkg.	8 1-oz. sq.
Coffee, Ground	1 lb.	80 tbsp.
Cream, Heavy	1 pt.	2 cups (4 cups whipped)
Flour		
All-purpose	1 lb.	4 cups (sifted)
Cake	1 lb.	4½ cups (sifted)
Lemon, Medium-sized		
Juice	1	2 to 3 tbsp.
Rind, lightly grated	1	1½ to 3 tsp.
Sugar		
Granulated	1 lb.	2 cups
Brown	1 lb.	2¼ cups (packed)
Confectioners'	1 lb.	3½ cups (sifted)
Walnuts		
In Shell	1 lb.	1⅔ cups nut meats
Shelled	1 lb.	4 cups nut meats

COMMON ABBREVIATIONS

tsp.	teaspoon
tbsp.	tablespoon
pt.	pint
qt.	quart
sq.	square
min.	minute (s)
hr.	hour (s)
mod.	moderate (ly)
med.	medium
doz.	dozen
pkg.	package

SIMPLIFIED MEASURES

dash—less than ⅛ teaspoon
3 teaspoons = 1 tablespoon
16 tablespoons = 1 cup
1 cup = ½ pint
2 cups = 1 pint
2 pints (4 cups) = 1 quart
4 quarts (liquid) = 1 gallon
4 quarts (solid) = 1 peck
4 pecks = 1 bushel
16 ounces = 1 pound

The Fourth Meal

What is the "fourth meal"? It is the meal that people eat for fun.

For breakfast, lunch and dinner you eat the things you think you *should* eat. But in between, you eat the things you like.

In the following pages you'll find suggestions for dozens of satisfying, delicious, often casual little lunches and between-meal refreshments for any hour of the day—from the time your neighbor drops in for morning coffee to that bedtime hour when you raid the refrigerator for a snack. And they're all easy, and take little time to prepare.

We hope these suggestions will add to the enjoyment of life in your home—for every member of your family and for the friends who drop in to share your hospitality.

GOOD AND EASY—WITH COFFEE

One of the pleasant interludes in busy mornings and after-noons is having friends drop in for coffee. The food served may be crackers out of the box. Or, you may prepare some-thing ahead, or something special, with little work. The cof-fee hour is primarily a time for both hostess and guest to relax and visit.

BLUEBERRY BUCKLE

¾ cup sugar
¼ cup soft shortening
1 egg
½ cup milk
2 cups sifted Gold Medal
    Flour
½ tsp. salt
2 tsp. baking powder
2 cups drained blueberries

Heat oven to 375° (quick mod.). Mix thoroughly sugar, shorten-ing, egg. Stir in milk. Sift to-gether and stir in flour, baking powder, salt. Blend in berries. Spread in greased and floured 9″ sq. pan. Sprinkle with Crumb Topping. Bake 45 to 50 min., un-til toothpick thrust into center comes out clean. *9 3″ squares.*

Crumb Topping: Mix ½ cup sugar, ⅓ cup flour, ½ tsp. cinna-mon and ¼ cup soft butter.

FRENCH BREAKFAST PUFFS

Like glorified doughnuts.

⅓ cup soft shortening
½ cup sugar
1 egg
1½ cups sifted Gold Medal
    Flour
1½ tsp. baking powder
½ tsp. salt
¼ tsp. nutmeg
½ cup milk
6 tbsp. butter, melted
½ cup more sugar
1 tsp. cinnamon

Heat oven to 350° (mod.). Mix shortening, sugar, egg. Sift to-gether flour, baking powder, salt, nutmeg and stir in alternately with milk. Fill greased muffin cups ⅔ full. Bake 20 to 25 min., until golden brown. Immediately roll in melted butter, then in mixture of sugar and cinnamon. *12 medium puffs.*

ALSO GOOD WITH COFFEE

Tarts (p. 193)
Little Sandwiches
Cheese Biscuits (p. 156)
Hot Gingerbread (p. 81)
Apricot-Nut Bread (p. 63)
Muffins (p. 25) with Jelly or Jam
Toasted Raisin Bread

Cookies (pp. 82-83, 194-199)
Quick Coffee Cakes (p. 25)
Easy Butterscotch Pecan Rolls (p. 29)
Cinnamon Rolls (p. 29)
Brown 'n Serve Sweet Rolls (p. 26)
Double-quick Coffee Bread (p. 16)
Doughnuts (p. 30)

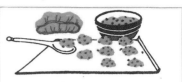

VELVET-CRUMB CAKE
See picture, p. 233.

1⅓ cups Bisquick
¾ cup sugar
3 tbsp. soft shortening
1 egg
⅓ cup milk
⅓ cup more milk
1 tsp. vanilla

Heat oven to 350° (mod.). Grease well 8x8x2″ sq. or 8x1½″ round pan and dust with Bisquick. Mix Bisquick and sugar. Add shortening, egg, milk. Beat vigorously. Gradually stir in additional milk and vanilla. Beat ½ min. Pour into pan. Bake about 30 min., until top springs back when lightly touched. While warm, cover with Broiled Icing (p. 166). Serve warm.

SCOTCH SCONES

2¼ cups Bisquick
2 tbsp. sugar
⅔ cup milk
1 egg
½ cup currants, if desired

Mix ingredients to make a soft dough. Roll or pat out ¼″ thick. Cut into rounds or triangles. Bake 10 min. on ungreased electric grill or heavy skillet; turn and bake 10 min. more. Or brush tops with milk, sprinkle with sugar, bake 10 to 12 min., until golden brown, in hot oven (450°). Serve warm. *12 to 16 scones.*

COOKIES-IN-NO-TIME

Warm and fresh from the oven. Make up your own favorite cooky dough and keep it chilled and covered in refrigerator. Or keep on hand ready-to-bake packaged cookies from your grocer. Just before or as soon as guests drop in, pop the cookies into the oven and put on the coffee pot.

HERMITS

Keep dough covered in refrigerator. Bake as needed.

½ cup soft shortening
1 cup brown sugar (packed)
1 egg
¼ cup cold coffee
1¾ cups sifted Gold Medal Flour
½ tsp. each soda, salt, nutmeg, cinnamon
1¼ cups halved seeded raisins
½ cup broken nuts

Mix thoroughly first three ingredients. Stir in coffee. Sift together and stir in flour, soda, salt, spices. Mix in raisins and nuts. Chill. Bake when needed. Heat oven to 400° (mod. hot). Drop dough with teaspoon 2″ apart on lightly greased baking sheet. Bake 8 to 10 min., just until a light touch with finger leaves almost no imprint. *About 3 doz. cookies.*

When you want to entertain nicely, with your best china and linen and a pretty table setting, but still want to keep things simple, a dessert party is the answer. Invite guests for dessert after lunch or dinner; they have their main course at home before they come. You serve a good and easy dessert and coffee, and are free to enjoy the party with your guests.

CREAM PUFFS

1 cup water
½ cup butter
1 cup sifted Gold Medal
   Flour
4 eggs

Heat oven to 400° (mod. hot). Heat water and butter to boiling in saucepan. Stir in flour, stirring until mixture forms into ball, leaving sides of the pan (about 1 min.). Beat in the eggs, one at a time. Beat mixture until smooth. Drop by spoon onto ungreased baking sheet. Bake 45 to 50 min., until puffed and dry. Cool slowly. Cut off tops and scoop out any soft dough. Fill with sweetened whipped cream (cut-up fruit may be added) or Custard (p. 172). Replace tops. Or fill with ice cream; top either with sweetened fruit or berries or with Chocolate or Butterscotch Sauce (p. 170).

FORGOTTEN MERINGUES

They bake while you sleep.

6 egg whites (¾ cup)
1½ tsp. lemon juice or
   ½ tsp. cream of tartar
2 cups sugar

Heat oven to 400° (mod. hot). Beat egg whites with lemon juice or cream of tartar until frothy. Gradually beat in sugar a little at a time. Beat until stiff and glossy. Drop by small spoonfuls in circles on brown paper on baking sheet, or heap into high mounds and hollow out with back of spoon. Put into oven, close door, turn off oven. (Don't peek!) Let stand overnight in oven. *12 meringues.*

To Serve: Fill Meringues with ice cream; top with fresh fruit or with Butterscotch or Chocolate Sauce (p. 170) and salted pecans or almonds.

 PERFECT FOR DESSERT PARTIES

DESSERT ON ICE

Dramatic way of serving molded fruit or other gelatin dessert puddings: Pack finely crushed ice in cake pan. Freeze. Unmold by dipping pan quickly in and out of warm water. Turn onto chop plate and top with molded dessert.

TO SAVE TIME

Buy marshmallow, chocolate or butterscotch sauce canned or in jars. Use canned or frozen fruit and berries.

ICE CREAM SUNDAE CAKES
See picture on p. 239.

Top squares of fresh cake with ice cream and your favorite sauce.

CALIFORNIA FIESTA

2 layers of Spice Cake (p. 161)
vanilla-flavored pudding mix
    (prepared as directed on
    pkg.)
sweetened sliced peaches
    (fresh, frozen or canned),
    well drained

Put layers of cooled cake together with cooled pudding and peach slices between. Spread pudding over top, decorate with peach slices.

RAINBOW BUFFET
Guests take their choice.

On large chop plate, arrange balls of ice cream in different flavors, such as vanilla, strawberry, chocolate, pistachio, pineapple, orange. Garnish with banana halves and maraschino cherries or whole strawberries. Surround with bowls of toppings, such as crushed pineapple, sweetened sliced peaches or berries, chopped or salted nuts, Chocolate or Butterscotch Sauce (p. 170) or Easy Marshmallow Sauce (below).

EASY MARSHMALLOW SAUCE

Cook ½ cup sugar and ⅓ cup hot water together just until sugar dissolves. Take from heat, stir in 16 finely cut-up marshmallows (¼ lb.) until melted. Pour slowly into unbeaten egg white, beating with electric or rotary beater until mixture thickens. *2 cups sauce.*

ANGEL FOOD DESSERTS

Serve slices of Angel Food (p. 162) with favorite Topping (p. 168) or Sauce (p. 170).

Cut Angel Food Cake crosswise into layers. Put together with Lemon, Orange or Strawberry Cream Filling (p. 169) between layers and over top and sides.

Singed Angel Wings (p. 205) with Hidden Fruit (p. 172).

INFORMAL AFTERNOON TEA

A small informal tea has the charm of easy hospitality. Set the tea table in the living room with the tea or coffee service near your chair, as hostess. Guests sit informally around the room. The accompanying refreshments may be simple, but they should be attractively arranged and served.

> **SMALL INFORMAL TEA**
>
> Tea (p. 219) or Coffee (p. 219)
> Some Special Tea Bread or Treat
> Cookies, Cupcakes or Cake

Small biscuits, rolls, muffins, cakes or cookies warm from the oven are delicious. Have them all ready to bake or heat so you can pop them into the oven just before, or as soon as, your guests arrive.

Your neighborhood baker has delicious breads, cookies and cakes to help you make afternoon tea enjoyable.

SPECIAL TEA BREADS

Split tiny rolls or Biscuits (pp. 28-29, 154-156), spread lightly with butter, toast on buttered side.

Serve Biscuits plain, with orange or strawberry marmalade or Canapé Spreads (p. 93).

Cinnamon Toast: Sprinkle hot buttered toast strips, rounds or triangles with mixture of 3 tbsp. sugar and ½ tsp. cinnamon.

Orange Toast: Spread hot buttered toast strips with orange marmalade.

Honey Toast: Spread hot toast with equal amounts of butter and honey creamed together.

SIMPLE, QUICK TEATIME TREATS

Toasted English Muffins (p. 62) and Jam, Tiny Hot Biscuits (pp. 28-29). Sweet Rolls (p. 18). Muffins (p. 25), Dainty Sandwiches (p. 220). Parmesan Rounds (p. 38), Top-a-Cracker (p. 39), Cheese Crackers (p. 39). Spread crackers with cream cheese, put red jelly or a slice of stuffed olive in center.

FORMAL TEA OR RECEPTION

The dining table is used and arranged with simple elegance. The tea service is at one end, the coffee at the other. Two friends of the hostess pour.

> Tea and Coffee
> Floating Island Punch (p. 224)
> Special Party Sandwiches (p. 220)
> Little Cakes Fancy Cookies
> Salted Nuts Fondant Mints
> Salads or ices (in paper cups) may be offered in addition.

HOT TEA

1 tsp. tea per cup
boiling water, as needed

Put tea in scalded earthen or china tea pot. Pour over it freshly boiling water. Let stand in warm place 3 min. Strain. Serve at once. Have pot of hot water to dilute tea as desired. Serve with thin half slices of lemon or milk and sugar. The lemon slices may have whole cloves stuck in them. Or thin half slices of orange may be used.

Note: Tea ball or bag may be placed in cup and boiling water poured over. After 3 min. or less, remove tea bag or ball.

ICED TEA

Fill glasses ⅓ full with cracked ice, strain fresh tea over. Serve with lemon or lime.

COFFEE FOR A CROWD

1 whole egg and shell
1¼ lb. regular grind coffee
9 qt. cold water

Mix egg and shell with coffee. Add 1 cup cold water. Tie coffee in cheesecloth bag large enough to allow room for coffee to swell. Measure water into large coffee pot. Immerse coffee bag in water, bring to boil. Remove pot from heat. Leave bag of coffee in water 3 to 4 min., remove and stir. If preferred, use boiling water to start, bring to boil. Stir. Remove from heat. Let stand 10 min. Remove bag. Serve. *Serves 25 (48 6-oz. cups).*

> **SERVING NOTE**
> Cream (1 tbsp. per cup): 1½ cups.
> Sugar (1 tsp. per cup): ½ cup or 25 cubes.

OPEN-FACED SANDWICHES

Cut thin bread slices with shaped cutters — flowers, diamonds, hearts, rings. Spread lightly with butter and any of the Canapé Spreads on p. 93. Decorate with sprigs of watercress, sliced olives, minced parsley or green pepper or pimiento. Little bunches of sweet green grapes, and grape, strawberry or mint leaves on the sandwich plates add a festive touch.

ROLLED SANDWICHES

Spread thin slices of fresh bread (crusts removed) with butter and colorful sandwich spread. Roll up; fasten with toothpicks to be removed before serving. Tuck bits of parsley or watercress in each end of the rolls.

RIBBON SANDWICHES

Butter ½″ thick slices of white and dark bread. Put together, alternating white and dark. Wrap in waxed paper, then in damp towel; chill; slice ¼″ thick.

FROSTED TEA CAKES

Make oblong cake, using Betty Crocker White, Yellow, Chocolate Devils Food, Angel Food or Honey Spice Cake Mix. When cool, cut into 1″ squares or fingers. Spread soft Butter Icing (p. 166) of your choice over tops, letting icing run down sides.

CHICKEN SALAD PUFFS

Follow recipe for Cream Puffs on p. 216 except—make 18 puffs size of a walnut. Bake 30 min. Or buy tiny puffs. Fill with Chicken Salad (p. 60).

MOLDED SALADS

Make as directed on pkg. of flavored gelatin. Unmold on large chop plate. Garnish with crisp lettuce, curly endive or lacy watercress. Offer mayonnaise with whipped cream added.

Molded Fruit Salad: Use any flavored gelatin. Add well drained cut-up fruit of your choice.

Molded Chicken-Almond Salad: Use lemon-flavored gelatin and 2 tbsp. lemon juice. Add 1 cup diced cooked chicken, ½ cup mayonnaise, 1 tsp. salt, ⅓ cup toasted slivered almonds, ½ cup halved sweet green grapes or canned pineapple.

Sea Food Salad Mold: Use lemon-flavored gelatin and 3 tbsp. lemon juice. Add ½ tsp. prepared mustard; dash of salt; paprika; 1 cup drained flaked crabmeat, lobster, shrimp, tuna or salmon; ½ cup thinly sliced celery.

HOLIDAY OPEN HOUSE

Holidays are happy days — times you wish to share with family, neighbors and friends. An open house is one of the easiest and most pleasant ways to have guests drop in. An attractive good-and-easy table setting for the holiday buffet is shown on pp. 236-237.

HOLIDAY OPEN HOUSE

Wassail Bowl
Cold Cider (for the children)
Fruit Cake   Christmas Cookies
Stuffed Dates   Nuts   Cream Mints
Kix Cone Trees (for the children)

KIX CONE TREES

¼ cup butter
½ lb. marshmallows
5 cups Kix
wooden skewers
colored sugar or fine colored
   candies

Stir butter and marshmallows over low heat until syrupy. Pour over Kix in greased bowl; stir briskly. Pack lightly into greased paper cone-shaped drinking cups. Insert skewers for trunks of trees. When cool, remove paper cups and roll cones in sugar or tiny candies. Push end of skewer into large gumdrop or thick slice of apple. *9 to 10 Christmas trees.*

Pinning gumdrops to candles.

WASSAIL BOWL

whole cloves
1 orange
2 qt. cider
stick cinnamon
brandy flavoring
rum flavoring
slices of lemon and orange

Stick whole cloves in orange about ½" apart. Place in baking pan with a little water. Bake in slow mod. oven (325°) 30 min. Heat cider with stick cinnamon to boiling. Add brandy and rum flavoring. Place in punch bowl with orange and a stick of cinnamon. Stick cinnamon may be used in cups as muddlers. *16 servings.*

Serving Note: Keep hot over low heat or heat in small batches as guests arrive.

C·A·N·D·L·E·S

HOLIDAY BUFFET

For a more formal open house at holiday time, with guests invited for definite hours, fancier foods are often served. Have a punch bowl with Eggnog (p. 65) or Festive Tomato Cocktail and an assortment of canapes and sweets.

SWEETS

Fruit Cake
Assorted Cookies
Rum-flavored Cakes
    (from bakery)
Date and Cream Cheese Sandwiches
Millie's Peanut Brittle (p. 224)
Party Mints

NIPPY BITS

Shrimp with Cocktail Sauce
Olives, Salted Nuts
Broiled Cocktail Sausages
Dried Beef Rolls
Wedgies
Cream Cheese Spreads (p. 93)
Crackers and Potato Chips

FESTIVE TOMATO COCKTAIL

4 cups tomato juice
3 small bay leaves
½ tsp. whole cloves
⅛ tsp. peppercorns
¾ tsp. salt
1½ tsp. diced onion or minced chives
3 tbsp. sugar

Simmer together ½ hr. Strain. Taste and add more ground cloves, sugar or other seasoning as desired. Serve either hot or cold. *8 servings.*

WEDGIES

Spread 4″ circles of bologna with cream cheese seasoned with prepared mustard, horse-radish and minced onion. Stack 6 slices with plain meat circle on top. Chill 2 hr. or more. Cut in small wedge-shaped pieces. Stick toothpick through each Wedgie.

Note: See Hors d'Oeuvres (p. 223) for other ideas.

ANCHOVY-OLIVE ROLLS

Wrap an anchovy fillet around each large stuffed olive; secure with toothpick.

BUTTERED OR CHEESE KIX

Melt in heavy skillet 5 tbsp. butter. Remove from heat. Stir in 5 tbsp. grated Parmesan-type cheese, if desired. Add ¼ box Kix (4 cups). Sprinkle with ½ tsp. salt. Stir well.

DRIED BEEF ROLLS

Spread dried beef with cream cheese seasoned with horse-radish and minced onion or chives. Roll up, chill, then slice.

WRAPPED OLIVES

Roll stuffed olives in half slices of bacon; secure with toothpicks. Broil until bacon is crisp. Serve hot.

BACON ROLLS

Roll shrimp or pineapple wedges in half slices of bacon; secure with toothpicks. Broil until bacon is crisp. Serve hot.

ANGELS ON HORSEBACK

Wrap half strips of bacon around small oysters; secure with toothpicks. Place in shallow pan. Bake in mod. hot oven (400°) until bacon is crisp. Serve hot.

CHEESE-BEEF STICKS

Cut American cheese in sticks 2 x ¼". Wrap each in dried beef slice. Broil until cheese is slightly melted. Serve hot on toothpicks.

APPETIZERS ON PICKS

Tiny onion, browned mushroom, cube of Swiss cheese.

Stuffed olive, browned mushroom, cube of Swiss cheese.

Cube of Swiss cheese, pickled onion, stuffed olive.

Maraschino cherry, pickled onion, sweet gherkin.

MORE HORS D'OEUVRES QUICKIES

Tiny Cream Puff Shells (p. 216) filled with Chicken or Sea Food Salad (p. 60).

Deviled Eggs (p. 85).

Balls of softened cream cheese on toothpicks, rolled in minced olives, parsley, dried beef or grated carrot.

Pineapple chunks rolled in softened cream cheese, then in finely minced mint leaves.

SHRIMP

Fresh cooked or canned, on toothpicks; serve with well seasoned Cocktail Sauce (p. 91).

SEASONED CHIPS

Spread potato chips on baking sheet. Sprinkle lightly with garlic or onion salt, grated cheese, lemon juice, minced parsley or chives, or any other flavor-adding condiment you wish. Slide into hot oven a few minutes and serve piping hot.

COCKTAIL SAUSAGES

Sauté in skillet or bake in mod. hot oven (400°) until golden brown. Serve on toothpicks.

STUFFED DATES

⅔ cup sweetened condensed
   milk (not evaporated)
4½ cups sifted confectioners'
   sugar
1 tsp. vanilla
1 tsp. almond extract
2 doz. pitted dates

Blend milk into sugar; add flavoring. Knead until smooth and
creamy. Cover with damp cloth
and store in refrigerator 24 hr.
Stuff dates with the mixture
above. Roll in granulated or
confectioners' sugar.

Easy Bonbons: Filling for
stuffed dates may be colored,
formed in balls or patties and
decorated with fruit or nuts.

TING-A-LINGS

2 6-oz. pkg. semisweet
   chocolate pieces or equal
   amount milk chocolate
4 cups Wheaties, Cheerios or
   Kix

Melt chocolate over hot water.
Cool at room temperature. Gently stir in cereal until well
coated. Drop with tbsp. onto
waxed paper. Place in refrigerator until chocolate is set, dry and
hard (2 hr.). *3 to 3½ doz.*

MILLIE'S PEANUT BRITTLE

3 cups sugar
1 cup water
½ cup white corn syrup
¼ cup butter
1 lb. raw Spanish peanuts
   (round, with red skins on)
1 tsp. soda
1 tsp. vanilla

Boil sugar, water and corn syrup
until it threads. Add butter and
peanuts; cook slowly to 300°,
stirring occasionally. Add soda
and vanilla. (It will foam up.)
Turn out on buttered baking
sheet; pull out thin as it cools.
When cold, break into pieces
with knife handle.

FLOATING ISLAND PUNCH

½ cup sugar
1 cup water
6-oz. can frozen lemon juice
3 6-oz. cans frozen orange
   juice
1 qt. ginger ale
1 qt. sparkling water or
   white grape juice
4-oz. bottle maraschino
   cherries and juice
1 orange, sliced thin
1 pt. lemon or orange sherbet
ice cubes

Heat sugar and water until sugar
dissolves; cool. Combine fruit
juices, ginger ale, sparkling water and fruit. Add syrup. Pour in
punch bowl. Add ice cubes. Drop
in sherbet by spoonfuls or in
small balls using an ice cream
dipper. *20 to 25 servings.*

Everyone enjoys being remembered with a birthday celebration, either with friends or with just the family present. Highlight it with a birthday cake, the favorite of the birthday boy or girl. Decorate it for the occasion, with candles on or around it.

FLOWERY ANGEL FOOD CAKE

In center hole of frosted Angel Food (p. 162), put fresh flowers in tiny vase; arrange clusters of them, without stems, around base of cake. Use sweet peas, violets, lilies of the valley, rosebuds, larkspur, apple blossoms, etc.

BIRTHDAY PIE

Make father's favorite pie—Lemon Meringue, Blueberry, Pumpkin, Apple or whatever his choice is (see pp. 186-192). Just before serving, place candles on top and light them.

PANSY CAKE

Leave only tiny stems (¼″) on pansies and press them into icing as a border or in an all-over pattern. In same way, you may use individual blossoms of hyacinths, violets, sweetheart roses.

A-DAY-AT-THE-ZOO CAKE

Arrange candles in rectangle in center of frosted oblong cake. Decorate around top edge with line of chocolate-frosted animal crackers set 1″ apart.

FOR MOTHER OR SISTER
Chicken Salad (p. 60)
Little Lettuce Sandwiches
Flowery Angel Food Cake
Fruit-cube Punch (p. 230)   Coffee

FOR FATHER OR BIG BROTHER
Shrimp Boats (p. 230)
Birthday Pie   Coffee

FOR GRANDMOTHER OR GRANDFATHER
Pansy-decorated
Orange LoveLight Chiffon Cake (p. 163)
Hot or Iced Tea (p. 219)

FOR SMALL CHILDREN
Sandwiches in Fancy Shapes
Ice Cream
A-Day-at-the-Zoo Cake
Pink Lemonade (p. 227)

YOUNG TASTE TEMPTERS

Brighten the days for your children with simple treats. A little extra thought on your part can make the plainest between-meal snack an adventure to build happy memories.

> ### HOME FROM SCHOOL
> A Milk Drink (p. 65 or below)
> Bread   Spreads   Cookies

PARTY MILK SHAKES

Blend into milk crushed fruit or fruit juice, chocolate syrup or other flavoring. A beaten egg may be added. Serve with colored straw.

LET THEM SPREAD THEIR OWN

Have sliced bread, butter, jelly, peanut butter on table. Children like to help themselves.

STRAWBERRY ICE CREAM SODA

¼ cup crushed strawberries
1 tsp. sugar (omit if frozen
    berries are used)
carbonated water
1 scoop strawberry or vanilla
    ice cream

Mix strawberries and sugar in tall glass. Fill glass ⅔ full with carbonated water. Add strawberry ice cream; stir vigorously. Fill to top with carbonated water.

Chocolate Ice Cream Soda: Make same as Strawberry except —use 3 tbsp. chocolate syrup in place of strawberries, chocolate ice cream instead of strawberry.

BANANA-CHOCOLATE LOLLIPOP

Peel bananas. Spear each with wooden skewer, dip in melted milk chocolate. Place in freezing compartment until chocolate is firm.

CAKE LOLLIPOPS

Put frosted cake square on end of lollipop stick. Arrange several in a flower holder in center of large serving platter, with balls of ice cream around.

ICE CREAM LOLLIPOPS

Write name on handle of each wooden teaspoon. Insert bowl of spoon into square (individual serving) of brick ice cream. Place in freezing compartment until hard. Dip in melted milk chocolate. When chocolate is partially set, dip in chopped nuts or chocolate shot.

VALENTINE CAKES

Frost with pink icing. In center, outline a heart with silver dragees. Or mark chocolate icing diagonally into diamonds with tip of knife. Press small heart into each.

GELATIN EASTER EGGS IN CAKE NEST

Break some egg shells so carefully that just the tip of the shell is broken when the egg is removed. Dry the shells; pour fruit gelatin of different colors into them. Set the filled egg shells upright in custard or muffin cups and chill until gelatin is firm. Then break away egg shell and put the bright colored "eggs" in a "nest" of hollowed-out angel food, sponge or chiffon cake, covered with Butter Icing and green-tinted coconut.

CIRCUS ICE CREAM

Put cone "hat" on ball of vanilla ice cream. With colored candies, make face on ball of ice cream.

JACK-O'-LANTERN CAKES

Frost Chocolate Cupcakes with Orange Butter Icing. With melted chocolate, draw a Jack-o'-Lantern face on each.

CHRISTMAS CANDLE CAKES

See p. 160. Serve with green ice cream or sherbet.

REFRESHMENTS IN BED

Use a nice shiny muffin pan for a tray. Put small helpings of food in some of the cups and stand a small glass of milk or juice in one. Tuck a surprise trinket or toy into one of the empty cups. Serve milk with a colored straw for a "circus" treat, or color the milk pink (see below).

COLOR MAGIC

Pink applesauce is much more tempting to children than brown. Add a drop of pink food coloring to servings.

Multi-colored tiny candies in bright designs make applesauce a new treat.

Pink Milk or Lemonade: A glass of pink or chocolate milk often wins a child who refuses milk in its natural state. Add a drop of food coloring or a little strawberry or raspberry juice to tint milk or lemonade pink.

Keep it simple; make it hearty; fix it quick. With a few combinations that fill this bill, you're set for teen-age entertaining any number, any time.

AFTER THE GAME
California Hamburgers (p. 44)
or Tuna Burgers (p. 229)
French Fried Potatoes
Catsup   Pickles
Brownies à la Mode

TELEVISION PARTY
Hollywood Dunk
Potato Chips   Corn Chips
Soft Drinks   Milk

AUTUMN AND
WINTER NIGHTS
Cider
Doughnuts
Basket of Fruit

HOME FROM THE MOVIES
Cheese Dreams
Olives
Applesauce   Celery
Ginger Cookies (p. 83)
Cocoa or Milk

WARM WEATHER
GET-TOGETHER
Cold Soft Drinks
Pretzels   Potato Chips or Popcorn
—
Fruit-cube Punch (p. 230)
Peanut Butter Cookies (p. 83)

BROWNIES À LA MODE

Bake batter for Brownies (p. 197) in 9" pie pan. Cut in pie-shaped pieces. Top each wedge with peppermint ice cream and Glossy Chocolate Sauce (p. 170)

CHEESE DREAMS

Put American cheese slices between 2 slices of bread. Butter outside of both bread slices generously. Just before serving, brown lightly in heavy skillet (low heat) or electric grill until cheese melts.

HOLLYWOOD DUNK

Mix 4 tbsp. deviled ham, 4 tbsp. horse-radish, 2 tbsp. minced chives, 1 tbsp. grated onion, 1 cup cream whipped stiff.

Serving Note: Place Dunk bowl in center of large round platter. Surround with chips. Let guests serve selves by dipping one end of chip into mixture.

STONEWALL JACKSONS

Place scoop of ice cream in bottom of tall glass. Fill with root beer.

**ACCOMPANIMENT TO
RECORDS**

Stonewall Jacksons
Cheese Kix (p. 222)

BATTER FRANKS

1 cup Bisquick
2 tbsp. yellow corn meal
¼ tsp. paprika
½ tsp. dry mustard
⅛ tsp. cayenne
1 egg
½ cup milk
1 lb. frankfurters (8 to 10)

Heat deep fat to 375°. Mix Bisquick, corn meal and seasonings. Stir in egg and milk until well blended. Dip frankfurters into batter. Fry until brown, 2 to 3 min. Push wooden skewer into end.

INDOOR PICNIC

Batter Franks   Baked Beans
Vegetable Relishes (p. 92)
Bowl of Fruit
Chocolate Chip Cookies (p. 83)
Beverage

TUNA BURGERS

6 hamburger buns
7-oz. can tuna fish
1 cup celery, chopped
½ cup diced American cheese
½ cup chopped ripe olives
¼ cup mayonnaise
1 small onion, minced

Mix all ingredients for filling. Salt and pepper to taste. Split buns, butter and sprinkle with paprika. Fill with tuna mixture, replace tops, put in waxed paper sandwich bags. Fold and fasten tops of bags with paper clips. Just before serving, heat on baking sheet in mod. oven (350°) 15 to 20 min. *6 tuna burgers.*

SHRIMP TOWERS

English muffin half, split and
  toasted on bottom side
tomato slice
cheese slice
4 or 5 shrimp
2 pieces partially cooked
  bacon (2")
pimiento-stuffed olives

Butter untoasted side of muffin half. On it place in following order: tomato slice, cheese slice, shrimp and bacon. Keep in refrigerator until just before serving. Then place under broiler until bacon is crisp and cheese melted. Plunge 3 olive-topped toothpicks through each "tower" to hold it together. Serve piping hot. Pass mayonnaise.

SWEET ENDINGS

Fruit Gelatin   Chocolate Cake

Pie à la Mode (Apple, Cherry, Blueberry)

Fruit Salad with Whipped Cream

Angel Food or Chiffon Cake or Gingerbread with Whipped Cream and Fruit or with Lemon or Orange Sauce

Cream Puffs filled with Ice Cream, topped with Chocolate or Butterscotch Sauce

A DUTCH LUNCH
See picture on pp. 234-235.
Quails (p. 107)   Baked Beans (p. 54)
Potato Salad (p. 61)
Dill Pickles   Rye Bread   Carrot Sticks
Crackers and Cheese
Brownies   Beverages   Apples

LATE BUFFET FOR YOUNG MODERNS
American Pizza Pie (p. 135)
Tossed Greens with Ripe Olives
LoveLight Chiffon Cake with
Fruit and Whipped Cream Topping
(p. 163)

HAM-CHEESE TOASTWICHES

8 slices buttered bread
4 slices boiled ham
(fat removed)
4 slices Swiss cheese
about ½ cup softened butter

Make 4 sandwiches from buttered bread, ham and cheese. Spread outsides of sandwiches with butter. Cut in halves. Brown slowly on both sides on electric grill or in skillet. Serve at once. *8 toastwiches.*

YEAR-ROUND SHORTCAKE

See picture, p. 238.

Spread Sweetened Whipped Cream (p. 168) between and on top of layers of tender, fluffy Yellow Cake (p. 159). Top with fresh, frozen or canned fruit.

What goes with what? Combine colorful foods with pale foods, something crisp with something soft. And serve it on a pretty plate.

SHRIMP OR CRAB BOATS

Hollow out long, crusty rolls (save crumbs for toppings, stuffings, meat loaves). Spread with softened butter. Fill with Shrimp or Crabmeat Salad (p. 60).

CHOCOLATE ICE CREAM

1 pt. heavy cream, whipped
1 cup prepared Chocolate
Sauce (p. 170 or canned)

Blend sauce into cream. Freeze 1 to 2 hr. *4 to 6 servings.*

FRUIT-CUBE PUNCH

Pour fruit juice into ice cube trays and freeze. At party time, put cubes in punch bowl or glasses and pour ginger ale over them. Garnish with mint, fruit.

SUNRISE SPECIAL

Denver Sandwiches (p. 46)
Fresh Vegetable Relishes (p. 92)
Jelly Pears or Peaches (p. 69)
Chocolate Chip Cookies (p. 83)

0

HEARTY PARTY

Cavatzone
Hot Chili Sauce   Crisp Celery Hearts
Flaming Peaches (p. 175)
Jubilee Jumbles (p. 195)
Coffee

LAZY DAY REFRESHER
See picture, p. 240.

Lemonade (use frozen concentrate)
Slices of Angel Food Cake (p. 162)

CAVATZONE

1 lb. ground lean pork
½ cup chopped onion
¼ cup grated Parmesan
cheese
½ cup grated Swiss cheese
1 large egg, beaten
¼ tsp. Tabasco sauce
1½ tsp. salt
2 tbsp. minced parsley
Mayonnaise Biscuit Dough
(below)

Heat oven to 400° (mod. hot).
Cook pork and onion over low
heat until no longer pink. (Do
not brown. Stir with fork to
break up as it cooks.) Cool.

Mix in rest of ingredients. Make
Mayonnaise Biscuit Dough,
spread half of it in well greased
sq. pan, 8x8x2". Spread meat mixture over dough. With fingers,
spread rest of dough over mixture. (The top will even out during baking.) Brush with beaten
egg yolk to give crusty glaze.
Bake 25 to 30 min. Cut in slices
about ½" thick and serve hot or
cold.

Mayonnaise Biscuit Dough:
Add ⅔ cup milk and ¼ cup mayonnaise to 2 cups Bisquick. Mix
well with fork.

EASY ENTERTAINING

SNACK SHELF SURPRISES
Build-your-own Sandwiches
Hash Hats (p. 50)
Quick Baked Beans (p. 54)
Top-side Peach Cobbler (p. 71)
Velvet-Crumb Cake (Bisquick
pkg. or p. 215)

DO-AHEADS
Saucy Sandwich Rolls (p. 232)
Tuna Burgers (p. 229)
Cavatzone (left)
American Pizza Pie (p. 135)
Coconut Angel Cake (p. 162)

KITCHEN QUICKIES
Chinese Chicken Goulash
  (p. 232)
Sure-fire Special (p. 46)
Southern Burgers (p. 84)
Supper Sandwiches (pp. 45-46)

LOADED LAZY SUSAN
Cream Cheese Spread (p. 93)
Carrot Cheese Sticks (p. 92)
Seasoned Chips (p. 223)
Buttered or Cheese Kix (p. 222)

CHINESE CHICKEN GOULASH

¼ cup butter or chicken fat
1 small onion, sliced
1 cup fresh or 4-oz. can mushrooms
2 cups chicken broth
1 cup washed uncooked rice
1 green pepper, cut in thin strips
½ cup diced celery
2 cups cut-up cooked chicken
¼ cup rich milk
salt and pepper to taste

Melt butter in heavy skillet, add onion and mushrooms; cook until golden. Pour in chicken broth and heat to boiling. Stir in rice, cover and simmer gently 10 min. Add rest of ingredients, cover and cook 10 to 15 min. more. *6 servings.*

SAVE TIME AND WORK

Use canned cooked chicken (two 6-oz. cans) for Chinese Chicken Goulash. For the broth use canned chicken broth (13¾-oz. can) or 2 or 3 chicken bouillon cubes dissolved in 2 cups hot water.

RAINBOW 'ROUND THE CAKE

Around Orange Cake (p. 159) on large chop plate, arrange balls of ice cream which have been rolled in tinted coconut (green, lavender, pink, yellow, etc.), alternating the different colors.

REFRESHMENTS, CHINESE STYLE

Chinese Chicken Goulash
Tossed Salad   Poppy-Seed Rolls
Orange Sherbet
Chinese Almond Cakes (p. 198)   Tea

SAUCY SANDWICH ROLLS

Serve a snack in a sack.

12 hot dog buns
1 lb. wieners, chopped or sliced
1 medium onion, chopped fine
3 tbsp. hot bacon fat
¼ cup Gold Medal Flour
¾ tsp. salt
dash of pepper
½ tsp. each dry mustard and Worcestershire sauce
½ cup each catsup and water
1 cup chopped celery
½ cup grated cheese

Brown wieners and onion in fat. Take from heat. Blend in rest of ingredients except cheese. Cook until celery is tender, about 5 min. Add cheese; heat until cheese melts; take from heat. Remove some of soft centers from buns. Fill pockets with mixture. Wrap in heavy waxed paper or foil, twisting ends tightly. Just before serving, heat in shallow pan in mod. oven (350°) 10 to 15 min. *12 sandwich rolls.*

Velvet-Crumb Cake

A delicious accompaniment for an afternoon
coffee party. See recipe on p. 215.

Dutch Lunch

Quails (p.107) Baked Beans (p.54)
Potato Salad (p. 61)
Dill Pickles Rye Bread Carrot Sticks
Crackers and Cheese Apples
Brownies Beverages

Holiday Open House

Share your Christmas cookies and fruit cake
with your friends (see p. 221).

Cake Mix Magic

A variety of delectable desserts that look hard to make are easy and so good with a mix.

Glamorous Year-round Shortcake (p. 230).

Old-fashioned Marble Cake (p. 159), always a favorite.

Ice Cream Sundae Cake (p. 217) as you like it.

Angel Food Cake

Refreshing with lemonade. Delicious with ice cream (p. 162)

INDEX